Top Ten Reasons to Buy This Book

SO HERE YOU ARE.

You could be in a bookstore, reading this and deciding whether this book is for you. You could be at home, or in your office, or maybe even reading a sample chapter online.

Wherever you are, you want assurance that this book, *Putting the Tarot to Work,* will make a difference in your life and career. For those with short attention spans and long to-do lists, here's the scoop:

1. *No focus on hocus-pocus.* Belief in the supernatural is not necessary. These processes work. Why they work—whether their effectiveness is practical or mystical—is for you to decide. But rest assured: no wearing of turbans, chanting to crystals, or burning incense is required. This book isn't about fortune telling . . . it's about fortune *making.*

2. *The "least you need to know" approach.* You won't have to spend hours studying the history of the Italian Renaissance before getting started. This book covers the basics, then offers step-by-step exercises that produce benefits you can enjoy right away.

3. *Use any deck—or no deck at all!* The techniques in this book work with any Tarot deck. Later chapters guide you in choosing the deck that's right for you—but, if you don't have access to Tarot cards, many of the methods described here can be adapted to use images from magazines, photographs, or even clip art!

4. *The Rat Race.* When you forget to forge a link between your job and your dreams, you get caught up in the Rat Race. The techniques in this book will help you align your dreams and sense of personal purpose with the work you do.

5. *Advantage: you!* The techniques in this book teach you to ask questions others haven't considered, approach problems from surprising new perspectives, and make connections others will overlook. These skills greatly enhance your value to your company!

6. *Simple for beginners, surprising for experts.* Even if you've never touched a deck of Tarot cards in your life, you can use the simple, step-by-step exercises in this book. If you're familiar with Tarot, the approaches and spreads in this book suggest new directions.

7. *The forest* and *the trees.* We're overwhelmed with information: advertising, the media, the market, the Internet. The most successful business people sift through this information, isolate what's really important, and comprehend how these facts impact and influence each other—something the techniques in this book help you do.

8. *Everyday insights.* This book shows you how to use Tarot to solve problems faster, make better decisions, generate new ideas, communicate more clearly, and act with greater confidence. Your job presents opportunities to employ these skills every day!

9. *A lot of book for the buck.* This book offers basic card meanings, the least you should know about Tarot, powerful exercises designed to expand your awareness and deepen your insights, and suggestions for those who want to know more! Everything you need to get started is here.

10. *One small step.* If reading this book motivates you to take just one action with potential to enhance your satisfaction with your career, your work environment, or your life . . . isn't it worth the cover price?

With more than two decades of experience as a training consultant, **Mark McElroy** has developed courseware and multimedia for SkyTel, MCI, Office Depot, Staples, Manpower, and others. Today he works as a writer, voice actor, and brainstorming consultant through his websites at www.hiremark.com and www.tarottools.com.

Forthcoming by Mark McElroy

Putting the Tarot to Bed

The Idea Deck—A Brainstorming Tarot

MARK McELROY

PUTTING THE TAROT TO WORK

CREATIVE PROBLEM SOLVING, EFFECTIVE DECISION MAKING, AND PERSONAL CAREER PLANNING

2004
Llewellyn Publications
St. Paul, Minnesota 55164-0383, U.S.A.

First Edition
First Printing, 2004

Book design and editing by Michael Maupin
Cover photo © 2004 by digitalvision
Cover Tarot image from *The Nigel Jackson Tarot*
Cover design by Gavin Dayton Duffy

Image from *The Alchemical Tarot* copyright © 1995 Robert M. Place. Used with permission. Image from *Classic Tarot* and *Universal Tarot* used with permission from the Italian publisher Lo Scarabeo.

The Nigel Jackson Tarot, The Robin Wood Tarot, The Sacred Circle Tarot, and *The World Spirit Tarot* are available from Llewellyn Publications.

Library of Congress Cataloging-in-Publication Data
McElroy, Mark, 1964–
    Putting the tarot to work / Mark McElroy.—1st ed.
        p.   cm.
    Includes index.
    ISBN 0-7387-04444-X
        1. Tarot cards. 2. Business forecasting—Miscellanea. I. Title.

BF1879.T2M43 2004
133.3'2424—dc22   2003065900

Llewellyn Worldwide does not participate in, endorse, or have any authority or responsibility concerning private business transactions between our authors and the public.
    All mail addressed to the author is forwarded but the publisher cannot, unless specifically instructed by the author, give out an address or phone number.
    Any Internet references contained in this work are current at publication time, but the publisher cannot guarantee that a specific location will continue to be maintained. Please refer to the publisher's website for links to authors' websites and other sources.

Llewellyn Publications
A Division of Llewellyn Worldwide, Ltd.
P.O. Box 64383, Dept. 0-7387-0444-X
St. Paul, MN 55164-0383, U.S.A.
www.llewellyn.com

♻ Printed in the United States of America on recycled paper.

For Clyde,

who always believed I could do it.

Contents

Acknowledgments

MY THANKS GO TO Carl Weschcke, for his faith and vision; Barbara Moore, for approaching, guiding, and encouraging me; Michael Maupin, for making this book the best it could be; and cover designer Gavin Duffy.

Other Llewellyn troopers: Sandra Weschcke, Gabe Weschcke, Beth Scudder, Lisa Novak, Nancy Mostad, Nanette Peterson, Mark Combes, Rhonda Ogren, Brenda Jokisalo, Jerry Rogers, Karen Karsten, Drew Siqveland, Kate Brielmaier, Eric Sneve, Hollie Kilroy, Meg Bratsch, Tom Bilstad, Josie Christopherson, Jenny Gehlhar, Jennifer Spees, and Lisa Braun.

And to Tarot artists, authors, and friends who inspired me: Valerie Sim, Diane Wilkes, Sandra Thompson, Tracy Hite, Teresa Michelsen, Rickey Hite, Joan Bunning, Mary Greer, Rachel Pollack, Robert O'Neill, Jana Riley, Nina Lee Braden, Andreas Schroter, Richard Jefferies, Chris Asselin, James Wells, Rachel Nguyen, Paula Gibby, Liz Hazel, Brigit Horner, Janet Selman, Debbie Lake, Saskia Jansen, Kevin Quigley, Dan Johnson, Sally Anne Stephen, James Revak, Wald and Ruth Ann Amberstone, and Janet Berres.

Introduction

QUICK—MAKE A LIST of indispensable tools for executives, corporate employees, and small business owners. Ready? *Go!*

Let's compare lists. A powerful computer? Check. A cell phone? Check. A pager? Check. A Palm Pilot? Check.

Tarot cards? Check!

Wait a minute—*Tarot cards?* Yes, Tarot cards—the same seventy-eight pieces of laminated cardboard used by that television psychic who exclaims in her fake Jamaican accent, "Honey, dat man is cheatin' on you!"

Tarot cards in the work place? What's next? Changing the corporate dress code to gold turbans, silk pajamas, and curly-toed bedroom slippers? Reading tea leaves in the break room? Replacing sales forecasts with astrological charts? (Actually, most managers I know could learn a thing or two about sales forecasting from astrologers . . . but that's another story.)

Don't panic. Reading this book won't cause you to chant to crystals or strike a yoga pose atop your manager's desk. What reading this book will do, though, is change forever the way you think about creativity, brainstorming, and problem solving!

The Future: Who Needs It?

As it turns out, the fortune teller at the corner coffee shop isn't the only person downtown who's interested in the future. Sales managers log monthly forecasts, trying to predict revenue for the coming quarter. No one raises an eyebrow when the marketing department engages in a little prophecy: "Sixty-five percent of our current base will purchase this product, increasing revenue by seven million dollars!"

At least they're trying. Many companies large and small, propelled forward by the hectic, day-to-day rat race of making a buck, give up on the future entirely. They scramble to put out the latest fires with no regard for how today's actions influence tomorrow's realities. They make snap decisions without pausing for reflection. They obsess on one dimension of a problem to the exclusion of all other options. They work without a plan.

Sound familiar? The fact is, almost every executive, corporate employee, or small business owner I meet is too busy surviving the day to pause even five minutes to reflect on tomorrow. As burn-out sets in, creativity, intuition, and insight evaporate. All businesses preach appreciation for creative approaches and "out of the box thinking," but faced with compressed schedules and lengthy to-do lists, most are too harried to put these into practice.

Thinking outside of the box becomes very difficult when you live in a cube. If we truly value creativity, we must schedule time to reflect—even briefly—on how our work impacts others. In simple terms: we must stop and think about the future.

Seeing the Future Through Visual Brainstorming

My experience managing a training design and production team provides a ready example. Members of our group felt positioned at the bottom of a huge pipe. Every day, new work came out of nowhere, spewing down from the pipe onto our heads. We scrambled to assemble some kind of response, and then shoved our output down other pipes to other faceless teams. What was the context of our work? How was it received? What impact did it have? We had no idea. We lived in the perpetual present, with no future in sight.

Our lives changed when we adopted a simple practice: we insisted on time for creative thought. The amount of time we demanded varied by assignment. Sometimes we needed an hour. Sometimes we needed a day. But ultimately, once we drew a line in the sand and said, "We're going to think before churning something out," our jobs, our output, and our lives improved.

Our primary tool for thinking turned out to be brainstorming. Assembled in an abandoned conference room, three or four of us would gather with packs of sticky notes in hand. We started by defining our challenge. That done, we asked ourselves a flurry of questions. What do these people need? What will happen if they keep working the way they work now? What changes might we suggest? How would those changes impact performance? What other factors could be influencing performance? What do these people need to know? What do these people have to achieve?

We jotted down every answer we could think of and plastered the bare walls with our little yellow notes. After ten or twenty minutes, patterns emerged. Sometimes we arranged our ideas into categories and columns. Other times, we used them to create an impromptu timeline. In all cases, our brainstorming process fulfilled two important functions—we developed a clearer picture of the present, and we explored several strategies for altering the future.

The first time the VP over our team visited one of our sessions, he expected to find us gathered soberly around a conference table, neatly outlining ideas in our Franklin planners. When he found four adults laughing, shouting out ideas, and slamming dozens of sticky notes against the wall, he thought he'd caught us engaged in some kind of rebellion against the establishment. ("Wasting valuable corporate resources! And laughing about it!")

He continued to be skeptical until he saw the results. Soon, our VP could see that this visual brainstorming method allowed us to see our ideas take shape—and made it easier to identify the holes in our thinking.

Craving Creative Fuel

After adopting a creative, visual approach to brainstorming, our work, our output, and our attitudes improved. We used the sticky note strategy successfully for several months—until it, too, became routine. Once the same group began doing the same thing in the same way over a long period of time, we began taking tried-and-true approaches and stopped seeing our challenges from fresh perspectives.

Our brainstorming process needed fuel—some kind of input that would force us to make surprising associations or unexpected connections. One day, on a lark, I pulled an evocative image from Visionary Network's *Oracle of Changes* software program, and asked the team, "How does this picture relate to the problem we're solving?"

The rush of new ideas caught me off guard. People immediately locked on to different aspects of the image: the colors, the weather, the horses, the placid lake, the full moon. They related these parts of the picture to our problem, making leaps of logic in the process.

"The sales reps in this new hire class feel isolated and cut off, just like the horses in this picture," said one member of our team. "They need some kind of regular contact with each other in order to feel . . . a part of the herd."

Another team member nodded. "See the full moon? How about a group that meets via conference call once a month?"

"Maybe we could position it as a kind of virtual retreat together," the first team member said. "A one-hour call that amounts to a 'day at the lake' with other reps—a time to exchange stories and ideas and talk about what's working!"

Before looking at the picture, we had three or four lonesome sticky notes on the wall, and our spirits sagged. After using the image to refresh our creative fuel, our ideas came so quickly, we almost had to find a room with bigger walls!

Seventy-Eight Full-Time Consultants for $12.95

Image-based brainstorming dramatically enhanced the creativity of our group. I started using the process personally—when planning presentations, meetings, or training modules. The quality of my ideas increased, but the time it took to generate them decreased. Being basically lazy, I decided this was a wonderful thing.

Eventually, I discovered that other people—including some high-profile creative firms—were using image-based brainstorming in their work. One article (shared in detail in this book's chapter on the brainstorming process) mentioned a group of high-priced creative consultants who based their brainstorming sessions on magazine photos: opening the magazine, flipping to a random image, and generating a list of possibilities.

I started gathering magazines for this purpose, but immediately encountered obstacles. First, the penny-pinching company I work for refused to purchase magazines of any sort. ("You should be working, not reading magazines!") I tried bringing in magazines from home, but brainstorming with *Time* and *Newsweek* skewed all our ideas toward war and crime metaphors ("End Border Skirmishes with the Competition! Call a Sales Summit Now!"). Worse, a stack of magazines, besides being bulky and heavy, never seems to be around when needed.

Then, when doing some personal research, I stumbled on the answer: Tarot cards.

In most Tarot decks, each card bears a deliberately evocative image, packed with symbols, metaphors, literary allusions, numbers, and keywords. A deck of cards slips easily into a pocket or purse (try that with a stack of magazines!). Lose a carefully-assembled collection of slick color advertisements, and you'll spend weeks (and big bucks) replacing them. Lose your deck of cards, though, and you can replace them faster than you can say, "Take me to your local bookstore!"

Another advantage: the seventy-eight cards found in most Tarot decks possess an internal structure—the cards relate to each other in meaningful ways. Random ads torn from magazines lack this relationship, limiting their usefulness.

And finally with Tarot cards, the price is right. Instead of spending $78,000 to have creativity consultants spend twelve hours with my team, I could hire seventy-eight creativity consultants for just twelve dollars!

Whatever your position, whatever your goals, whatever your situation, you can change your career and life for the better by *Putting the Tarot to Work*. You don't have to know anything about Tarot—the only requirements are an open mind, and a willingness to experiment and observe the results. Take what works for you! And don't forget to let me know how things go.

Mark McElroy
mark@tarottools.com
Summer 2002

CHAPTER

Playing for Keeps

Preview: What to Expect in Chapter One

This chapter explores:

☞ How business is waking up to the value of creative brainstorming

☞ Why the Tarot works so well as a brainstorming tool

☞ How to overcome common objections to the use of Tarot

Playing with Ideas

ON THIS BRIGHT, SUNLIT morning, the brainstorming team at Play—a consulting firm whose clients include American Express, the Weather Channel, Calvin Klein, Nationwide Insurance, Oscar Mayer, and Disney—prepares for a session. Confronted with a challenge, most corporate problem solvers retreat into a locked, windowless conference room to deliberate for hours. Instead, the folks at Play:

> . . . grab a stack of magazines to flip though to "force connections." The point is to come up with ideas—no matter how silly, bad, or inappropriate—from random input. This exercise in free association both removes penalties for "bad" ideas and guarantees exposure to unrelated and offbeat sources of inspiration . . . The team flips through magazines, calling out ideas . . . Play believes that the more connections you make between seemingly unrelated concepts and the more perspectives you have on a problem, the more likely you are to hatch a winning creative solution.[*]

This process forces people to connect unrelated ideas in unexpected ways. An example: the Weather Channel asks Play to come up with creative ways the company can make more money. During today's creative session, a magazine ad for men's clothing raises the idea of Weather Channel ties featuring weather-related themes. A picture of raindrops on a windowpane suggests an "Adopt a Raindrop" program for the cable channel's web site. Registered viewers follow a raindrop from its inception in a cloud, through its lifecycle in streams and rivers, to its ultimate destination in the sea . . . and the registration process provides the Weather Channel with a mailing list of potential customers interested in weather-related products.

Pay special attention to the Play team's process! First, the team accesses a "random resource"—in this case, a set of pictures with no clear or obvious connection to the problem

[*] Cheryl Dahle. "Mind Games," *Fast Company*, Jan/Feb 2000, 168.

at hand. Next, participants leaf through random magazine images, forging links between the pictures they encounter and the issue under consideration. The media praises this process—generating solutions with the help of random input—as a bold, innovative strategy.

Tarot readers, however, have done this for decades.

When I share that last observation with a live audience, the giggling begins. "Come on!" people say. "The Tarot? You're seriously suggesting business people work with *Tarot cards?* What's next—replacing laptops with crystal balls? Sacrificing goats on conference-room tables?"

Let me reassure you: no goats will be harmed by any process in this book. Crystal balls are not required. Belief in the supernatural is not a factor. I don't focus on hocus pocus.

That's because the processes outlined here, while based on Tarot cards, are practical, not mystical. Instead of teaching fortune-telling, we're discussing *fortune-making*—demonstrating how introducing a deck of Tarot cards into your creative process enhances the quality and variety of ideas you generate. Once you learn how to use Tarot as a focusing and brainstorming tool, you'll make better decisions, achieve broader perspective, and find more satisfaction in your career.

Why the Tarot?

Like the folks at Play, you could use magazine photos as your source of inspiration. (In fact, if the use of Tarot cards becomes an obstacle, every technique in this book can be adapted for use with pictures of any kind.) But when used as a creativity tool, Tarot cards possess distinct advantages over pictures from magazines.

It's Only a Game

We associate cards with games, and games with "playing." Being dealt a hand of cards presents a challenge: how many winning combinations can you assemble? Magazine ads and other images lack this critical association.

The Magical Mindset

People associate Tarot cards with fortune telling or foreseeing the future—even if they don't believe the cards can actually be used for these purposes. Something about the Tarot attracts attention. Everyone (including skeptics!) expects *something* to happen when the cards hit the table!

Because we associate the cards—even frivolously—with psychic processes, we *expect* the pictures to suggest ideas and generate insights. These expectations set the stage for brainstorming in a way that magazine photos never will.

Inspiration Through Illustration

Many magazine ads feature one large, central image that, by design, points to one object or idea: the product. Most Tarot decks, however, compress a wealth of images and symbols onto every card in hopes of generating a multitude of associations and responses.

Structural Support

Images pulled from magazines lack any connection to each other. As a result, each image stands alone, and all images command equal weight.

By contrast, Tarot cards possess an underlying structure. Some cards are trumps, commanding more authority and attention. The four suits of a Tarot deck remind us to approach solutions from a variety of perspectives. The numbers on each card suggest ways ideas can be ranked, put in order, or evaluated. Court cards (Kings, Queens, Knights, and Pages) remind us of people we know or approaches we've tried. This built-in structure allows the Tarot to support associations and connections in ways that random images never will.

Spread the News

Before drawing Tarot cards, most people select or define a specific layout for the cards. These layouts, called spreads, guide the placement of Tarot cards into predefined positions. Spreads assign special meaning to each position. We might say, "This card will represent the true cause of our situation," or, "This card represents our best possible course of action."

The use of spreads relates each card's general meanings to specific aspects of the problem under consideration. As a result, even very familiar cards suggest unique approaches and conclusions. You could enhance the value of magazine photos by using spreads, but a spread of more than two or three images would require you to work on the floor (and you can completely forget about working on one of those cramped airline tray tables!).

At Least They're Consistent

Different decks by different artists render cards in different ways. Even so, a consistency exists across many decks, with similar symbols appearing on corresponding cards. As a result, the cards create a kind of symbolic shorthand between people who use them—even when different groups use different decks.

Imagine five people sitting at a table, engaged in hot debate. If familiar with Tarot, one member of the group might remark, "Well, this is a real Five of Wands moment, isn't it?" (The Five of Wands, by the way, associates with conflict and opposition.)

No matter which deck they use, members of this group will grasp the importance of the comment and, perhaps, consider moving from the chaos of the Five to the cooperation and victory of the Six. Groups using different sets of random magazine images never develop this kind of shared response . . . and never reap the benefits associated with it.

They're Everywhere

As recently as the 1970s and 1980s, Tarot cards were relatively rare. Today, even chain bookstores stock a dozen different decks. Good metaphysical bookstores stock as many as a hundred.

If you have trouble finding cards in your area, the Internet connects you with dozens of vendors. I recommend a number of good brainstorming decks at www.tarottools.com. In addition to the deck previews and reviews on my site, you'll also find links to sites which allow users to "shuffle," select cards, and read their associated meanings . . . for free!

Forget to bring your own Tarot cards? A quick trip to the bookstore averts disaster. If you left your library of magazine ads at home, you'll have lots of shopping and ripping and tearing to do!

Unbeatable Bargains

A standard deck of Tarot cards costs between $10.00 and $20.00.

On the other hand, subscriptions and magazine purchases become expensive. If you buy just three or four magazines a month, you spend more than you would for one Tarot deck. Collect images aggressively, and you spend a fortune in no time.

Losing your magazines could set you back a small fortune. Lose a Tarot deck, and, on average, you'll be back on track for less than twenty bucks.

No Extra Luggage Required

Want to lug a stack of laminated magazine pages on the flight from Atlanta to Chicago? No thanks. Want to use them on the flight? Not without stacking them on your neighbor's lap!

A Tarot deck fits in a briefcase, pocket, or purse. Some paperback novels dwarf the largest deck available, and miniature decks make the Tarot even more portable. This compares very favorably with the size of a stack of magazines. For that matter, how many other creativity tools come in a package this small?

All Things to All People

Certainly, magazines come in all shapes and sizes, and there are magazines designed to appeal to every possible audience.

Tarot decks match or exceed this variety. These days, decks are available for almost any group, ethnicity, or purpose you can imagine: black and white decks, handmade decks, collage decks, decks you can color yourself, decks featuring animals, decks based on historical periods and figures, specialty decks based on movies and television programs, science-fiction decks, fantasy decks, comic-oriented decks, sports decks—the list goes on and on. While some are better than others for our purposes, rest assured . . . your deck is out there.

Objections—Overruled!

When adopting Tarot cards as a personal or professional creativity tool, you may face some opposition. Most of this has nothing to do with Tarot—people oppose innovation in general, because new ideas threaten the status quo. Even so, I suggest you meet this opposition as eloquently as possible by anticipating the most common objections before they're made.

Objection One: You Should Be Working, Not Playing Cards

About the only time creative play is tolerated in most corporate settings is during training sessions. In fact, trainers are expected to use "ice breakers"—games, really, but we're afraid to call them that—to start a session. All too often, though, the games played are unrelated to the subject matter being studied. Having launched the session, the trainer puts games aside. The clear message: when the serious business starts, the games stop.

That's unfortunate, because integrating creative play into our work leads to innovation and success. In my own workgroup at a telecommunications company, we noticed immediate gains when we insisted on scheduling time to "play" with ideas—brainstorming, anticipating issues, and tossing around solutions—as part of every project plan. By playing our way through a project before working on it, we save time and money, anticipating obstacles before they arise.

In the same way, playing with the Tarot can help you explore:

- The root cause of a problem
- The differences in perspective between two or more parties
- The hindrance of progress
- The right time for action, or
- The political importance of an event

By its nature, Tarot encourages reflection and analysis. The resulting insights and solutions usually dispel any confusion over the value of working with Tarot. Even if you only focus on the cards for five or ten minutes, the Tarot can be a valuable and practical resource.

Objection Two: Religion Doesn't Belong in the Workplace

Some HR types may wonder whether the use of Tarot raises issues of religion in the workplace. For both ethical and legal reasons, special care must always be taken to respect the faiths of all employees. However, any religious objections to applications in this book lack a basis in either reason or fact.

Tarot imagery draws on a wide variety of sources, including mythology, Christianity, Eastern religions, nature religions, and others. The Tarot itself, however, is not associated with any particular religion, and the uses suggested in this book require neither religious faith nor mystical inclination. In fact, Tarot cards themselves were created for playing a game much like modern Bridge. The fortune-telling and spookiness now associated with Tarot began several hundred years after Renaissance Italians invented the cards.

Even so, anyone who plans to introduce Tarot in the workplace should ask directly and specifically whether other employees object to using the cards as brainstorming and creativity tools. In my experience, the use of Tarot intrigues most employees. Those few who *do* feel their beliefs conflict with the use of Tarot cards generally do not consider the matter open for discussion. As a result, I recommend this rule of thumb: if the cards raise concern or make any member of the workgroup uncomfortable, they should not be used.

When this is the case, you may find that even these objections disappear if you introduce Tarot images and techniques *without using cards*. Consider scanning images from the deck, cropping out the numbers and titles associated with the Tarot, and incorporating the pictures into presentations or posters. Should Tarot images themselves prove problematic, you can still incorporate the "random images torn from magazines" approach with most exercises in this book and achieve a degree of success.

Objection Three: What Will the Boss Think?

What your boss thinks about your use of the cards relates directly to the results you achieve with them.

If you gather a group of employees in a break room, giggle like schoolgirls at a slumber party, ask questions about office romances and the lottery, and produce nothing over the course of the next two hours, your boss will likely discourage the use of Tarot cards.

If your group defines clear, work-related questions, generates innovative, "out of the box" answers to critical corporate challenges, and develops action plans or practical solutions, your boss will be delighted.

Naturally, when you plan to use the cards in a workgroup, you should assure your boss that no members of the group object. You might also consider giving him a copy of this book in advance of your request, with relevant passages marked or highlighted.

Objection Four: Won't People Think I'm Weird?

Or, more diplomatically phrased, this objection might become, "I like the idea of using Tarot as a creativity tool, but don't think others in my office will understand."

Actually, while many of the methods outlined in this book were designed with group work in mind, all work equally well for individuals. Feel uncomfortable introducing the Tarot to your workgroup? Make it your own little secret! Before a meeting or prior to a call, you can put the Tarot to work, achieving useful insights and participating more fully in the session to come.

Objection Five: We've Gotten This Far Without Tarot Cards!

For just a moment, forget about the cards.

What would happen if you made an appointment with yourself to sit down and focus on these questions?

- To what degree am I doing what I really wanted to do?
- How fulfilling is my job? How could it be made more fulfilling?
- What was my "dream job" when I was a kid?
- How can I arrange things so I'm more likely to get a promotion or raise?
- What can I do to have more control over my future?

Would your career benefit as a result?

What would happen if, before each meeting or conference call, you sat for ten minutes and focused on these questions?

- What's the goal of this meeting or call?
- What role do I play in reaching this goal?
- What obstacles might interfere with reaching the goal?
- How can we get around those obstacles?
- What do we need to know that we haven't anticipated?

Would this short session have impact?

The unfortunate truth: our break-neck business routine doesn't lend itself to contemplation and reflection. We rush from meeting to workgroup to meeting without pausing for water, much less introspection or planning. Like leaves in a swift stream, we allow the current to carry us to whatever destination lies ahead.

The Tarot cards provide an excuse to pause, to think, to reflect on your goals and the company's goals, to consider options, to generate new ideas. Committing to work with the cards draws a line in the sand. You tell the world and yourself: *I am going to make time for contemplation, concentration, creativity, and reflection.* Sitting down, shuffling the deck, and dealing the cards becomes a calming ritual that clears you, calms you, and focuses you on the work you need to do.

Used intelligently, the seventy-eight cards of the Tarot become seventy-eight creative consultants you can pop in your pocket and consult anytime. Maybe your work together will produce just one great idea. Maybe you'll see just one way to align your career path more closely with your dreams.

Wouldn't that justify the cost of a deck of cards?

Summary: Chapter One in a Nutshell

ASSOCIATING BUSINESS CHALLENGES WITH randomly selected images enhances the creative brainstorming process. While any images can be used—even ads torn from magazines!—Tarot cards make especially good brainstorming tools.

Because we associate Tarot cards with magical, creative play, ideas occur more freely. The vivid images on Tarot cards spark the imagination, and the underlying structure of the Tarot prompts us to see relationships between our ideas we might otherwise overlook. Few other brainstorming tools are as portable, affordable, or easy to find.

By carefully positioning your work with the cards as serious business, you'll be able to incorporate them into your creative process without raising any objections from others.

CHAPTER

The Least You Should Know About Tarot

Preview: What to Expect in Chapter Two

This chapter explores:

☞ A quick overview of the Tarot

☞ How to discover meanings for each card

☞ How spreads and reversals enhance the meanings of the cards

☞ How to select the deck that's right for you

The Absolute Least You Should Know About Tarot

IF YOU CAN:

- Look at pictures
- Point to picture elements (people, objects, symbols, or colors) that catch your eye
- Describe what you see
- Associate these elements with information from your experience and memory
- Relate this information to your current situation or challenge

. . . you can start *Putting the Tarot to Work* today!

This intuitive approach—looking at the cards and making connections to your question—offers several advantages. Right away, you can use this visual brainstorming method to generate new ideas, broaden your perspective, and deepen your understanding. In fact, you can use almost every technique in this book without studying Tarot history, structure, or traditional meanings.

That said, I still believe the information in this chapter—a brief history of the Tarot, a discussion of the structure of the deck, suggestions for selecting a deck, and exercises designed to enhance your ability to associate ideas with the images on the cards—offers real value. As you'll see, every fact you learn about the Tarot creates an additional "hook" capable of catching additional associations and realizations.

This chapter, then, gives you a quick but thorough tour of the basics: the least you should know before using Tarot.

Aliens, Egyptians, & Secret Societies—Not!

Most books on the history of the Tarot repeat stories like these with a straight face:

- Aliens created Tarot, then gave it to the Egyptians, along with plans for the pyramids.

- Tarot cards are the only remaining artifacts to survive the destruction of the lost continent of Atlantis, and were distributed throughout the world by Gypsies.

- The Tarot was created by a secret organization more than 3000 years ago, and the symbols on the cards contain all of that group's magical secrets!

The facts: all evidence suggests Tarot cards appeared in Italy in the fifteenth century, apparently as part of a game to amuse royalty. Featuring images influenced by Renaissance Christianity, Greek mythology, figures from royal families, and other themes of interest at the time, the original cards lack any documented connection with fortune telling.

In fact, the best available evidence suggests Tarot cards weren't used as fortune telling props until hundreds of years after their invention. This comes as a great surprise to most Americans, who rarely associate Tarot with anything *but* fortune telling.

A more detailed history of the Tarot than this lies outside the scope of this book. However, if you want to know more about the origins of Tarot, I strongly recommend the concise History Information Sheet available from the Internet-based discussion list, Tarot-L. This resource, compiled and edited by Tom Tadfor Little, can be found in "Further Reading and Resources" on page 225.

What Cards Make Up a Tarot Deck?

While decks vary, most consist of seventy-eight cards. When used for brainstorming purposes, each of these seventy-eight cards can represent or suggest:

- An approach to problem solving

- An action to be taken

- A person (or type of person)

- A moment or situation from everyday life

- Information about an issue or situation

- A factor or influence that creates, perpetuates, or could resolve your situation.

Like a standard deck of playing cards, a Tarot deck features four suits, each containing cards numbered from one to ten. Also within each suit are court cards—though the Tarot features a Page, Knight, Queen, and King instead of the more familiar Jack, Queen, and King. In addition to these, the deck includes twenty-one additional trump cards, plus a special card called the Fool.

Fortune-telling books will usually lump the trumps and the Fool into a group of cards called the Major Arcana, or the "Great Mysteries." For our purposes, though, we'll just call this group of twenty-two cards the trumps. (You'll get extra points in *Trivial Pursuit,* though, if you remember that, technically, the Fool is not one of the trumps.) The same books will call the other fifty-six cards the Minor Arcana, or "Little Mysteries." (Sounds spooky, eh?)

Pay Attention to Trumps!

When using the deck as a brainstorming tool, the appearance of a trump indicates an idea or influence in need of special attention.

Let's say you ask a question like: *What two factors played a role in creating this mess I'm in?* To guide your brainstorming, you draw two cards, one of which is a trump. In this example, the trump would represent the more influential of the two factors.

Numbered from zero to twenty-one, the trumps are:

0—Fool

1—The Magician	8—Strength	15—The Devil
2—The High Priestess	9—The Hermit	16—The Tower
3—The Empress	10—Wheel of Fortune	17—The Star
4—The Emperor	11—Justice	18—The Moon
5—The Hierophant	12—The Hanged Man	19—The Sun
6—The Lovers	13—Death	20—Judgement
7—The Chariot	14—Temperance	21—The World

The order of the trumps varies from deck to deck. None of these variations impact the way the cards are used in *Putting the Tarot to Work.*

You'll also notice some Tarot decks call trumps like Death or The Devil by less creepy names, like *Transition* or *Addiction.* If these or any other cards bother you, just remove them from the pack. (Be aware, though, that these cards represent important ideas, and that removing them robs you of the opportunity to make potentially valuable connections.)

Put Your Best Suit Forward

Most decks divide the fifty-six remaining cards into four suits: Wands, Swords, Cups, and Coins. For brainstorming purposes, these suits represent four ways of dealing with, understanding, or exploring an issue:

Suit	How the issue relates to or is influenced by . . .
Wands	. . . intentions, goals, agendas, desires, business concerns, management, and creativity
Swords	. . . decision-making, logic, mathematics, strategies, responses, judgment, and reason
Cups	. . . emotions, feelings, perceptions, intuition, reactions, and prejudices
Coins	. . . practical matters, all physical objects (including the human body), material resources, employees, the five senses, and, of course, money

Drawing a majority of Cups cards during a brainstorming session prompts participants to focus on how emotions or feelings create, complicate, or perpetuate a situation. A mixture of Swords, Coins, and Cups might suggest an exploration of how decisions (Swords) made strictly to save money (Coins) could impact the morale (Cups) of a company's employees.

In her book *Tarot Mirrors,* Mary K. Greer positions the four suits as four unique perspectives or four dimensions. I believe we increase our chances of success when we adopt these perspectives and assume a "four dimensional" approach to solving corporate and small-business problems. Random magazine ads don't usually remind us to examine the conflicting goals, decisions, feelings, and practical considerations inherent in every situation.

Some deck creators abandon these suits for new ones, or substitute crystals for Wands, pentacles for Coins, or vessels for Cups. Whatever they're called, the primary benefit of suits is their ability to remind us to examine a challenge from multiple perspectives.

Order in the Court!

Four court cards—usually a King, Queen, Knight, and Page—appear within each suit. For our purposes, these cards refer to specific kinds of people (controllers, collaborators, extremists, and beginners) or the methods these people tend to employ.

Kings approach others and attempt to resolve situations by assuming authority over, taking control of, or imposing order upon the qualities associated with their suit.

Queens approach others and attempt resolution by building consensus, encouraging collaboration, and using psychology through their suit's unique perspective.

Knights approach others and attempt to solve problems by embodying the extremes of their suit in positive or negative ways.

Pages represent individuals who want to, are beginning to, or have potential to express the qualities associated with their suit.

To discover what qualities a particular court card represents, pair the approach associated with the court card in question with the perspective represented by its suit.

Example One: King of Cups

A King represents an approach to problem solving through the assumption of control, exercise of authority, or imposition of order. The suit of Cups deals with prejudices, relationships, emotions, feelings, or responses.

Combine the approach of a King with the subject matter of the suit . . . and *voilá!* The King of Cups could represent the desire to solve a problem or control a situation by enforcing prejudices, controlling relationships, limiting feelings, or ordering and organizing perceptions and responses. In a business setting, this card could refer to any effort to control or manipulate people's reactions by limiting the range of appropriate or acceptable responses.

Is the King of Cups, associated with authority, control, and limitation of emotion, a negative card? Not necessarily. Imagine a layoff in which a company reduces its workforce by half. A King of Cups-style manager would treat departing employees with dignity (to limit unpleasantness). He would also keep remaining employees well-informed of their status (to prevent unnecessary flight from disabling his department).

In the same situation, the King of Cups might also represent a manager (or even the need for a manager) who keeps a stiff upper lip, controlling his emotions while doing what has to be done during a difficult time.

Example Two: Knight of Coins

The Knight of Coins represents the desire to solve a problem or approach a situation by embodying extreme financial, material, or traditional values in positive or negative ways.

If the issue is financial, the Knight may represent a person, organization, or plan primarily dedicated to restricting expenses. If handled positively, we experience this Knight's actions as frugal or financially conservative. If executed badly, we perceive the Knight to be a stingy penny-pincher exalting profit above all else.

The Knight could also represent a person, organization, or plan dedicated to solving problems by spending a great deal more money. If handled positively, we might experience this Knight's actions as generous or liberal. If executed badly, this Knight appears careless with money and wasteful of precious resources.

When a court card appears in your brainstorming session, consider it an invitation to identify people, organizations, or programs that embody the approaches and attitudes suggested by the card.

The Pips (Without Gladys Knight)

Each suit also contains ten pip cards, numbered from one to ten. Modern playing cards feature pips: on the ten of diamonds, for example, you'll find ten diamond-shaped pips.

Nonillustrated Pips

In most early Tarot decks, the pips worked the same way: the six of swords featured six swords, and the eight of cups featured eight cups. Several decks today continue this practice. Since no pictures or illustrations appear on the pips, we say these decks contain "nonillustrated pips."

When brainstorming, decks with nonillustrated pips pose a challenge. Consider this card from a deck with nonillustrated pips—the *Classic Tarot*, at right.

Asked to guess the meaning of this card, most people fail to say, "Distraction, boredom, or the desire for change"—a traditional interpretation for the Four of Cups—unless that describes their feeling after spending several minutes staring at the card!

People who prefer decks with nonillustrated pips generally depend on number symbolism to determine the meaning of the card. Number symbolism associates each number with specific themes:

Four of Cups— Classic Tarot

Number	Associated Meanings
1	**Opportunity.** Singularity of purpose. Unity. The essence or "seed" of the suit.
2	**Duality.** A crossroads. The need for balance. Combinations. The influence of "the other."
3	**Productivity.** The physical expression of an idea. Creativity. Achievement.
4	**Stability.** Permanence. Dependability. Stagnation. Stillness.

Number	Associated Meanings
5	**Instability.** Chaos. Loss. Transition. Breakdown. Opportunity for change.
6	**Flexibility.** Charity. Cooperation. Collaboration. Acceptance. Impermanence.
7	**Psychology.** Internal work or the inner world. Motives. Attitudes. Decisions. Dreams.
8	**Activity.** External work in the outer world. The need for action. Results. Products. Change.
9	**Totality.** Achieving what can be achieved. Fullness. Fruition. Attainment.
10	**Finality.** Ultimate outcome. End result or endpoint. Conclusion. Completion.

To determine the meaning of a nonillustrated pip card, combine the theme of the card's number with the unique perspective of its suit. In the case of the Four of Cups:

Four	=	Stability / Stagnation / Stillness
Cups	=	Emotion / Feeling / Spirit
Four of Cups	=	Stagnation of Spirit and / or Unchanging Emotion, or a feeling of boredom and / or a desire for change

An awareness of number symbolism also encourages exploration of how a situation changes over time. If your situation is represented by the Four of Cups, for example, you may be experiencing stagnation or boredom. Through number symbolism, however, the Four of Cups encourages a look back at the Three: what past efforts, rooted in a unity of spirit, made this stability possible? What prompted your situation to move from the celebration of reaching a milestone to the stagnation that haunts you now?

In addition, the Four of Cups also points to the Five: what events might upset or interfere with the stability of your current situation? What would be the emotional impact of that instability? What would you lose? What might you gain?

Understanding how to combine number symbolism with the perspective of each suit enhances your experience of the pip cards—whether the deck you use illustrates them or not.

Illustrated Pips

Decks with illustrated pips feature pictures on every card, including the pips. In many decks, these images represent the artist's attempt to capture the traditional meaning of the card with a memorable visual image. By way of illustration, consider the artwork from *The Robin Wood Tarot* Four of Cups, as shown below.

Generally, even people unfamiliar with Tarot understand this card suggests boredom, distraction, or a desire for something more.

In the corporate arena, I suggest using a deck with illustrated pips. Most busy employees lack the time or inclination to memorize a table of numbers and their associated meanings, rendering a nonillustrated deck almost useless. People respond more strongly to images than they ever do to an arrangement of pips, making fully illustrated decks the tool of choice for brainstorming sessions.

Four of Cups—
Robin Wood Tarot

What Does My Card Mean?

Every card in the Tarot deck, from the highest trump to the lowest pip, suggests an entire spectrum of ideas, approaches, attitudes, or actions. Over the years, many different meanings have been suggested for each card.

Most Tarot decks come with little white booklets (more recently, some decks come with full-sized, full-color handbooks) defining meanings for each card. Some authors preserve traditional meanings; others change them to suit their personal perspective.

In addition to the little white book that comes with your deck, Appendix A of this book lists brief, "business-flavored" meanings for each card. For further reading, consider purchasing the larger book associated with your deck, or try Jana Riley's *Tarot Dictionary and Compendium* (Samuel Weiser, Inc., 1995), an excellent resource that compiles, for each card, the interpretations of a dozen different Tarot scholars.

Resist the compulsion to look up the meaning of every card. Before looking up a commentator's meaning for a card, always spend some time deciding what the card suggests to you. When brainstorming, that suggestion may be far more important than any meaning in any book!

Spread the News

When drawing cards from a Tarot deck, you might lay them out, one after the other, in a straight line. On the other hand, you might position the cards into rows, one above the other, or arrange them in the shape of a circle. Any deliberate arrangement of cards creates a *spread*.

In addition to guiding the layout of the cards, spreads assign specific meanings to each position in the layout. The dealer assigns positional meanings before dealing or revealing the cards. These meanings assist in associating a particular card with some aspect of your situation. Generally, the shape of a spread reflects some aspect of your challenge, question, or issue.

Consider a simple Past-Present-Future spread:

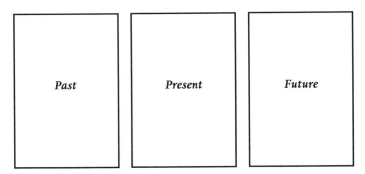

In the example above, the leftmost card represents the past, the center card represents the present, and the card on the right represents the future. The meaning of the first card would be examined in light of past events. The other two cards characterize the present or suggest a possible future.

Consider how the shape of the simple five-card spread below reflects the meanings assigned to each position:

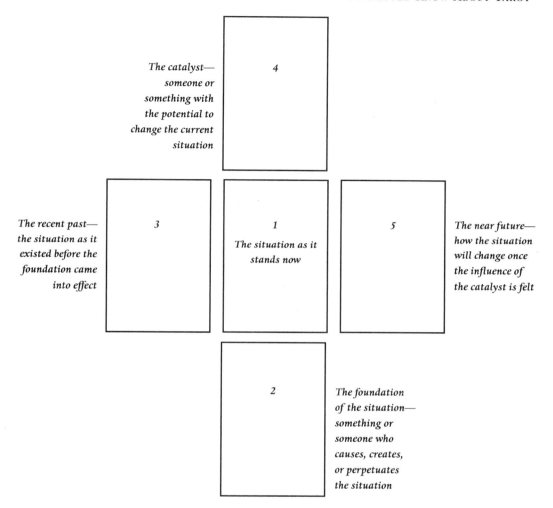

The catalyst—someone or something with the potential to change the current situation

4

The recent past—the situation as it existed before the foundation came into effect

3

1

The situation as it stands now

5

The near future—how the situation will change once the influence of the catalyst is felt

2

The foundation of the situation—something or someone who causes, creates, or perpetuates the situation

Putting the current situation in the center of this spread makes logical and visual sense, as does putting the past to the left, the future to the right, the foundation beneath, and the catalyst overhead.

When your question concerns the way a manager treats her employees, you might base a spread on an org chart, with the Manager Card at the top, and direct reports arranged beneath her.

When resolving a difference of opinion between two people, you could draw a card to represent each person's viewpoint, then place a "bridge" card between them to signify the information needed to bring the dispute to a close.

This book includes a number of spreads for you to use or adapt when working with business questions, but designing spreads of your own quickly becomes second nature.

Reversals

In the process of shuffling and dealing, some cards turn upside-down. In Tarot, the inversion of a card is called a *reversal*.

When brainstorming, many people simply ignore reversals. When a reversal appears, they turn it right side up and continue. This time-honored, legitimate approach to reversals proves useful to most beginners, who may struggle to recall a single meaning for a card.

However, just as many people see a reversed card as an opportunity to see the card in an entirely new way. Some people suggest the reversal of a card reverses its meaning: a reversed Death card, for example, may herald the beginning of a new project or the start of a new venture (as opposed to the upright Death card, which suggests endings or closure).

Others take a more subtle approach to reversals, suggesting that inversion sublimates the energy of a card, obstructing or suppressing it. They may also believe a reversed card's qualities haven't yet been expressed or discovered, or that the activity represented by the card is declining.

If the idea of reversals intrigues you, Mary K. Greer recently published an entire book packed with suggestions for working with reversed cards (*Tarot Reversals,* Llewellyn, 2002).

What you do with reversals is entirely up to you!

Selecting a Deck

When selecting a deck for personal or business use, consider these three factors: the style of the artwork, the text on the cards, and the structure of the deck.

Artwork

When selecting a deck for personal use, let personal preferences guide you. Find a deck with artwork that you respond to or enjoy. To help you pinpoint a deck you like, many stores offer a "card album"—essentially, a photo album packed with sample cards from every deck in inventory.

Think twice before selecting an *affinity deck*—cards designed to appeal to special interests—as your business deck. *The Baseball Tarot,* for example, adapts Tarot concepts to baseball terminology (The Fool, associated with beginnings and naiveté, becomes The Rookie). Your co-workers may not share your enthusiasm for baseball or cats or cute dragons, limiting their ability to respond to the cards. Consider, too, the impact of Anglo-centrism (the depiction of all human figures as Caucasians). If your company values diversity, you might select a deck that reflects a multicultural approach, such as Llewellyn's *World Spirit Tarot*.

The Internet also offers a broad variety of resources when you're browsing for a deck. In the "Further Reading and Resources" section of this book (see page 225), I provide addresses for several excellent web sites. Diane Wilkes' excellent Tarot Passages web site offers several hundred reviews featuring photos of trumps, court cards, and pips. Another good resource is Aeclectic Tarot, which features short reviews and six images from each deck. The Comparative Tarot web site features cards from many decks paired with descriptive essays written by passionate deck collectors. I also recommend and preview a number of decks at the web site associated with this book: www.tarottools.com.

Finally, with an eye toward using the cards in a business setting, it's good to be aware that certain card images in some decks may incorporate full or partial nudity. In many cases—as with the *Universal Tarot* or the *Alchemical Tarot*—the cards depict the human form in much the same way a fine sculpture might. Other decks, including the *Phantasmagoric Theatre* and *Navigators Tarot of the Mystic SEA,* feature nonhuman or androgynous characters, and might be prove to be better choices when working in diverse or sensitive groups.

In most decks, nudity appears on the Lovers, The Star, The Sun, and The World. In today's lawsuit-happy environment, I recommend erring on the side of caution by removing these cards if you sense any potential for offense within your work group.

Keywords and Help Text on the Cards

At first, a keyword—text defining the meaning of a card—sounds like a good idea. Why struggle, when a well-chosen keyword or paragraph of text can define the meaning instantly?

The value the Tarot offers you, however, hinges on the process of linking the image to a matter of personal concern. Keywords interfere with this process. For example, if the word "Ungratefulness" appears on the Four of Coins (as it does in the *Tarot of the Master*), alternative meanings for the card—selfishness, greed, financial conservatism, control, tradition, or hidden talents—may not occur to you.

Other decks go so far as to include tiny paragraphs at the top and bottom of each card, like this text from the *Quick and Easy Tarot:*

> **Judgement (Trump 20):** Arguments, legal, and contractual issues resolved to your favor. If you have wronged someone, seek reconciliation and forgiveness. Forgive those who have hurt you and move on with your life. Find a new career. If you have been in a low period, this card signifies a turnaround.

These definitions limit the brainstorming process, discouraging the exploration of other meanings. (You may also hesitate—and rightly so—to use a deck in a business setting that advises your employees to "Find a new career"!)

Especially since the processes in this book depend heavily on making unlimited associations with the cards, I recommend you select a deck without keywords or help text. Since the goal of brainstorming is to generate as many associations as possible, why choose a tool that places limits on imagination?

The Seventy-Eight Card Structure

Choosing a deck with a popular structure—78 cards, 22 trumps, and 56 Minor Arcana cards—takes advantage of a balanced, time-tested system of meanings. Decks with more or fewer cards depart from this system, and, in these cases, you must determine whether the author's changes suit your purposes.

Many decks sold as Tarot cards are not, in fact, Tarot decks at all. *Soul Cards*—a collection of evocative, primal paintings sold as a deck of cards—present intriguing artwork, but lack Tarot's structure and symbolism. You may also see *Angel Meditation Cards* and other decks which, while personally appealing, may have limited application when used with the exercises in this book or deployed in a business setting.

In my experience, the structure and balance of a seventy-eight card Tarot deck offers significant value.

Summary: Chapter Two in a Nutshell

IF YOU CAN LOOK at pictures and associate them with aspects of your situation, you're ready to start *Putting the Tarot to Work*. Even so, knowing more about the history, structure, meaning, and symbolism of the cards enhances your ability to make important connections and achieve new insights. Spreads—structured layouts with specific meaning assigned to each card position—provide additional opportunities to relate the cards to the issue under consideration, as do reversals.

When selecting cards for business use, select a deck with artwork appropriate for your group. Think twice before adopting decks with keywords or help text that may place limits on your creativity, or that depart from the time-tested seventy-eight card structure common to many Tarot decks.

CHAPTER

All Hands on Deck!

Preview: What to Expect in Chapter Three

This chapter explores:

☞ Why "playing" with the cards is serious business

☞ How to play a series of games promoting imaginative interaction with the Tarot deck

☞ How to associate actions, attitudes, approaches, and ideas with the images found on Tarot cards

Encountering the Cards

ONE MORNING, YOUR BOSS stops by your desk. In his arms, he carries a stack of brightly colored boxes—new software packages, sealed with shrink-wrap.

He plops one on your desk. "We're requiring everyone in the office to learn to use this program. No money for training, so you're on your own!"

As he walks away, what do you do?

A few of you—and you know who you are!—tuck the box in a desk drawer and go on about your business.

Some of you methodically open the box, remove the CDs, place them to one side, inventory the various booklets and collateral material, and actually pause to read the "Read Me First" instructions printed on canary yellow paper. After following the installation instructions to the letter, you take the manual home and read each section. The next day, you step through the tutorials, in order.

Those of us who have lives, however, toss the in-box material to one side, slap the CD into the drive, step through the installation process on the fly, and plow ahead. We learn by tinkering and experimenting. We bring a real project to the table and explore how the program impacts its completion. Handed a new tool, we test it by putting it to work.

In my experience, people respond to brainstorming with Tarot cards the same way they respond to new software. Some people dismiss the potential benefits of using Tarot as a creative tool. If given a deck, they peek at a card or two, but ultimately stuff them in a drawer. Unable (or unwilling!) to see practical applications, they move on to other things.

Others—usually out of a need to be "right" or "correct"—seek out an authority (often, the first Tarot book they find). They spend a great deal of time reading, studying, and memorizing card meanings. They spend more time poring over a card's description in a book than they do exploring the card itself. After a period of initial excitement over the cards, these people some-times exhaust themselves. For some of them, the work involved in getting to know the sev-enty-eight cards and all their potential combinations becomes overwhelming.

Still others jump right in. Curious by nature, they unwrap the deck, fan out the cards, and start relating to the images and symbols right away. "Look at that hat! Why are some cups on this card turned over? What do these dogs mean? This picture reminds me of my mother! I tried to tell the future with these yesterday, and it didn't work!"

I understand the strategy of the first group—they need to understand the practical benefits of a tool before adopting it. I understand the motives of the second group—they want to know as much as possible about a new tool's potential before they "get behind the wheel."

Learning by Playing

I wish more people, however, understood the value of the approach the third group adopts—an approach rooted in "play." Anyone in business (especially business for themselves!) knows the importance of practicality and preparedness, but so few understand the value of play!

Experience convinced me: to get the most out of your first brainstorming sessions with Tarot, you have to play with the cards. That's right—*play*. Mix them up! Shuffle them! Look for cards that appeal to you. Try a game or two! My advice to all newcomers: set aside the rules, open your mind, and invest at least half an hour in creative play.

Corporate types in starched shirts resist this approach. "Who's got time for games? I'm here to start *Putting the Tarot to Work* . . . not to have recess!" I remind such people that games play a critical role in the learning process.

How do we teach children important basic concepts? We sing songs, we read light-hearted books, and we play games. How do cutting-edge corporate training programs presenting mis-sion-critical information? More and more frequently, through interactive games!

This chapter encourages you to approach visual brainstorming through creative play. Before you calculate the practical value of adopting Tarot as a creative tool, and before you memorize your first canned card meanings, I urge you to play at least three of the following games—by yourself or (preferably) in a group.

Note: While these games can be played with nonillustrated pips, they work best with decks featuring a picture on every card. If you happen to be working with a nonillustrated deck (a deck that shows, for example, nothing but four cups on the Four of Cups), I suggest using only the twenty-two trump and sixteen court cards when working with these exercises.

By design, the games in this chapter introduce the cards and illustrate their use. In addition to encouraging interaction and building familiarity, they teach critical brainstorming and creative techniques—and these have value, whether you choose to adopt the cards as a tool or not! In short, these games provide valuable creativity training, but package that training in the form of engaging entertainment.

Ready to start *Putting the Tarot to Work?* Then, for the moment, put your work away—and start playing cards!

The Games

The Movie Game

When people begin brainstorming with Tarot, they tend to shuffle, deal cards, turn them face up . . . and stare. Uncertain how to get started, they ask, "What's next?"

The Movie Game gives beginners something to do with the cards. Playing the game teaches players to look for details on the cards . . . but also to look for connections between the cards. (Both are valuable brainstorming skills!)

From a shuffled facedown deck, draw four cards. Turn them over as you draw them, placing them in a row. Explain the cards represent single frames of film, cut from a movie at half-hour intervals.

Ask the following questions, recording answers on a flip chart:

- What is the movie about?

- Who is the main character?

- Are there other characters?

- Does a character from one part of the movie appear in another?

- What happens in the opening scene? What is at risk?

- What kind of obstacle challenges the hero in Card Two?

- What kind of solution does the third card represent?

- How does the movie turn out?

- What's the title of the movie—and why?

- In the final analysis, is this a movie you would pay to see? Why or why not?

The Story Game

Like the Movie Game, the Story Game engages the imagination and urges players to explore relationships among the cards. It encourages beginning brainstormers to associate images from the cards with people, situations, or actions. It's also a lot of fun!

Select three cards from a shuffled, face-down deck. Place these in a row. Designate the first card as "The Beginning," the second card as "The Middle," and the third card as "The End."

Tell a story out loud, with the first card representing the setting—the situation as the story begins. The second card represents an incident or action that changes everything and turns the world upside down. The third card represents how the characters overcome the problem.

In groups, expand this game by allowing each person to draw a card and add to the progressive story. Alternatively, begin with a story, fable, fairy tale, or movie familiar to everyone in the group, build an outline of the main points of that story, and then pick out cards from a face-up deck that illustrate the points in the story outline.

The Name-Tag Game

The Name-Tag Game prompts players to associate specific card images with people, personalities, attitudes, or actions. It also encourages players to see themselves (or qualities or attitudes they possess) in the symbolism of each card.

Ask each person to draw a card, explaining that this card serves as a "name tag." In sequence, ask each participant to explain how his or her name can be connected with the image on the card. Connections need not be direct: McElroy, an Irish name, may suggest someone with red hair, which may connect with a red-haired figure on the card. This exercise works especially well as an icebreaker exercise in newly organized groups.

After this exercise, return the cards to a pile, drawing one occasionally and asking the group to identify the participant with whom this card is connected. Award bonus points if players recall the nature of the connection between the card and the participant's name.

When groups know each other well, change this game by drawing one card at random for each participant. Allow players to study the selections. After five minutes, ask players to associate each card with someone in the group and explain why that card describes that person.

Depending on the nature of the groups you work with, you may wish to remove "dark" or potentially upsetting cards from the deck before playing this game. (Not many people's ego can deal with being named "Death"!)

The Details Game

The Details Game explores the difference between "looking" and "seeing"—an important skill for visual brainstorming. The game requires players to go beyond immediate impressions and make more sophisticated associations.

Draw a card. Invite the group to catalog this card, identifying every possible concept contained within or associated with the card. To do this, ask questions like these:

- What's happening on this card? What has happened just before? What will happen next?

- What colors are present? What are these colors associated with? What do they remind you of? How are they used here?

- What objects or symbols are there? Where have you seen them before? What emotions, memories, or ideas are associated with these symbols?

- What people are on the card? Do they remind you of anyone? What about them suggests people you know? How are they different from people you know? How do the people on this card feel? What would they say, if given the chance? What advice would they offer? What warnings? What compliments? What career advice?

- What is the setting of this card? What is the time of day? What is the weather like? What temperature is it? What sounds would a person in this card hear? What smells might he or she notice?

- What physical materials would be used to build an authentic life-size replica of this card?

- What details are most likely to be overlooked at a glance?

Keep answers to these questions on a flip chart. If working with a group, divide into teams and award a prize for the group creating the longest list of associations.

The Interview Game

The Interview Game helps players begin to associate the wide range of Tarot images with familiar, everyday aspects of the workplace.

Draw between three and five cards. Imagine each card represents a candidate for an open job in your department. What qualities would this candidate offer? What strengths? What weaknesses? What skills? To what extent would this person make a good manager? A good team member? A good CEO? A good CFO?

How do you think this person would fit in with your team right now? What would this person bring to the team that's missing? What qualities does this person have that are already represented on your team?

Would you hire this person? Why or why not?

The Moments Game

The Moments Game enhances the players' abilities to make associations by reversing the usual process. Instead of moving from image to idea, players begin with ideas, then choose images that represent them. This game is especially good at helping new players learn to see cards in the context of a given situation—a critical skill when using the deck to generate solutions for specific business challenges.

Make a list of "moments." Some may be personal:

- going to the grocery store
- shopping at the mall
- attending church
- commuting
- riding the subway
- eating lunch at your desk
- watching television
- going to the movies

Some may be professional:

- being asked to produce too much in too little time
- layoffs
- bonuses
- promotions
- working with problematic employees
- struggling to meet an aggressive deadline

Spread the deck out, face-up, and choose cards capturing or representing these moments.

The Messaging Game

Beginning brainstormers quickly become skilled at spotting image details—colors, symbols, numbers, or objects—and associating these details with ideas, concepts, or memories. More sophisticated brainstorming, however, requires perceiving these details as a kind of coded language—a message the brainstormer must attempt to understand. The Messaging Game sharpens a player's ability to extract meaning from a series of images by asking the question, "What are these cards trying to say?"

Pretend that one day, all pagers stop working. All phones go permanently dead. For mysterious reasons, email disappears the moment you send it, never to be seen again.

Now imagine that sending Tarot cards becomes the only means of communicating with distant friends, family, and coworkers. Which cards send which messages?

If working with a group, ask someone to choose a card representing their day, or their romantic life, or their career, then pass that card to an uninformed person. How successfully does that person associate the card with the information the sender hoped to express?

Invite all participants to explain what led them to their choices and interpretations.

The Résumé Game

In addition to helping players associate images with work-related concepts, this game aids players in associating visible images with invisible emotions and states of mind. Brainstormers who learn this valuable skill go beyond the obvious connections, making larger intuitive leaps as a result.

Invite each person in the group to write down a list of every job he or she has ever held. For each job, participants should choose two Tarot cards: one to represent the job, and one to illustrate how the participant felt about that job. (In some cases, one card can represent both ideas!)

Invite other members of the group to examine the cards, allowing them to guess the occupation and define its emotional impact.

The Org Chart Game

An important part of brainstorming is learning to associate card images with people (or with the attitudes, approaches, and actions of people). Players who learn to do this will make better, faster connections between cards in a spread and real-life "players" in a business challenge.

Build your company's organizational chart, from the CEO, down through his or her direct reports, to theirs, to you. Select a card to represent each person on the chart, using meanings in the back of this book or your impressions of what each card might mean.

Alternatively, use this same exercise to build a Tarot "family portrait," selecting a card to represent each member of your work group, team, or department.

If working alone, you might also choose a card depicting your relationship or feelings toward each person in the diagram.

The Goals Game

This game aids players in linking visual images with activities and strategies—important, since most brainstorming sessions are designed to suggest both!

Perhaps the worst interview question in the world is: "What do you want to be doing five years from now?" Even so . . . what *do* you want to be doing five years from now? Can you locate a card that describes where your career will take you in half a decade?

Find a second card representing your strategy—what you will do to attain your five-year goal. What strategy does the card represent?

Summary: Chapter Three in a Nutshell

"PLAYING" WITH SOFTWARE—CLICKING menus, tweaking settings, experimenting with options—can be a very effective way to learn practical applications of new programs. In the same way, playing with Tarot cards familiarizes you with their content and prepares you to use them effectively as a brainstorming tool. The games in this chapter encourage players to interact with the images on the cards. By linking the images to real-world actions, attitudes, and approaches, these games expand a player's ability to associate images with meaningful ideas.

CHAPTER

Making Sense of the Message

Preview: What to Expect in Chapter Four

This chapter explores:

☞ How to prepare for a brainstorming session

☞ How to phrase questions for effective brainstorming sessions

☞ How to select a layout, or spread, for the cards

☞ How to shuffle, cut, and deal the cards

☞ How to pull messages, meanings, and ideas from the images on the cards

Making Meaning

CURIOUS ABOUT THE HABITS of our company's most successful sales reps, my boss assigned me the responsibility to develop, implement, and analyze a "Survey of Sales Force Excellence." Developing the survey took several days; delivering it to reps across the country took several more.

During that time, my boss would stick his head in the door and ask, "Is it done yet?" at least once a day. Finally, on the day the last survey form returned to my office for processing, my boss appeared, asking to review the results.

"I plugged the raw data into a spreadsheet," I said. "But I haven't done any analysis."

"I can't stand the wait!" my boss said. "Let me see what you have so far!"

I pulled up the spreadsheet. My boss scanned the neat columns of figures, squinting and nodding. "Lots of numbers here," he said. He pointed to a group of fives. "Does that mean something? That doesn't look good to me."

"You have to be careful not to draw conclusions based on a few numbers," I explained. I went on to talk about standard deviations and correlations, margins of error and skew.

My boss shook his head, disappointed and frustrated. He knew the numbers on the screen told a story and contained a message, but lacked any means of making sense of that message.

Many beginning brainstormers experience the same issues with Tarot images. Vaguely aware the cards can be used to answer questions or explore ideas, they shuffle the deck and arrange it into little piles. They choose one card, and then another, and then another. They squint at the symbols and pictures. "Ah," they say, "A Death card. This can't be good."

They know the cards on the table contain a message, but they lack any means of making sense of that message.

Learning to Read

This process of extracting meaning or messages from the Tarot is called "reading the cards." In addition to the playful exercises offered in chapter 3, this chapter offers a more structured approach to the entire process of card reading. Designed to be followed step by step, the process in this chapter can be used by anyone—including those with little or no experience using Tarot—as a brainstorming tool.

Until your own reading style evolves, this simple method provides you a window on the process. But be prepared: once you learn to read the cards, what used to look like a line of vague images printed on rectangles of cardboard suddenly becomes a billboard emblazoned with a message just for you!

Most people's idea of Tarot reading comes from watching a telephone psychic with a kerchief on her head flip rapidly through a deck. In almost every case, no matter what cards appear, she extracts one message: "Honey! Dat man is cheatin' on ya!"

Don't let television psychics set your expectations! Solving corporate problems and brainstorming creative solutions requires neither kerchiefs nor fake Jamaican accents. Instead, I suggest you follow these seven simple steps for extracting meaning from the cards:

> *Step One:* Prepare for the Reading
>
> *Step Two:* Phrase a Question
>
> *Step Three:* Select a Spread
>
> *Step Four:* Shuffle the Deck
>
> *Step Five:* Cut the Cards
>
> *Step Six:* Deal the Cards
>
> *Step Seven:* Interpret the Message

Step One: Prepare for the Reading

Any successful effort—from an effective business meeting to an efficient project plan—requires preparation. Brainstomring sessions with the Tarot are no exception to this rule. But how do you prepare for such a session?

Many books about Tarot describe elaborate rituals, like the one suggested in a Tarot book I read years ago: "Light a red or white candle, and open all doors and windows. Lift the cards carefully by their edges, placing them gently on a table made of wood, stone, glass, or some other natural element so their vibrations will be untainted." Other books teach new decks must be blessed, balanced, or cleansed (usually by rubbing them with sea salt or passing the cards through sweet-smelling smoke).

If one of these rituals puts you in a creative frame of mind, go for it! In most cases, though, complex rituals involving candles and incense strike me as inappropriate in business settings. (They're probably against office fire codes, too!) In their place, I recommend this very practical five-step "ritual" essentially, the same preparations you should make before launching any creative session: limit distractions, suspend the inner critic, think quantity, not quality, set a time limit for the work, and encourage creativity.

Limit Distractions

A little-known fact: phones and pagers emit electronic signals that disrupt the cosmic Tarot Information Field!

Or . . . maybe not. But these electronic signals (also called "rings" and "beeps" and "alerts") do disrupt the focus and attention of everyone in a creative session. A single phone call or page shatters an entire group's concentration and creative flow.

To enhance the quality of your results and boost productivity, limit distractions. Close the door. Transfer phones to voice mail. Turn off pagers and cell phones—even if you work for a pager or cell phone company!

Suspend the Inner Critic

Some people make light of the Inner Child Tarot, a deck using images from fairy tales, claiming its imagery is too positive, warm, and fuzzy to be useful. In many business meetings over the years, my more pessimistic coworkers have inspired me to envision a deck embodying the opposite extreme, capturing their nay-saying and negativity in a deck I'd call the Inner Critic Tarot!

The Inner Critic slams the door on creativity by analyzing, editing, or critiquing creative output. Express an idea, and those in touch with their Inner Critic say, "We've done that before," or "That'll never work," or, "That's too expensive."

The Inner Critic makes valuable contributions when the time comes to refine or refocus ideas. During the creative process, though, you must repress him at all costs. After all, bizarre, silly, or impractical ideas often inspire valuable, serious, and practical solutions later on.

Think Quantity, Not Quality

Remember those television psychics? They burn through those cards as fast as they can, calling out associations and impressions as quickly as possible. While I question their sincerity (and fashion sense), I admit their method offers an advantage: one fake Jamaican "shaman" serves up more ideas in five minutes than some people generate in hours!

In a creativity session, fling associations and sling ideas just as fast as you can. Instead of trying to come up with The Idea, pretend the company pays $500 for every idea, whether it's good, bad, useful, dangerous, or insane. When working with a group, use the theme "Fifty Ideas in Fifteen Minutes" to set an aggressive target and reinforce the concept of quantity over quality.

Tip: unless your team includes someone very quick with a keyboard or proficient with a pen, consider tape recording your sessions. (Nothing stifles creativity faster than a slowpoke at the flip chart.) The team can transcribe the recording later, preserving every precious idea!

Set a Time Limit for the Work

Everyone panics when the Death card (Trump 13) appears in a reading. Despite its name, the Death card really only reminds us of a reassuring fact of life: namely, that all things (including, thankfully, those excruciating meetings with Mr. Monotone from Information Services) must come to an end.

With this lesson in mind, always schedule a maximum time limit for any creative session. Scheduling an open-ended session risks ending the meeting on a low note, when ideas and energy have fizzled out. In my experience, a thirty-minute session works well.

The time limit also adds a sense of urgency to your work, prompting participants to pick up the pace as the end of the session draws near. When on a roll, the group can always vote to extend the session another fifteen minutes.

Encourage Creativity

Corporations claim to value creative thinking, but in practice discourage it. Management dismisses people with new ideas or alternative methods, calling them "upstarts" or "kooks." In the meantime, brown-nosers who regurgitate the same old ideas fly up the corporate ladder.

The result? Many business people back away from creativity. When *Putting the Tarot to Work,* you affirm the value placed on creativity. Reinforce that message with the following rewards:

- Offer pre-printed certificates for various kinds of ideas: the wackiest idea, the idea most likely to succeed, the idea requiring the most inventive use of ketchup, the most practical idea, the least practical idea, the Little Idea that Could, etc.

- Review earlier sessions, showing how creative approaches produced real world solutions.

- Illustrate respect for unbridled creativity by tossing in wacky and unrealistic ideas without hesitation.

- Fill a sterile conference room with objects designed to appeal to the senses: a bowl of mints, a set of rainbow-colored spring toys, intriguing photographs, a table-top fountain, a board game, or even several decks of Tarot cards. Put a sign on the door transforming the conference room into a Creativity Center.

- Start with a simple creative game: free association. Draw a few cards and ask people to tell a story about what they see. Relate the cards together in some way, making them frames from a movie or chapters in a book. Reward early efforts, then reveal a larger prize for the most creative idea.

Step Two: Phrase a Question

With the creative juices flowing, the most important step in the reading process begins: phrasing your question.

Thoughtful questions produce clear answers. Imprecise questions produce vague answers. Your degree of success with Tarot as a creativity tool hinges on developing effective questions.

To create the most effective question possible, always be specific, focus on personal responsibility, write your question down, and be aware of the many types of questions at your disposal.

Be Specific

I once participated in a problem-solving session in which a management team asked twenty people, "What's going on with our company right now?" The group's vague, unfocused answers surprised management. Given the question, what did they expect?

The management team started with a broad question designed to hide their real concern. Revising for precision requires honesty and introspection. They should have asked a question addressing what was on their minds: "Why is our stock value falling so rapidly?" An even better question might even be: "What will drive the stock price up again?"

Specific questions require more work and candor to author, but offer far more potential for meaningful exploration.

Take Personal Responsibility

"What can increase the value of our stock?" fails to address a critical issue: not everything impacting stock prices falls within a company's control.

The best questions acknowledge this by focusing on personal responsibility. After all, the only things you can control . . . are the things you can control! With this in mind, we can refine and expand the question even further:

"What can *each person* here do to increase the value of our stock?"

"What can *management* do to increase the value of our stock?"

"What can *Marketing* do to increase the value of our stock?"

"What can *Training* do to increase the value of our stock?"

"What can *Sales* do to increase the value of our stock?"

Whenever possible, relate the question back to what you control. The resulting answer reinforces the role of personal responsibility in creating successful outcomes.

Write the Question Down

Writing down your question crystallizes your idea. Frequently, discussing the meaning of various cards leads the group in several directions at once. The conversation wanders. People begin working on one issue, and wind up talking about another.

A written question gives your discussion context. When minds wander—and they will!—the written question becomes a creative lifeline, reminding group members to channel their attention back toward the subject under consideration.

Consider Many Types of Questions

Four general types of questions come up again and again in corporate problem-solving sessions: 1) Yes/No; 2) Information Questions; 3) Process Questions; and 4) "What If?" Questions.

Yes/No Questions. Remember the Magic 8-Ball? Ask a question, shake the ball, and, the answer emerges from the murky depths: Yes! No! Ask again later! If you limit your work with the Tarot to Yes/No questions, you might as well buy a Magic 8-Ball (or save the money and just flip a coin!).

Asking Yes/No questions abdicates all responsibility for the future. Asking the Tarot "Should I leave my job?" puts your career at the mercy of seventy-eight pieces of laminated cardboard. How empowering is that?

Answers to Yes/No questions also offer limited value. Imagine asking, "Will this project be successful?" What if the answer is yes? Should the team simply kick back, do no work, and wait for success to come? What if the answer is no? Should everyone quit?

I suggest you revise Yes/No questions into open-ended inquiries. Some examples:

"Will this project be successful?"

- How can we maximize the success of this project?

- What portions of this project are critical to its success?

- What kind of environment should we create to ensure the success of this project?

- Who plays a role in the success of this project?

- What factors influence the success of this project?

"Should I take this new job?"

- Why does this new job appeal to me?

- What benefits does this new job offer?

- What benefits are associated with my old job?

- How can I know whether this new job is the right one for me?

- What will help me decide which job is the best one for me at this point in time?

- What kinds of questions should I be asking about this new job possibility?

"Will I be laid off tomorrow?"

- What thinking guides the selection of people being laid off?

- What can I do to maximize my chances of keeping my job?

- How can I set aside my fears of layoffs and focus on my work?

- What will be the outcome of all these layoffs? How will the layoffs impact me, personally?

Note how the above questions empower the person asking them. Instead of generating pat answers, they open doors to new thoughts, ideas, and approaches.

Is a Yes/No question the first inquiry that comes to mind? Revise it into an open-ended question, and watch doors open to new ideas and approaches!

Information Questions. Corporate problem solving usually begins with an information safari. A problem-solving team interviews subject-matter experts, gathers documentation, and organizes research efforts to define what can be known. This process broadens perspective—a good thing, since what you don't know *can* hurt you!

Information questions request or examine information, encouraging participants to challenge their assumptions. They begin with the words reporters use most: Who? What? When? Where? Why?

These kinds of questions can be particularly valuable when planning a project. What have we overlooked? What influences are we unaware of? What aspects of this situation are we blind to? Who benefits from this arrangement? What does this information mean? What pieces of the puzzle are we missing?

Want to probe for blind spots and eliminate assumptions? Ask information questions!

Process Questions. Process questions begin with the words "How do I?" or "How can we?" These questions examine what needs to be done and explore a way to do it.

When companies pay high-priced consultants to perform a gap analysis, they're hiring people to make observations and ask process questions: "The company is here. The company wants to be over there. How can we get from A to B?"

On my thirty-fifth birthday, I paused to take a look at my career satisfaction. My goal, all my life, has been to be a writer. Had I reached the goal?

I was doing a lot of writing: scripts, presentations, storyboards, speeches for CEOs. I had written a great deal of documentation, step-by-step instructions and other kinds of technical material. I made a comfortable salary.

But where were the books I dreamed of writing? The non-fiction books on subjects that excited me? The novels I planned to write?

My dream remained unfulfilled. So how could I get from here (the present, which was pleasant enough, but not what I had hoped) to over there (the future I wanted)? What steps should I take? What actions, taken each day, would move me closer to my goal?

I asked a process question: "How can I get from where I am to the future I want?" That brainstorming session changed my life—and led to my writing the book you're reading now!

Need to get from Point A to Point B? Ask a process question.

"What If?" Questions. "What If?" questions explore multiple choices, drawing cards to represent options known and unknown.

If you're faced with multiple choices, use a What If? question to explore options, drawing a card for each option. You may also want to draw a card to represent one or more options you haven't considered, and allow the cards to give you ideas for new directions or innovations you didn't generate on your own.

What If? questions allow you to experiment with options before taking action. Want to explore possible futures without risk? Use the Tarot to answer your own What If? questions!

Step Three: Select a Spread

With your question firmly in mind, select a spread or layout with appropriate structure and balance. When generating answers and ideas with Tarot cards, selecting the right spread makes all the difference. With time, you'll design and develop your own spreads. To start off, however, you may find the following spreads useful.

One-Card Spread

Best for beginners, the one-card spread consists of exactly what the title implies: one card, drawn from the deck and placed face up on the table. This spread offers little when examining how things change over time, or when examining a situation from multiple perspectives. The one-card spread is perfect, though, for focusing thoughts and generating quick solutions.

What should be the goal of this meeting? Draw a card. What question should I remember to ask in this interview? Draw a card. What can I do to make this situation resolve itself quickly? Draw a card. When you need to isolate a key piece of information, the one-card spread is hard to beat.

In her book, *Learning the Tarot,* Joan Bunning suggests a variation of this spread: the Card of the Day. Especially helpful for beginners, Card of the Day involves drawing one card in the morning, then watching for that card's influence throughout the day. What events, incidents, or encounters reflect the meaning of your card?

Yes If and No If

While "yes and no" questions are best left to coin-tosses and Magic 8-Balls, the Yes-If and No-If spread makes it possible to consider these questions without giving up your responsibility to make good choices.

After framing your yes or no question ("Will I get a raise this year?"), select two cards, designating one as a "yes-if" answer, and the other as a "no-if" answer. Use the "yes-if" card to explore strategies for increasing your chances of getting a raise. Use the "no-if" card to explore attitudes or actions to avoid (because they don't help you reach your goal).

The Crux of the Problem

So many situations in life result from the collision of opposing forces. Our ideals collide with our desires, our dreams disrupt our intentions, or our goals conflict with the agenda of another coworker or our manager.

The Crux spread represents a crossroads made of cards: one card crossed by another, so the two cards resemble a plus sign. This simple spread can yield profound insight into the nature of a problem—the factors coming together to create and perpetuate a situation.

Sales in a slump? Try the Crux spread—you might receive the Seven of Cups and the Five of Coins, and understand that your situation has been created by your having been guided by fantasies and rosy outlooks instead of the cold, hard, financial facts.

Past, Present, Future

Often, conquering a challenge requires insight into how a situation has changed over time. What happened before? How does that influence what's happening now? What will happen if things go on, undisturbed and unattended?

The three-card Past, Present, Future Spread helps you answer these questions. Draw three cards, and place them in a line from left to right. The card to the left represents the past, the card in the center represents the present, and the card on the right represents the future.

If you already know the past or the present, the cards appearing in these positions may surprise you, as they tend to be photographs of events you've observed. If the cards in these positions seem entirely divorced from what you know, this as a tip that you need to re-examine the situation from a new perspective.

Don't like the future portrayed in the future card? Keep in mind this card represents how the future plays out without action on your part. Your actions could change the future! Let the cards prompt new ideas and new approaches.

Step Four: Shuffle the Cards

With preparations complete, a question selected, and a spread mapped out, shuffle the cards. Shuffling randomizes the cards, but also provides an opportunity to focus on your question. For me, shuffling takes on a zen-like quality. The sound, the tactile feedback, and the repetitive nature of the process clear my mind.

I shuffle Tarot cards the same way I shuffle playing cards: I split the deck in two, then riffle the two halves of the deck together. Doing this ten to twelve times completely randomizes the deck.

Others feel this shuffling method damages or bends the cards, so they use the "finger-painting method"—spreading the cards into one large mass, swishing them around, then squaring up the deck.

Step Five: Cut the Cards

Cutting the cards further randomizes them. In addition, cutting reassures others that the deck has not been "stacked" to produce certain cards.

As you start *Putting the Tarot to Work*, you will notice an uncanny connection between the content of your question and the images on the cards. Others will notice this, too, and may suspect you of manipulating the deck. Allowing others to cut the cards relieves this fear, and allows others to participate in the randomization process.

Even when working alone, I cut the cards. For me, cutting defines the transition from shuffling to dealing.

Step Six: Deal the Cards

As you deal the cards, you must decide two things:

- Do you deal the cards face up or face down?
- How do you deal with reversals, or "upside-down" cards?

Face Up or Face Down?

Some people enjoy the drama of face-down cards. The hidden information generates tension and anticipation. The act of flipping the card over focuses attention. When using a multi-card spread, turning the cards over one-by-one marks your progress through the reading.

Others prefer to deal all cards face-up. Revealing the cards makes exploring their relationships easier. When all cards are face-up, people notice details—"See how that man on that card seems to be pointing to the door on the other card?"—they wouldn't notice otherwise.

In my opinion, face-up cards encourage people to consider more holistic answers. You should choose the approach, however, that works best for you.

Reversals

People handle reversals in one of two ways: they ignore them, or they assign meaning to them. Most beginning readers ignore them. Faced with an upside-down card, the dealer simply turns it right-side up.

A few readers believe reversals literally reverse the meaning of a card. An upside-down Devil, instead of suggesting bondage, addiction, or selfishness, might indicate freedom, recovery, or generosity.

Others assert an upside-down card suggests something blocks or represses the qualities associated with that card. An upside-down Sun card, for example, might suggest that you want to be happy and joyful, but something prevents you from expressing that joy.

As a beginner—and, frequently, in group sessions—I ignore reversals. In my private practice with the cards, I use them. What you decide to do with reversals is up to you—just make up your mind before you see the cards. Anyone who sees a few upside-down "negative cards" and suddenly embraces reversals to make those into "positive cards" is cheating!

For more ideas about creative ways to use reversed cards, see Mary K. Greer's *Tarot Reversals* (Llewellyn, 2002). While not written from a business perspective, the approaches to working with reversed cards are easily adapted for the brainstorming process.

Step Seven: Interpret the Message

Remember my boss and the spreadsheet? Motivated by an eagerness for answers, he approached my computer and delved into the raw data. The longer he stared at those figures on the screen, the more frustrated he became. He knew the information he wanted lurked in those rows and columns of digits. He simply lacked a method for interpreting the message.

With the cards shuffled, cut, and dealt into a spread, the time comes to interpret the meaning of the images on the table. Some people do this quite naturally. Others don't.

Chris, a bright, athletic man in his early forties, expressed curiosity in my methods and wanted insight into his career. We phrased a question, shuffled and cut the *Osho Zen Tarot*, and dealt the cards into a simple spread.

Chris looked at the images, looked at me, and asked, "Now what?"

I gestured to the spread. "Which of the cards stand out to you? Do any draw your attention?"

Chris scanned the line of cards again. "Not really, no."

I shrugged. "Let's start with the first one, then: Stress. What does it suggest to you?"

"That I'm stressed?" Chris asked.

I nodded. "Are you?"

Chris rolled his eyes. "Isn't everyone?"

"But this card doesn't turn up for everyone," I explained. "It did turn up for you. What role does stress play in your life right now?"

"You're the fortune teller," Chris said. "You tell me."

"I'm *not* a fortune teller . . . and this isn't a guessing game," I explained. "I'm not trying to shock or surprise you with what I can reveal about your life. Instead of telling you what the cards mean, my role is to help you explore what they mean to you. What do you see on the card?"

Chris frowned. "A man."

"What do you notice about the man?"

"He's on a card."

This went on for twenty painful minutes. Like many in the corporate world, Chris has been conditioned to think exclusively in linear, logical, or informational mode. As a result, he neglects his ability to make associations and think on an intuitive level.

Exercise: Looking, Seeing, Associating

Fortunately, most of us aren't as creatively challenged as Chris. Even so, almost everyone who brainstorms with Tarot cards recalls at least one time when the ideas and associations refused to flow. When I find myself combating "brain freeze," I revert to a set of simple, but often neglected, skills: looking, seeing, and associating.

This exercise, designed to jumpstart the brainstorming process, asks you to look at a card, write down what you see, and associate those observations with memories, ideas, and information. I've chosen a card for you at random—in this case, the Eight of Vessels from one of my favorite decks, Robert Place's *Alchemical Tarot*, at left.

Look closely. What attracts your attention? What associations spring to mind? I invite you to invest ten minutes exploring the card, listing every object, symbol, or image you notice. When you're done, take an additional five minutes to list at least one association for each object, symbol or image. Here's one to get you started:

Object, Symbol, or Image	Association
A man making pottery . . .	. . . God. ("Thou are the potter, I am the clay.")

Eight of Vessels—
Alchemical Tarot

My own list of associations appears in the table on the following page. Put the book down now, make your own list, and then compare it to mine. No fair peeking!

Just out of curiosity: did you stop and make your own list, or did you move immediately to mine? If you didn't make your own list, you might ask yourself why. After all, if you're motivated enough to read this material, why aren't you motivated enough to put it into practice?

Consider this question carefully, since your success with the Tarot corresponds directly with your ability to link information with action. The more details you notice, the more associations you generate—and the more opportunities you create for insight and creative thinking.

Other Strategies for Making Meaning

When you use Tarot to brainstorm answers to your questions, dealing cards from the deck presents you with a series of images and symbols. Reading the cards is really nothing more than allowing the images to prompt associations and ideas.

Object, Symbol, or Image	Associations
A man making pottery	God. ("Thou art the potter, I am the clay.")
Unused clay	Potential, resources, raw material, mankind, children (who remain impressionable).
Clay vessels of different shapes and sizes	Previously completed work. Different tools are needed for different purposes. Different people have different needs. Offering customers a choice. Value of trying different ideas until you get the right one. If at first you don't succeed, try and try again.
The alchemical symbol for water	Changing, shifting, emotions, feelings, ideas, refreshment.
Another symbol I don't recognize	Infinity? Personal infinity? The unlimited range of choices we make every day? The unknown? Information we can't use because we don't fully understand it?
A pot being formed on the wheel	The moment a goal or idea becomes a reality, our achievement may be very different from our plan. Work. The necessary drudgery of work.
The potter's red cap	Red equals stop. Anger. Dissatisfaction. Embarrassment. Who else wears a red cap? Santa Claus.
The expression on the potter's face	Disappointment. Boredom. Work being productive, but not satisfying.
The fact the potter is alone and isolated	Sometimes, to get work done, you have to withdraw. Being good at what you do can make you feel isolated and alone—or make others jealous, who might then exclude you. Perhaps he expected others to appreciate his work, but it has only alienated them. Maybe he wishes he could work in a group.
The fact the potter faces the corner	Suggests punishment.

But, if you lack an innate ability to intuit the meaning of the resulting message, don't despair. Almost anyone can learn to interpret a spread using the following methods: 1) Describing; 2) Associating; 3) Personalizing; 4) Dramatizing; and 5) Referencing.

Describing

Especially when confronting Tarot cards for the first time, some people sit and stare, uncertain how to proceed. Both in her book *Tarot Mirrors* and on her website, Mary K. Greer stresses the value of describing the card aloud, as though speaking to someone who cannot see it.

Describing the card ("I see a woman. She carries two vases or urns. She kneels beside a stream at night. She pours water from one of the urns into the water.") breaks the silence and starts the brainstorming process.

Greer takes this even further, suggesting that participants write or record their descriptions, then rework them into the first person: "I am a woman. I carry two vases or urns. I kneel beside a stream at night. I pour water from one of the urns into the stream."

I assign tremendous importance to the process of describing the cards, especially when reading from a deck rich with symbols and images. If I've taken time to phrase and focus on my question, the elements I notice first almost always become the seed of the idea I need!

If you need some questions to help you get started describing the card, try these:

- What is the name of the card?

- What number is associated with the card? What suit? What keywords or titles?

- Who or what is on this card?

- If a person, how is this person dressed?

- What is this person doing? What activity does the card represent?

- What is the setting? Where does the action take place?

- What colors stand out?

- What are the most important elements or symbols on the card?

- Why do these elements or symbols seem more important than others?

Associating

Association links one idea with another. Over the course of years, we build up deeply personal associations with every object we encounter. Take a pocket watch for example. To one person, the pocket watch suggests nothing more than the obvious: a way to keep track of time. To another, the watch recalls a grandfather who used to carry a similar timepiece. To someone else, the watch symbolizes the approach of retirement.

For each object on the card, ask yourself, "What ideas connect to or are suggested by this object?" Some associations you make may feel entirely disconnected from the question under consideration at the time. Go with it! Exploring these unexpected associations sparks new ideas!

Use these questions to explore associations for each element on the card:

- In what places have you encountered this object? Where are these objects found?

- What memories do you have about objects like these?

- Does the object or person on the card remind you of someone? Who? Why?

- Do you connect the object with an event? With a special place or time?

- Can this object be used to perform work? Have you performed a task with an object like this one? What were the circumstances? How did you feel about the work? What was the outcome?

- Imagine this picture is meant to call up a memory of some kind. What memory would it point to from your own experience? What was the situation?

- What kind of objects or tools that you work with on a daily basis are like the objects or tools seen on this card? What kind of work do you do with them?

Personalizing

When you personalize the card, you imagine that the people or beings on the card are real. You use your imagination to explore what the beings on a card think or feel, in an attempt to identify or empathize with them in some way.

Some questions to get you started:

- What is the person or being on this card thinking or feeling? What makes you think so?

- Why does the person on the card feel that way?

- If no one is on the card, what would a person arriving here think or feel upon arrival? If you walked into the scene, what would you think or feel?

- What advice would you give to the person on this card? What advice about your situation would this person give you?

- If the person on this card could speak, what would the person say about your question or concern? Why would he or she say that?

- Do you deal with people on a regular basis who are like the people on this card? When do you encounter these people? How do you feel about them? What kinds of thoughts or actions are associated with these people?

Dramatizing

Dramatizing involves telling the story of a card. Using your imagination, you work to determine the events before and after the moment depicted on the card.

The following questions can help you dramatize a card:

- What kind of place is suggested by the environment of the card? Have you been to this kind of place? What happened there?

- What's happening on this card, right now?

- What events led up to the event depicted on the card?

- Imagine this card can be set in motion. What will happen in the next several minutes?

- How would an audience feel as they watched this scene being performed on stage or on screen?

- What could have been done in the past to prevent the event depicted on this card?

- What can be done in the future to prevent the event on this card from happening again?

- In what way could the event on this card be depicted as good or profitable?

- In what way might the event on this card be bad or negative?

- Does this card present the beginning, middle, or end of a story? How can you tell?

Referencing

After generating your own intuitive meanings for each card in the spread, you might also want to investigate other meanings. The "little white book"—or, these days, the full-color glossy book—included with each deck often defines what a given card meant to its designer. A good Tarot dictionary (I use Sandra Thompson's *Pictures from the Heart*) suggests dozens of traditional meanings for each card. Appendix A, a table of business-related meanings in the back of this book, may also prove helpful.

When the meaning of any card in your spread escapes you . . . look it up!

Summary: Chapter Four in a Nutshell

READING THE CARDS—ESSENTIALLY, extracting meaning from the images you draw from the deck—is the first step in effective brainstorming.

Before using the cards as part of a creativity session or problem-solving exercise, prepare yourself and the space around you by limiting distractions. Choose your question carefully, being as specific as possible. Select a spread—a layout for the cards—that connects to your question in some way. Then, after shuffling and cutting the deck, deal the cards into the spread and interpret their meaning by exploring the content of each card and linking your associations together. This simple method facilitates the process of connecting your question with the cards in front of you.

CHAPTER

Basic Brainstorming with the Tarot

Preview: What to Expect in Chapter Five

This chapter explores:

☞ How to use a single card to generate dozens of insights and solutions

☞ How to enhance your brainstorming ability by making just one association per card

☞ How to use twenty-two cards from a Tarot deck to generate twenty-two solutions in ten minutes or less

Living What You've Learned

IF YOU'VE READ THE first four chapters, you're now familiar with the basic structure of a Tarot deck. You've played several games designed to enhance your creative thinking skills, and you've learned how to associate the numbers, colors, images, and symbols on a Tarot card with situations, actions, and ideas in your every day world of work.

With that experience under your belt—it's time to start *Putting the Tarot to Work!*

This chapter offers you three simple—but powerful—brainstorming strategies. These three strategies are flexible—they can be tailored for use in any situation. They are powerful, allowing you to generate dozens of ideas in minutes. Best of all, they're easy to use—so easy, in fact, you can use them the minute you finish this chapter. With nothing but these techniques and a pack of seventy-eight Tarot cards, you'll be ready to surprise yourself and impress everyone else with your virtually unlimited creative reservoir!

A Tale of Two Sessions

The Official CEO Brainstorming Session

The executive boardroom buzzed with excitement. The CEO himself wanted a brainstorming session! Drooping pager sales meant the company needed fresh ideas for distributing its products.

Assistants brewed coffee, arranged flip charts, and placed platters of chalky miniature donuts in strategic locations. A secretary positioned blank sheets of paper and colored markers within reach of every seat. Members of the executive team filed in, clutching lists of ideas.

By reflex, all took their seats when the CEO sat at the head of the table and cleared his throat. "We have a four-hundred member nationwide sales force. We have distribution agreements with two major retail chains. We sell our product at trade shows, and our events van travels to all kinds of events, from college graduations to golf tournaments. Still, we need to sell more pagers. I've asked for your best ideas. Let's hear them."

Silence settled over the room. Finally, one senior executive spoke. "We could do more trade shows."

The CEO nodded. "Okay. Anything else?"

A second officer opened his leather-bound folder and placed it on the oak conference table. "Let's get more of those distribution agreements with more retail chains."

The CEO nodded harder. "Very good, very good. And?"

"We could make better use of the events van," suggested an executive in a starched shirt and conservative suit. "Take it more places."

By the end of the four-hour session, the meager contents of every flip chart in the room boiled down to this idea: *Let's do more of the same old thing.*

A Simple Game of Cards

The training team gathered around the cramped conference room table. Someone tacked a single sheet of flip-chart paper to the faded walls. Another member of the team fished a tin of mints from her purse and passed it around the room. The team leader shuffled a deck of worn, dog-eared cards and drew three:

Two of Swords   *Eight of Wands*   *King of Pentacles*

The group crowded close and stared at the cards. Seconds later, the team leader started a stopwatch and shouted: "Go!"

"Sales reps feel torn in two directions, like the woman on this card," Sharron said. "The company tells them to do one thing, but they're being pulled in another direction . . . I don't know. Their managers send mixed signals? They aren't being paid enough?"

"Or maybe they're paid too much," Dan pointed out. "They're like that king. Maybe the base pay is so high they don't need commissions. Or maybe the king is a manager—as long as he has one or two star players, he's sitting pretty. There's no need to get other reps up to speed."

Connie pointed to the Eight of Wands. "But this means change, that change is coming, or that something needs to change. What's changing?"

"The market, for one thing," Shane offered. "Everyone has pagers. The easy fruit's been picked. They can't milk existing accounts anymore. They need to be going after new customers."

"We need to look at everything that could change their behavior," Sharron said, nodding. "Their comp plans, the way they cold call . . ."

"How often they cold call," Connie said. "How many calls they make."

Dan picked up the King of Coins. "Look at this guy! He hasn't gotten out of that throne in ages. Maybe we'd see better results if managers got off their butts, got out into the field, and saw what's really going on."

"So we need ride-alongs with the reps," Sharron said. "Managers who actually go on the sales calls. Do they do that now?"

"That works with the Two," Shane noted. "Both sides—managers and reps—influence what's happening to sales. Both have to be involved in the solution. Both have to take action."

"What actions can they take together?" Dan asked. "What actions could they take if they would just take off their blindfolds and see them?"

"Wait!" Connie shouted. "What if one of these cards represents the sales reps, one represents management, and one represents what the problem really is? Which card would be which and why?"

Ten minutes later, the group leader called, "Time!" In a quarter-hour, the brainstorming team generated more than thirty fresh ideas for impacting sales force performance.

Advantages of Putting the Tarot to Work

Both groups contained bright people with good heads for business. Both groups wanted to solve a problem, and both groups used brainstorming to do so. The second group, though, approaches the problem with a playful, risk-taking spirit. Instead of worrying about impressing the boss, team members feel free to open the mental floodgates and allow ideas to flow. As a result, group two gets a lot more done . . . and their work has a much greater potential to impact the company's bottom line.

In addition to their freewheeling attitude, the training group also employed a tool the officers in the boardroom overlooked: the seventy-eight cards of the Tarot. While the first group tip-toed around their session impressing the CEO with safe revisions of his ideas, the second group used a deck of Tarot cards to open their imagination, generate fresh insights, and examine their issue from a variety of new perspectives.

Learn to integrate the following three strategies into your brainstorming process, and your creativity will quickly rival that of the training team. Once you start *Putting the Tarot to Work*, the ideas you generate could gain you the admiration of your team . . . and the attention of the crew in the boardroom, too!

Strategy One: The Single Card Draw

What to Do. With the situation, issue, or challenge in mind, draw a single card in answer to the question, "What do I need to know most about this issue?"

And yes—this strategy is really that simple.

If you're new to the process (or if the ideas don't come of their own accord), invest a minimum of five minutes studying the card. On one side of a sheet of paper, list all symbols, images, colors, numbers, titles, and details that catch your attention. When five minutes are up, spend an additional five minutes recording an association for each element in the list—what the symbol, image, color, number, title, or detail suggests to you. Still not satisfied? Try one (or all!) of the approaches outlined in chapter 4 (describing, associating, personalizing, dramatizing, or referencing).

When done, relate the observations you've made to your situation, issue, or challenge. Beginners frequently find answering the four questions below helps them make the leap from observation to application.

1. How does this card relate to my situation? Do the items on your list seem to be associated with a person who is involved with or influencing your situation? Could these items somehow connect with the development of the issue—how it evolved, or how it is progressing? Might they relate to factors within or outside your control which influence, create, disrupt, or cause your situation?

2. How does this card relate to actions surrounding my issue? Perhaps an item on your list will cause you to see a past action in a new light. Perhaps you'll be prompted to consider an alternative course of action you've overlooked. Or maybe you'll suddenly see a great reason to take an action you've already come up with. At the very least, ask yourself how some of your observations might translate into tasks on a "To Do" list!

3. How does this card suggest an approach to my issue? Could any items on your list suggest a new way to think about or evaluate your situation? Do any suggest a new perspective, or a new "take" on the issue? What would happen if you adopted an approach suggested by your brainstorming list? Might any of your ideas represent an approach to recommend? To avoid?

4. How does this card suggest an attitude or prejudice influencing this issue? What conclusions have you already drawn about this situation? Are there items on your list that connect with those conclusions or assumptions in some way? Do they challenge them? Reinforce them? How might items on your list represent conclusions or judgments others have made with regard to this situation?

Practicing the Single Card Draw

The Situation. After a sales contest proved very popular in June, management extended it into July, August, and September. June and July sales figures climbed fifteen percent. In August and September, however, sales figures fell dramatically.

Management admires your creative approach, so they ask you to come up with some ideas for them to consider. Why are sales sagging? Why isn't the contest inspiring the level of activity it did in June and July? What can be done to reverse the decline in sales?

The night before the meeting, you pull out your Tarot deck and prepare to brainstorm. You decide to use the Single Card Draw strategy. After shuffling and cutting the deck, you draw your old friend from the last chapter's listing exercise: the Eight of Cups.

With this card in hand, you turn to a list of questions management supplied:

1. What are some possible reasons for the decline in sales activity?

2. What are some things management could do to reverse the downward trend?

3. What can be done to change the way the organization thinks about the contest . . . or about sales in general?

4. What recommendations do you have?

Put down the book and use the list of associations you created in chapter 4 to generate possible answers for these four questions. When you're finished, compare your answers to the ideas I offer you below.

Some Possible Answers. Right off the bat: your answers will likely differ from mine . . . and that's fantastic! No two people brainstorm alike. (In fact, that's the reason why group brainstorming sessions produce such great results!) That said, please approach the answers below as examples or alternatives. Rather than use my answers as a grading key, compare our responses with an eye toward enhancing your own brainstorming ability.

When I did this exercise, I pulled out my list of associations from chapter 4. In general, I connected the images and symbols on the Eight of Cups with resources, raw material, trying a series of ideas in search of the "right" one, boredom, isolation, and the necessary drudgery of work. With these associations in mind, I gave myself a jump start by answering the four basic brainstorming questions from earlier in this chapter, capturing my results as a series of questions:

How does this card relate to my situation? What resource limitations might sales reps be facing? Where are the sales people getting the "raw material" (qualified leads, names of customers to call on) they needed? What would happen if management offered a series of exciting sales promotions instead of repeating the same one over and over? What are the steps in the sales cycle—the current sales routine—and how might they be modified or changed to reinvigorate sales?

How does this card relate to actions surrounding my issue? Could we do a survey to find out why the sales promotion was so successful in June and July? Could the same survey ask people "What changed?" Could we shake up the drudgery of day-to-day sales by having managers ride along with reps to observe their sales process first-hand? Could we combat isolation by pairing reps and allowing them to share best practices with each other? Would a mentoring program help weaker reps learn from stronger ones?

How does this card suggest an approach to my issue? Instead of evaluating performance in terms of final sales figures, could we evaluate each rep's skill with each step in the sales process (cold calling, presenting the sale, answering objections, asking for business, closing the sale)? How are leads evaluated—do we know we're sending reps to well-qualified potential customers? What do managers think caused the downward trend in sales? How would they recommend we correct it?

How does this card suggest an attitude or prejudice influencing this issue? What role does morale play in this situation? What factors influence morale? To what extent did we assume a "Band-Aid" like a sales promotion would fix a deeper, more complex problem? To what extent is senior management making decisions (like extending the sales contest) in isolation, without talking to the field?

Not a bad list, for five minutes' work! After I finished patting myself on the back, I took a second look at the list of questions management supplied:

What are some possible reasons for the decline in sales activity? I suspected a successful sales promotion had been extended to the point it was no longer effective. I also wondered how much time had passed since the skills of the reps themselves had been evaluated, and what procedures were in place for coaching those skills and sharing best practices. All of these factors could easily influence performance.

What are some things management could do to reverse the downward trend? Management could offer a new sales promotion, or rotate through a scheduled series of sales promotions, providing variety and adding an element of urgency ("Take advantage of this promotion . . . before it goes away!"). Perhaps more importantly, management could take a fresh look at every step in the sales process with an eye toward discovering the deficit most likely responsible for declining performance.

What can be done to change the way the organization thinks about the contest . . . or about sales in general? The figure on the card strikes me as bored (at best) or dissatisfied (at worst). He's also facing the corner, which suggests punishment. It struck me that management and sales may be too obsessed with promotion ("Time for a new sales contest!") and punishment ("Who's the one doing something wrong here?"), when, in fact, they should concentrate on skills.

What recommendations do you have? Based on this brainstorm, I would go to the management meeting and share these ideas:

- Discontinue the existing sales promotion (it isn't generating any excitement anyway).

- Talk to reps about the promotion—why it seemed to work at first, and why, ultimately, it no longer produced results.

- Rather than depend on the promotion of the month to boost sales, focus on skills. Involve managers in evaluating every step in the sales process: acquiring leads, cold calling, pitching the product, asking for the sale, and closing.

- When the managers discover an area of weakness, have them pair the challenged rep with someone stronger. Encourage them to ride along with and learn from each other. Once a week, talk with challenged reps to find out what they learned.

- Reward this period of introspection with a new, short-term promotion designed to inspire competition and excitement among the reps.

These insights are neither earth-shattering nor revolutionary. The important thing? I came up with many concrete, practical ideas in about ten minutes. Would I have reached the same conclusions if I had brainstormed without Tarot cards? Maybe. But I know from experience that, when I use the deck, I always generate more ideas in less time. Why spend hours racking my brain, when I can spend ten to fifteen minutes brainstorming with the Tarot—and achieve better results?

And what about your ideas? Maybe you came up with solutions like mine. Maybe we saw similar themes in the Eight of Cups, and generated similar answers. Or maybe your response produced a completely new solution I would never have imagined in a million years! That's the beauty of *Putting the Tarot to Work*—working with the cards prompts each of us to see our issues in a new and unexpected light.

Strategy Two: Speed Reading

What to Do. Earlier, I mentioned one TV psychic who zips through her Tarot cards as fast as she can. In fifteen seconds, she'll go through ten cards, smacking them into piles and making up a story as she goes. "King of Cups! You're seeing an older man, aren't ya? Three of Coins! It's lots of work maintaining that relationship, eh? But here's the Eight of Coins, which tells me you stick with him 'cause he's paying your bills! Here's what you don't know, baby: Queen of Wands! Dat old man's also seeing your sister!"

While we'll leave the discovery of twisted trysts to the TV psychics, the method employed here—moving rapidly through the deck, tossing out one quick association per card, then drawing the next card—makes for a powerful brainstorming strategy. Especially when the idea is to generate the maximum number of ideas in the least amount of time, the speed-reading technique becomes my method of choice.

Practicing the Speed Reading Strategy

The Situation. I recently participated in a conference call concerning the launch of a new product: a discounted, "all-distance" telephone service designed to allow anyone in the country to call any other U.S. resident at any time of day for one low monthly fee. The marketing employee leading the call asked, "With this product in mind, what are some things we can do to maximize this product's success?"

I produced a Tarot deck, shuffled, and quickly dealt five cards (see following page): the Eight of Wands, the Six of Cups, the Hanged Man, the Queen of Wands, and the Nine of Coins from the Universal Tarot.

Quick! Just as I did, glance at these cards, then reduce each one to a single-sentence recommendation. Say yours out loud or write them down . . . but don't peek at my answers until you generate your own!

Eight of Wands   *Six of Cups*   *Hanged Man*

Queen of Wands   *Nine of Coins*

Some Possible Answers. Glancing at each card, I noted keywords, possible meanings, number symbolism, and images. Right away, I made these associations:

- ***Eight of Wands:*** rapid change, big news, speed.
- ***Six of Cups:*** sharing, giving to others, buying and selling.
- ***Hanged Man:*** turning things upside down, learning from mistakes.
- ***Queen of Wands:*** for this card, I drew a blank.
- ***Nine of Coins:*** having everything needed, being rich, money.

So, when the call leader asked for my recommendations, I said, "Because this product makes a fundamental change in how people use their telephone, I think you can expect a lot of interest from the media—so I'd have media packs ready to mail to reporters well in advance of the launch. People who switch to the service will want to tell family and friends about it, so I'd put a form on the website that makes it easy to invite others to join.

"I know it's early, but it's never too early to anticipate what can go wrong—so someone needs to sit down and think of all the systems impacted by this product, from lead generation to final fulfillment, with an eye toward anticipating glitches and challenges."

For some reason, I got no ideas at all from the Queen of Wands. Rather than let this break my flow, I went right on to the Nine of Coins.

"The idea of getting both local and long distance service for one rate per month is so new and unusual, people will be suspicious as to whether or not the offer is really as good as it sounds. Sales reps should prepare to help customers understand this product gives them everything they need in one package. As usual, the sales pitch should focus on the money people will save . . . but when we call, we should be prepared with hard dollar figures that help customers understand just how much money this plan will save them each month."

The phone line fell silent.

"Could you run over those ideas again?" the marketing rep asked. "I wasn't able to write them all down!"

How about your ideas? Did your recommendations parallel mine, or were they entirely unique? If one of the cards stumped you (as the Queen of Wands did me), did you give up . . . or keep right on going?

When speed reading, the key to success is keeping the ideas flowing! Even if you run through all seventy-eight cards and produce only five ideas . . . you'll walk away with five ideas you didn't have before.

Strategy Three: WWTD?

What to Do. From any Tarot deck, remove the Fool and the twenty-one trumps. Put these cards in order from zero (the Fool) to twenty-one (the World), and arrange them on a table so you can see each one.

Think of each of these twenty-two cards as twenty-two advisors who have been there and done that in the business world. No matter how complex your issue or difficult your situation, know that these twenty-two advisors have dealt with it dozens of times in the past. Whatever the issue, these advisors each confronted it, wrestled with it, and earned themselves a fat, luxurious bonus check for conquering it. Each has a unique perspective; each took a different approach. All, however, were incredibly successful.

Your goal is to tap into this collective reservoir of hard-won wisdom and practical experience. To do this, you must examine your situation or question from the perspective of each of these twenty-two successful mentors. With your decision or situation in mind, you start with the Fool and work your way down the line, asking, "In this situation, what would _____ do?" In other words, you start by asking, "What would this Trump do?" (WWTD?) and conclude with "What would the World do?"

Ask this question with each trump in mind, and soon, you'll have twenty-two options for action. Some of these will be outrageous. Some will challenge your sense of ethics. Some will be brilliant . . . and some, positively obtuse. But of the twenty-two options, at least one is bound to surprise or inspire you.

Give yourself no more than thirty seconds per card, and go with the first course of action that pops into your head. Practice this technique, and in less than fifteen minutes, you can generate twenty-two different options for action in any situation! Best of all, once you become proficient with this brainstorming strategy, you won't need to have the actual cards in front of you. As a result, you can use this technique anytime, anywhere . . . and amaze people with your ability to come up with an apparently limitless stream of intriguing alternatives.

Practicing the WWTD Strategy

The Situation. A music retailer has increasing problems with shrinkage—losses due to shoplifting. Management encourages employees to watch the store more carefully, but the problem only worsens. With valuable tapes and CDs walking out of the store on a daily basis, the time comes to take corrective action. But . . . what to do?

Use the WWTD strategy to brainstorm twenty-two courses of action. Be serious. Be silly. Be inventive. Be creative. Be open to any idea, no matter how strange or bizarre. Remember the goal: twenty-two ideas, no matter how outrageous or absurd, in fifteen minutes or less.

If you're new to the cards and can't come up with an approach based on a trump's label or appearance, refer to the table in the next section of this chapter (Reference: The Trumps, Their Expertise, and Their Attitudes) for a table of keywords and questions designed to boost your understanding of each card's perspective.

Before looking at the sample answers below, be sure to make out your own list!

Possible Answers

0. What would *the Fool* do? Accuse everyone who left the store of shoplifting until he finally got one right.

1. What would *the Magician* do? Learn how to be a great shoplifter in order to know what to watch for.

2. What would *the Priestess* do? Set up observation cameras.

3. What would *the Empress* do? Hold a workshop teaching employees how to catch shoplifters, and create a system for rewarding employees who finger thieves.

4. What would *the Emperor* do? Dispatch uniformed security personnel to handle the situation.

5. What would *the Hierophant* do? Post signs reminding people of the penalties of shoplifting.

6. What would *the Lovers* do? Form a partnership with other local shop owners to share best practices for defeating shoplifting and share information on the identity of shoplifters.

7. What would *the Chariot* do? Publicize cases in which shoplifters were successfully prosecuted to the fullest extent of the law as a way of defeating shoplifting before it begins.

8. What would *Strength* do? Wrestle the shoplifters to the ground before they left the store!

9. What would *the Hermit* do? Go away for a one-on-one seminar on stopping shoplifting.

10. What would *the Wheel* do? Research to see if shoplifting rises and falls according to a predictable cycle, then staff extra people specifically to watch the floor at those times.

11. What would *Justice* do? Hold court on the spot, sending the shoplifters directly to jail.

12. What would *the Hanged Man* do? Ask others how they whipped the problem, then learn from their mistakes.

13. What would *Death* do? Hand shoplifters merchandise and say, "Go ahead! Get it over with! No need to sneak around! Steal it!"

14. What would *Temperance* do? Educate customers on how shoplifting harms them, too (creating higher prices, for example), then enlist their help in spotting and catching the thieves.

15. What would *the Devil* do? Set a bounty for each shoplifter fingered (and then, maybe, wrongly accuse people in order to collect a big reward).

16. What would *the Tower* do? Clear out the store and completely rearrange the floor plan with prevention of shoplifting in mind.

17. What would *the Star* do? Set a goal for the reduction of shoplifting by a certain deadline.

18. What would *the Moon* do? Watch shoplifters over cameras, then announce to the entire store over loudspeakers, "Hey, you in the blue shirt! I see you! Put it back!"

19. What would *the Sun* do? Hold a big party for employees when the team reduced shoplifting to the point selected by the Star.

20. What would *Judgment* do? Send shoplifters a wake-up call by posting photos of previous shoplifters in the store, complete with "This is what happened to them, and it can happen to you" stories attached.

21. What would *the World* do? Make shoplifting obsolete by making everything in the store free for the taking.

Whew! That's a lot of ideas in a very little time!

When I started this exercise, I had no idea what my twenty-two answers would be. I generated the list in just over ten minutes, and reproduced it here with no editing at all.

As you can see, the degree of practicality varies from idea to idea. But, because I turned off my inner critic and kept working, I developed (without trying) a terrific anti-shoplifting strategy. The idea comes up again and again, in various forms, throughout my brainstorm: enlist the help of customers and employees . . . and reward those who catch thieves at work. Equally exciting ideas include: scheduling more employees at periods when shoplifting activity is known to be high, attending seminars to learn more about shoplifting techniques, keeping qualified law enforcement close at hand, and (my personal favorite) forming a coalition to share information with other vendors who are likely dealing with the same shoplifters. Combine these ideas with the Star's advice for setting a target date for reducing shoplifting by a given percentage . . . and the managers of this store have everything they need to launch and evaluate their anti-shoplifting plan.

And remember: your answers very likely differ from mine . . . and that's the way it should be. The goal isn't to mimic my ideas . . . it's to stifle your inner critic and come up with as many answers as possible in the shortest possible time.

Reference: The Trumps, Their Expertise, & Their Attitudes

Of course, your success with the WWTD strategy depends on how well you can envision the attitudes, approaches, and perspectives of your twenty-two advisors. (Otherwise, you'll limit yourself to asking, twenty-two times over, "What would this total stranger do?") I invite you to study each trump and determine for yourself, based on expressions, symbols, postures, or colors, what options the figure on the card would suggest.

Trump	Keywords	What Would _____ Do?
0—Fool	Enthusiasm, Inexperience, Playfulness, Trickiness	. . . a total beginner . . . . . . a practical joker . . . . . . a young upstart . . . . . . someone wanting to impress the boss . . . . . . someone just having fun . . .
1—Magician	Empowerment, Creativity, Awareness, Skill	. . . an action hero . . . . . . a person with magical powers . . . . . . someone in charge . . . . . . a "do it yourself" person . . . . . . a "whiz kid" . . .
2—Priestess	Reflection, Reception, Secrecy, Analysis	. . . an analyst . . . . . . a psychic . . . . . . a wise woman . . . . . . someone "behind the scenes" . . . . . . someone with a hidden agenda . . .
3—Empress	Development, Growth, Nurture, Productivity	. . . my mother . . . . . . an expert coach . . . . . . a productivity expert . . . . . . an environmentalist . . . . . . a nurturing mentor . . .
4—Emperor	Authority, Directives, Order, Organization, Control	. . . my father . . . . . . someone with rigid opinions . . . . . . The Boss or The CEO . . . . . . a "take control" person . . . . . . someone who delegates everything . . .
5—Hierophant	Externals, Regulations, Appearances, Standards	. . . a "by the book" person . . . . . . someone wanting to look good . . . . . . an expensive consultant . . . . . . a "goodie-two-shoes" . . . . . . a PR person . . .
6—Lovers	Affiliations, Partnerships, Networking, Team Spirit	. . . a good team player . . . . . . a great business partner . . . . . . my best friend . . . . . . a terrific vendor . . . . . . a group of friends . . .
7—Chariot	Victories, Triumphs, Competition, Excellence	. . . the "Employee of the Year" . . . . . . an undefeated quarterback . . . . . . a "take no prisoners" competitor . . . . . . my role model . . . . . . a ruthless military commander . . .

Trump	Keywords	What Would _____ Do?
8—Strength	Resolve, Focus, Dependability, Reserve	. . . Superman . . . . . . someone who thinks physically . . . . . . a "take action now" person . . . . . . a reliable, trusted worker . . . . . . a confident manager . . .
9—Hermit	Solitude, Isolation, Time, Experience	. . . someone with unlimited time . . . . . . a spiritual leader . . . . . . a wise old man . . . . . . a seasoned worker . . . . . . a one-person shop . . .
10—Wheel	Cycles, Fluctuations, Luck, Fate	. . . someone in tune with trends . . . . . . the previous manager or CEO . . . . . . someone taking a random approach . . . . . . a "best case / worst case" person . . . . . . someone motivated by habit . . .
11—Justice	Evaluations, Deliberations, Objectivity, Fairness	. . . a lawyer . . . . . . someone known for fairness . . . . . . King Solomon . . . . . . Mr. Spock . . . . . . someone honest to a fault . . .
12—Hanged Man	Trial, Transformation, Traitors, Hard Knocks	. . . the competition . . . . . . someone about to leave the company . . . . . . someone making a mistake . . . . . . someone experiencing deja-vu . . . . . . a person who shakes things up . . .
13—Death	Endings, Transitions, Finality, Conclusion	. . . someone determined to end this . . . . . . someone wanting to be fired . . . . . . someone with nothing to lose . . . . . . someone wanting to get on with it . . . . . . a person with a fatalistic attitude . . .
14—Temperance	Blending, Mediation, Averaging, Combining	. . . an arbitration expert . . . . . . someone "middle of the road" . . . . . . a politically correct person . . . . . . someone who values "getting along" . . . . . . an average Joe . . .
15—Devil	Manipulation, Callousness, Materialism, Profit	. . . someone valuing profit over all . . . . . . Machiavelli . . . . . . a "get-rich-quick" person . . . . . . a manipulative person . . . . . . a deceptive person . . .

Trump	Keywords	What Would _____ Do?
16—Tower	Destruction, Revision, Breakage, Failure	. . . a pessimist . . . . . . a "tear it down, start over" person . . . . . . a person new to this situation . . . . . . a destructive person . . . . . . a demolition expert . . .
17—Star	Hope, Goals, Dreams, Beauty	. . . an actor or actress . . . . . . an optimist . . . . . . a performance coach . . . . . . a person focused on the future . . . . . . a dreamer . . .
18—Moon	Illogic, Inversion, Madness, Romance	. . . a person doing the wrong thing . . . . . . a certifiably crazy person . . . . . . a wild man . . . . . . a trailblazer . . . . . . a risk-taker . . .
19—Sun	Celebrations, Satisfaction, Achievement, Appreciation	. . . a person seeking recognition . . . . . . a person intent on winning . . . . . . the best employee at the company . . . . . . a happy person . . . . . . the brightest person I know . . .
20—Judgment	Decisions, Conclusions, Opportunity, Reality	. . . a person with unlimited authority . . . . . . a historian looking back on this . . . . . . a general rallying the troops . . . . . . a person with the one right answer . . . . . . a decisive person . . .
21—World	Completion, Realization, Fullness, Joy	. . . a "tie-up-loose-ends" person . . . . . . a person who has it all . . . . . . a person with no financial limits . . . . . . a person with no limits at all . . . . . . someone with no agenda . . .

If you find yourself in a pinch, though, you can use the table below, which offers handy keywords and questions for each trump. If any of my keywords or questions restrict your creativity or fail to inspire you, always feel free to ignore mine and substitute your own.

Summary: Chapter Five in a Nutshell

SUCCESSFUL BRAINSTORMERS VALUE THE quantity of ideas over the quality of those ideas. Rather than try to impress others, they make associations on the fly—answers and ideas can be evaluated later. By design, the three strategies in this chapter help silence your inner critic and enhance your ability to generate insights as quickly as possible.

The Single Card Draw strategy focuses on a single card, encouraging you to determine how that card connects with your situation, actions you've taken (or could take), approaches you've tried (or could try), and attitudes or prejudices which may influence your judgment.

The Speed Reading strategy encourages you to burn through the deck as quickly as possible, making just one association per card.

The WWTD (What Would the Trumps Do?) strategy positions twenty-two cards (the twenty-one trumps, plus the Fool) as expert advisors. In each case, brainstormers imagine the mindset and approach of the Trump in question, then ask, "In my situation, what would _____ do?" The result: twenty-two courses of action—some wild, some crazy, and some downright outrageous—that may lead to valuable insights and solutions.

Employ these three brainstorming strategies when facing decisions or solving problems, and you'll amaze employers and coworkers with your insights and creative genius!

CHAPTER

Seventy-Eight Steps to a More Satisfying Career

Preview: What to Expect in Chapter Six

This chapter provides Tarot-based brainstorming strategies that:

☞ Define your level of satisfaction with your current job and career path

☞ Indentify your strengths . . . and opportunities for growth

☞ Set goals designed to motivate action and generate positive change

☞ Teach you to use Tarot cards as visual reminders of your goal

Getting Your Bearings

HOW MUCH CAREER PLANNING have you done? (Just for the record, pausing by the water cooler and musing, "I really ought to do some career planning!" doesn't qualify!)

Most of us are too busy meeting daily deadlines to pause for an objective look at where we are . . . and where we're going. All too often, our career paths get left to chance, simply because we lack the time to assess our current situation, identify a goal, and plot a course to take us there. As a result, our work lacks any relevance to the greater direction of our lives, and, as our work becomes increasingly divorced from our values and dreams, our jobs become drudgery.

Investing between thirty and sixty minutes in a career-oriented brainstorm provides an opportunity to get your bearings, restore a sense of context and meaning, and judge the degree to which your current work is building a bridge to the future you desire. For those already on the right track, this brainstorming exercise offers confirmation. For those uncertain of their path, the same exercise opens doors to a new attitude, a new approach . . . or even a new career.

Michael's Story

Michael topped the ridge and tied off his support line, his breath fogging the chilly air. With the line secured and tested, he stood, hands on hips, and relished the sensations of the world around him: the sharp scent of the snow-laden fir trees, the crunch of snow beneath his feet, and the sight of jagged peaks—the Tetons, orange with morning sunlight—in the distance.

Just months ago, he would have spent this morning hunched in a corporate cube, sipping bad coffee from a plastic cup and staring at a computer screen.

He walked to the edge of the steep slope, looking down. His group—six teens and two other counselors—made their way up: their arms trembling with exertion, their jaws clenched in determination. Michael paid special attention to Quinn, the inner-city kid who seemed especially uncertain of himself and his ability to climb.

Michael understood, on a very personal level, what Quinn was going through.

* * * * *

In the Beginning

Just eight months earlier, Michael faced an uphill climb of his own. AtlanTel, Mike's employer for the last five years, had been acquired in a merger. Soon, new executives roamed the halls conducting "process evaluations" designed to identify and release non-essential personnel.

Rumors characterized Mike's department as a sinking ship. Mike's best employees moved to other companies within a matter of weeks. Worse, Mike's counterpart—a manager from the parent company—met with members of Mike's team, identified the best workers, then hired them away. Mike found himself surrounded by a desperate, demoralized crew, waiting for the axe to fall.

Secretly, Mike half-hoped his position would be eliminated. Over the last few months, his job satisfied him less and less. He felt the need to do something that mattered, saying, "I always told myself I was going to make the world a better place. No amount of selling long distance is going to do that."

Brainstorming Career Options with the Tarot

Uncertain what else to do, Mike turned to a friend, Jenna, who seemed completely satisfied with and dedicated to her career. To his surprise, Jenna admitted she used Tarot-based brainstorming to assess her current situation, define her goals, and explore options for the future.

"I feel silly," Mike insisted. "I should be pounding the pavement, looking for work—not telling fortunes."

Jenna ignored him, laying out three cards from the *Universal Tarot*. "Pretend I'm on the phone with you, and need you to describe these cards for me. What do you see?"

"There's a woman, surrounded by swords. She's blindfolded and can't see any way out." Mike laughed out loud. "I know how she feels!"

"Look closer," Jenna recommended. "Is she really surrounded?"

Mike studied the card. "There might not be a sword behind her. Actually, she probably could move in a couple of directions, but when you're blindfolded and know you're surrounded by swords, you're less likely to make a leap just to see what happens."

"So is it better for her to just stand there?"

Eight of Swords   *Six of Cups*   *Wheel of Fortune*

Mike frowned. "Come to think of it, she's probably better off just making her move and taking a chance. The ropes tying her arms look loose. If the thought occurred to her, she could free herself, take off her blindfold, and find her own way out. At least that'd be better than standing there and waiting for someone to finish you off!"

"What would you tell her, if she could hear you?"

"Take that blindfold off and get out of there. No one's coming to rescue you, so you're going to have to do it yourself." Mike stopped suddenly. "That's pretty good advice."

Jenna made some notes. "And the next card?"

"I don't know. A guy is handing a cup to a little girl. Maybe she couldn't reach it herself. Does this mean I'm going to meet someone who hands me an answer and tells me what to do?"

Jenna shrugged. "Maybe. Try making this card into advice. What is it telling you to do?"

Mike shook his head. "I don't know. Work with kids? Get some kind of charity gig? I don't think I'll be leaving my job to go work at a soup kitchen, if that's what you're telling me."

Jenna laughed. "I'm not telling you anything! What about the third card?"

Mike sighed. "Wheel of Fortune. Doesn't look much like the television show. I don't know what kind of advice that would be. What goes around comes around? Wait for the time to be right before you make a move?"

"Could be," Jenna said. "Now, try stringing all three cards together to make a sentence. Start with the words 'To make my job situation better, I need to do three things. . .'"

"To make my job situation better, I need to do three things: realize I'm only as trapped as I think I am, look for ways to help other people, and not rush into anything. I should wait until the time is right."

"So how do you feel about that brainstorming session?" Jenna asked.

Mike shrugged. "There's some good advice. I mean, I've thought before about working with kids. My sister does it. But there's just no money in it. I don't think that part really applies to me."

Beyond the Brainstorm

The images from the cards stayed in Mike's mind over the next several days, especially at work. When his coworkers obsessed on rumors, worried about the future, but took no action to help themselves, Mike remembered the Eight of Swords. When another manager quit without bothering to arrange his next job, Mike thought of the Wheel of Fortune.

Then, out of the blue, his sister called. Anna and her partner, Christine, ran a wilderness adventure camp near Jackson Hole, Wyoming. Thanks to a government grant, they were expanding their program to include weekend encounter programs for troubled youth. Did Mike know of anyone qualified and willing to work on the camp staff?

Mike reeled off the names of two acquaintances.

"Mike!" Anna interrupted. "I'm not asking about people you know—I'm asking you!"

Mike blinked. "But I'm not qualified."

"Of course you're qualified! You love the outdoors. You're great with kids—and you used to talk about wanting to work with them. And from the sound of the last email you sent me, it's time for you to get away from AtlanTel and do something on your own!"

★ ★ ★ ★ ★

A flicker of motion at the lip of the ridge caught Mike's eye. Quinn, red-faced and huffing, pulled himself up and over the edge. He sat down hard in the snow, catching his breath. A few seconds later, the boy noticed the view—the Tetons, rising up into the morning sky like a wave of frozen stone. The sight took away the breath Quinn had worked so hard to catch.

Sensing the importance of the moment, Michael moved quietly to Quinn's side.

"I made it," Quinn said. "I didn't think I could do it."

Mike remembered his days at AtlanTel—the hectic pace, the pointless assignments, the days spent worrying about layoffs—and realized that world now seemed a million miles away.

He smiled and put an arm around the younger man. "Quinn, I know exactly how you feel."

Seventy-Eight Steps to Success

Michael's story combines elements from the lives and experiences of many people who, over the past several years, have learned to use the Tarot to brainstorm about their career options:

- Ethan spent years slaving away in an unrewarding job in his state's Tax Commission. When he started his search for a more fulfilling career, he invested a few hours in brainstorming his next steps. The cards drew his attention to his true passion—real estate—and helped him envision a step-by-step transition plan. Now, after completing his real estate classes, he's juggling as many clients as a part-time realtor can . . . and soon plans to leave the Tax Commission and realize his dream of being a full-time agent.

- Shandra loves children, but avoided working with them or having her own because she feared she would become the strict disciplinarian her mother had been. Brainstorming with the cards helped her confront her issues, identify critical differences between her and her mother's approaches to life, and identify a list of jobs in which she could provide children with the help and support she never received as a child.

- Nathaniel felt increasingly distanced from his telecom job. Inspired by his sister's work with youth, he began brainstorming about a possible career helping others realize their own best potential. At this writing, he's on the verge of launching his own company designed specifically to attune people to motivations, hopes, and dreams.

After earning degrees in creative writing and publishing several short stories, I was well on my way to realizing my own dream: walking into a bookstore and seeing my work for sale on the shelves. I wound up making a living by writing—writing scripts, authoring speeches, generating text for web sites, and creating the content for training manuals—but I never reached my goal of completing and selling a book. While brainstorming with the Tarot, I began paying closer attention to the obstacles impeding progress toward my dream, including worries about money and other people's opinions. In my work with the cards, I came up with ways to reclaim personal time formerly dominated by an all-consuming corporate job. I also cultivated the courage to ignore what others thought, focused my vision, and developed a plan for finishing this book.

Our brainstorming process helped us clarify career goals, explore options, and fulfill dreams. Handled properly, these seventy-eight cards become seventy-eight stepping-stones to the job you'll love.

The Benefits of Career-Oriented Brainstorming

What happens when you brainstorm career options with the Tarot? Different things happen for different people. You may decide you need dramatic changes—a new job, or a major move.

You may decide your best path involves changing your current job in small ways. The alternatives you generate will be unique to you. The goal here is to enhance your personal sense of pride, achievement, happiness, and accomplishment at work.

Using the information in this chapter, you can learn how Tarot cards can help you:

- Identify the kind of work that's best for you

- Plan a new career (or a change in your existing career)

- Establish and explore new directions with minimized risk

- Schedule your departure from a job you no longer find rewarding

- Generate exciting new job opportunities

- Unite your dreams and your employment opportunities

- Experience a greater sense of direction in your life

If you want to stay in your current position, you can use the cards to:

- Spark ideas that provide you with upward mobility

- Improve your chances of getting a raise or promotion

- Outline what's needed to make your current job even more rewarding

- Discover how to preserve your sense of achievement and satisfaction

- Explore how to carry these feelings into other areas of your life

- Define clear, achievable short- and long-term goals

I know the cards can help you with any of the tasks above—because I've used them for all of these purposes!

The Benefits of Using Tarot to Explore Your Career Options

Once you put the Tarot to work as a career-planning tool, you'll enjoy the following benefits:

- *You'll make your dreams into realities.* You'll learn how to translate your dreams into goals, then author a step-by-step plan for achieving those goals in record time.

- *You'll move from dissatisfaction to action.* Instead of complaining about your work, you'll clarify what motivates and satisfies you. Instead of daydreaming about a better job, you'll have a plan for finding one! Instead of just thinking about a better future, you'll create one.

- *You'll gain confidence.* Instead of blindly leaping into action, you'll develop several options and select the best one for you. Having explored situations in advance, you'll notice options and opportunities that others will overlook.

- *You'll broaden your perspective.* While others simply request raises, you'll broaden your understanding of the company's circumstances, anticipate possible objections to a raise, and prepare a point-by-point explanation of why you deserve higher pay. As you enhance your awareness, you'll develop a level of insight others will admire.

The Spreads

To aid you in your brainstorming process, this chapter offers three layouts—or spreads—designed to help you explore job-related ideas and information. These spreads include:

- The *Self-Portrait Spread,* designed to capture a "self-portrait" of where you are today in terms of your career.

- The *Strengths and Opportunities Spread,* which helps you to identify your own best qualities . . . and articulate options for growth.

- The *Goal-Setting Spread,* designed to aid you in defining and achieve your employment goals.

In addition to explaining the purpose and structure for each spread, this section includes examples of how the spreads can be used to brainstorm important ideas and insights. You can work with any of these spreads at any time . . . but, if this is your first time to use these techniques (or if you haven't taken time for any personal career planning in a while), you'll get the most out of them if you complete them in order.

The Self-Portrait Spread

What to Do. This deceptively simple five card spread serves as a photograph of your current employment situation. Contemplating the cards in this spread moves you beyond your feelings and builds an understanding of why you feel the way you do.

Use this spread to create a "baseline reading"—to capture where you are, where you're headed, and how you feel about it now. Months later, you can repeat this spread to get a dramatic sense of changes you've made in your life!

The spread consists of five cards (see following page).

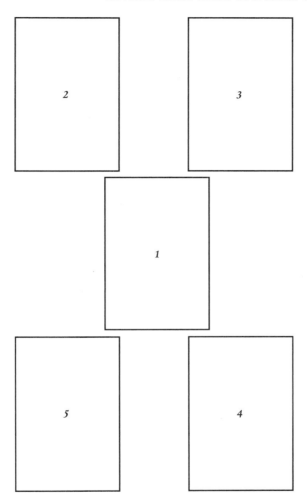

Card One: Yourself. Every portrait has a subject, and, since this is a self-portrait, the subject is you! Use this card to brainstorm a definition of where you are right now with regard to your work. In addition to the card itself, consider what the type of card suggests:

- A trump card indicates an important question you need to answer or a critical decision you need to make.

- A court card indicates a need to consider the role of a certain person (with some thought, you'll know who this person is!) in your work, and a need to consider how this person impacts your job satisfaction.

- A pip card is a snapshot of how your current job makes you feel on a day-to-day basis.

Card Two: Your Situation. Use this card as a springboard for exploring your environment at work. It may relate to anything that impacts your sense of the place: from management's most recent decisions to the outlook of your coworkers. As you explore the card, ask questions like these:

- If you were to describe your work environment with just five words, what five words would you select? To what extent are those words reflected in this card? What other words might this card suggest?

- How could your work environment be changed? What could you do to encourage those changes? What one change in your surroundings at work would greatly improve your work experience?

- If you were to ask this card what it thought of your work environment, what would it tell you?

- Name the images on the card out loud. What aspects of your work environment could these images represent?

- Finish this sentence: Your work environment is like the [name of card goes here] because . . .

Card Three: Your Approaches and Attitudes. Use this card to generate insights into what you're thinking and feeling about work. Your approaches and attitudes significantly color your work experience. Sometimes, changing your approach changes everything! Use this card to explore the glasses you look through—which may or may not be rose-colored—by asking these kinds of questions:

- How has your attitude or approach to work changed in the last six months? How might this card relate to those changes? What factors or decisions drove those changes?

- To what degree do you choose the way you feel about your job? How does this card capture those feelings? To what degree could you choose to change those feelings? How might this card suggest a strategy for change?

- What would the person or being on this card tell you if you asked, "What do you think about my on-the-job attitude?"

- Name images on the card out loud. How do these images relate to your approach to your job? To your satisfaction on the job? To your attitude toward the job?

- Finish this sentence: "My attitude on the job is like the [name of card goes here] because . . ."

Card Four: Your Blind Spot. Again and again, clients look at this card and ask, "What does this card have to do with me?" That's a natural reaction when confronting your own Blind Spot—an aspect of your situation you have extreme difficulty seeing or accepting.

Usually, the Blind Spot sprouts from a prejudice so ingrained in our way of thinking that we no longer understand its influence on our lives. Blind Spots also relate to information we discard or deny—facts we know, but prefer to avoid because they make us uncomfortable. As this card prompts you to consider your own Blind Spot, ask yourself these questions:

- What are the images on this card? What prejudices or attitudes do they suggest? How might they connect to something you're denying or not dealing with?

- What kinds of assumptions do you make about people? How are those assumptions influenced by factors such as race, sexual orientation, gender, nationality, or religion? To what degree do the images on this card point to or highlight those assumptions?

- As a way to move past the assumptions that prejudice your thinking, imagine this card has been deliberately devised to lead you to the worst possible career decision. What would its message be?

- If the person or being on the card could speak, what message about your Blind Spot would he or she offer?

- To what degree are your feelings about work rooted in assumptions or prejudices?

If you simply can't make sense of this card, don't force yourself to see the Blind Spot. Make a note of it, or put the card in a prominent place. Over the next several days, keep the Blind Spot card in mind, and see if situations arise that give you ideas.

Card Five: Your Actions. Whatever our situation, it does not exist independently of us! Our actions—things we do or fail to do—contribute to our experience. This isn't a matter of assigning fault or blame. Instead, this card reveals the role your actions play in your employment situation. Understanding that role can empower you to make important and much-needed changes in your career. As you examine this card, consider these questions:

- Have you stopped doing things you used to do? How does this card connect with or suggest those activities? What might it suggest about your reasons for stopping or curtailing certain activities?

- What responsibilities have been added? How do you feel about those additional responsibilities? What feelings might this card suggest?

- What actions have you taken lately to make your work more satisfying? To what degree is your satisfaction with your work impacted by what you choose to do or not to do? To what degree do the images on this card suggest actions you need to take? Actions you've taken lately? Actions you've been avoiding?

- Name the images on this card one by one. What actions are suggested by the images on this card? How are those actions associated with your work?

- If the image on the card is a person, what actions would that person recommend to you?

Practicing the Self-Portrait Spread

The Situation. At work, Sherrie is considered "Miss Dependable." She's always there and always ready to help others with any project. All the same, the work doesn't satisfy her the way it used to. Getting up and going to work becomes more of a chore every day. She misses feeling excited about her job . . . and is curious about this change in her attitude and what it might mean.

Sherrie decides to use the Self-Portrait Spread to explore the situation further, and deals the following five cards from the *Universal Tarot* (see the following page). Refer to the illustration on the following page—or, if you prefer, pull these same cards from your personal deck and arrange them into the self-portrait spread. What ideas do these cards give you? If you were Sherrie's brainstorming partner, what would you tell her?

Some Possible Answers. Remember: the goal of the exercises in this and other chapters is to enhance your own brainstorming ability through practice. Your answers may be very different from the ones offered in the following example . . . and that's just fine. In the meantime, seeing how Sherrie uses the images (and reading about the conclusions she draws) may inspire you to see the cards in a new light when you attempt this reading for yourself.

Card One: Yourself—Queen of Coins. Sherrie noticed this card, the Queen of Coins, was a court card. This prompted speculation about how people in her workplace might impact her job satisfaction.

At first glance, the woman on Queen of Coins reminded Sherrie of her mother, which, in turn, prompted her to think of her boss, Martha. When Sherrie joined the company, her boss, Martha, trained and nurtured her. Because the work group was new and small, Martha took special time with Sherrie, and became her mentor. Soon, Martha seemed more of a "mother" than an employer. The attention made Sherrie, who had been hired as an office manager, feel less like a secretary and more like a vital part of the team.

As the department's success grew and more employees were added, Martha's responsibilities also increased. Nine new employees joined the department, and all of them needed their manager's attention. Meetings with other managers and employees required more and more of Martha's time—and she had less to spend with Sherrie.

Brainstorming with the Self-Portrait spread helped Sherrie connect the change in Martha's role with the shift in her own enthusiasm for the work.

Card Two: Your Situation—Knight of Wands. Looking at the fiery Knight of Wands, Sherrie was reminded of the pace at work. Over the last several months, everyone's job had become more hectic. Sherrie realized that she started helping others with projects because she had the extra time to do so. "Now," Sherrie said, "I'm still expected to be everyone's knight in shining armor, even though my work load has increased. I've got more than I can do alone! Everyone expects me to help them do things they really ought to do for themselves . . . but no one volunteers to help me in return!"

Card Three: Your Approaches and Attitudes—The Lovers. "When I started this job," Sherrie said, "we were in a honeymoon period. The work was fun and easy. Everyone felt connected to everyone else. Now, my attitude has changed. I avoid people, because I know they're going to try to put their work off on me. I wouldn't mind helping, if I felt like I could get some help in return." Sherrie decided this card captured the fact that, in her mind, the honeymoon was over. The requests that used to make her feel so important now felt like attempts to take advantage of her difficulty with saying, "No."

"The people on this card are equals," Sherrie said. "They work together. One of them isn't pushing things off on the other."

Sherrie realized while looking at this card that her attitudes had also been influenced by Martha's withdrawal. "It's like this: why should I make time for everyone else, if my own boss won't make time for me?"

Card Four: Your Blind Spot—The Magician. This card proved most difficult for Sherrie to understand, so she began making associations out loud. "He's a magician. He does magic. Magicians make things appear and disappear. But it's not really magic—it just looks magical, until you understand how it's done."

Talking about the Magician led Sherrie to an interesting idea: "I keep wishing that things would go back to the way they were—that I could just walk in one day and everything would be like it used to be. You know—wave a magic wand and everyone would cooperate again. Could that be my blind spot? Waiting for magical changes instead of figuring out the trick and doing it myself?"

After some deliberation, Sherrie decided the Blind Spot card challenged her to think of what she could do to encourage better cooperation among her coworkers . . . and even with Martha. "I'll start looking for ways to share the work, or start coming to them first . . . and I'll also talk with Martha about the differences and ask her how she would go about getting people to cooperate more."

Card Five: Your Actions—Two of Swords. This card proved to be the easiest for Sherrie to understand. In fact, she laughed out loud in recognition. "There I am! Sitting on the rock in the dark, waiting for someone to take off my blindfold for me. I've got swords in my hand that I could use to defend myself, but I've got my arms crossed in front of my chest like I'm lying in a coffin! I've just given up . . . and that just makes things worse."

Sherrie determined that she would "get up off her rock" and start "poking around with swords" in an effort to restore a sense of camaraderie at the office. "I'll suggest we need some kind of outside event—a party, or a night out—so folks can get to know each other better. I'll offer my help . . . and feel better about turning things down when my workload is heavy."

Sherrie decided she'd also approach Martha, discuss how much she valued the other woman's assistance and input, and ask how the two of them might work together more closely.

Your Turn. Brainstorming is an intensely personal activity—your ideas may vary wildly from Sherrie's. If you were able to anticipate the answers she generated—congratulations! If your own answers differed dramatically from hers—congratulations! Again—the goal of an exercise like this one is to practice using the tool . . . not to regurgitate the possible answers you find in this book.

Of course, the real test comes when you start *Putting the Tarot to Work* in your own brainstorming session! Why wait? Before moving on to the next section, try painting your own "self portrait" with the cards.

The Strengths and Opportunities Spread

What to Do. Outside of cliché questions in bad job interviews ("What are your greatest strengths? And your greatest weaknesses?"), we rarely pause to consider what our personal strengths and opportunities for growth might be. When planning your career, you should concentrate on both: what you do well and what you could improve. This spread identifies your strengths, your opportunities for growth, and a factor you can use to balance these.

This spread consists of seven cards (see following page).

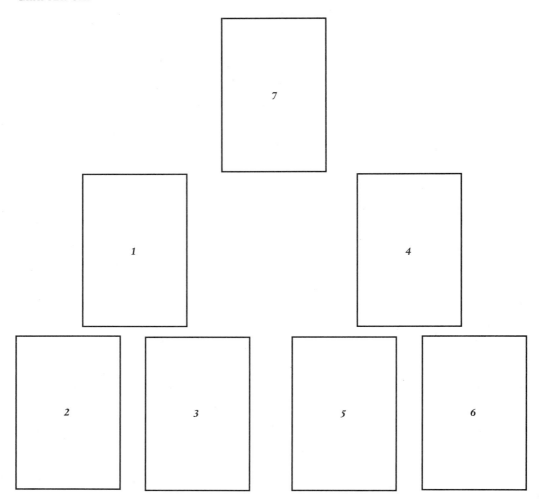

This spread arranges cards related to your strengths on the left and your growth opportunities on the right. The seventh card, at the top of the spread, represents a factor you can use to achieve a healthy balance of these two forces in your life and career.

Trump cards in any position indicate an especially powerful influence; spend extra time considering the meaning of these cards.

Court cards may refer to a specific person: someone who represents a strength you admire or a growth opportunity you need to identify. These cards may also prompt you to think of someone who possesses valuable insights into your strengths, growth opportunities, or career.

Card One: Key Strength. Use the people, images, scenes, meanings, and theme of this card to launch a brainstorm about your key strength—an ability, attitude, passion, perspective, or skill with potential for great influence on your work and career. As you work with this card, ask yourself questions like these:

- On this card, what work or process is beginning, in progress, or nearing completion? What are people on this card doing? What talents or skills would be required to complete the work being done here? To what degree does this activity point to a strength you possess?

- How would you describe the outlook of the people on the card—or the emotional tone of the card itself? When have you felt or dealt with that emotion in the past? What happened then? How might your skill in dealing with or maintaining that emotion point to a strength?

- To what degree do the images, symbols, people, places, or items on this card connect with hobbies, pastimes, or activities you enjoy or feel strongly about? Make a list of things you enjoy doing when you're "off work." To what degree does this card reflect or refer to these activities? How might these activities point to a strength?

- What advice would you give the people on this card? Have you encountered people in this situation? How did you help or assist them? How would you call attention to the way their situation is changing or could change? What aspects of your experience could be of value or assistance to these people? How might your ability to offer this kind of advice point to a strength?

Cards Two and Three: Supporting Strengths. These cards indicate additional strengths that interact with, support, or compliment your Key Strength. Brainstorming with these cards may give you additional insight when identifying and defining your Key Strength, or reveal dimensions of that strength which may not be apparent at first glance.

Explore Cards Two and Three using the same questions you used to explore your Key Strength. Be especially alert to repeating or related themes as you answer the questions.

Card Four: Primary Opportunity. The people, images, scenes, meanings, and theme of this card all point toward your primary growth opportunity—an ability or skill you may need to acquire, an attitude you should overcome or abandon, a passion which works against your advancement, or an unhealthy perspective which limits your vision. As you contemplate this card, ask yourself questions like these:

- How do you feel about the work that is beginning, in progress, or being completed on this card? What talents or skills would be required? What would you have to learn to be able to do this work well? What types of work are associated with the theme of this card? What types of activity are associated with the theme of this card? How might these activities or skills point to a growth opportunity for you? To what degree do the images or themes associated with this card point to activities or approaches you need to abandon or alter?

- How would you describe the outlook of the people on the card—or the emotional tone of the card itself? How well do you deal with this emotion? How might it work to distract you? How might it keep you from pursuing your dreams? How can you find ways to build your skill at channeling this emotion more effectively? To what degree does this emotion suggest a growth opportunity for you?

- What attitudes are evident on this card? What are the attitudes of the people on the card? What attitudes would their activities prompt in others? In you? If you fail to perceive any kind attitude associated with this card, what might that suggest about your sensitivity to those around you? How might these perceptions point to a growth opportunity for you?

- If the people on this card could speak, what advice would they offer you about something you should change in order to grow? What advice would you offer them as a means of changing or taking best advantage of their situation? How might these words of advice indicate changes you need to make in order to grow?

Cards Five and Six: Additional Opportunities. Use these cards to explore opportunities to interact with, support, or compliment your Primary Opportunity. Contemplating these cards may help you identify your Primary Opportunity, or reveal dimensions of the opportunity that may not be apparent at first.

Explore Cards Five and Six using the same questions you used to explore your Primary Opportunity. Be especially alert to repeating or related themes as you answer the questions. Watch, too, for themes, concepts, or insights that connect with your strengths in interesting ways. Often, a strength may point to a way to take better advantage of a growth opportunity.

Card Seven: Balancing Strategy. What's the key to balancing your strengths and opportunities? How can you moderate the degree to which your strengths and growth opportunities influence your life and career? The Balancing Strategy card suggests:

- A plan of action.

- A theme, situation, or environment.

- A goal.

- A way of thinking.

- An attitude.

- A direction with potential to bring your strengths and growth opportunities into a healthy, balanced state.

As you brainstorm with this card, ask yourself these questions:

- What actions might this card suggest? What kinds of tasks would fill your "To Do" list if this card became your focus?

- What kind of environment or situation might this card suggest? What would be involved in creating—or modifying—this situation? How might this situation impact your ability to express your strengths? To pursue growth?

- How might this card represent a goal? What goal would it be? How would reaching this goal alter the balance of your strengths and growth opportunities?

- How might this card represent a way of thinking or an attitude? In terms of your strengths and weaknesses, what would happen if you adopted that attitude? Abandoned it? Encouraged it in others?

- What kind of job or career might this card suggest? What sort of work might this card suggest? How would pursuing this line of work make use of your strengths or offer opportunities for growth? How would contact with people in this line of work impact your strengths or opportunities?

Practicing the Strengths and Opportunities Spread

The Situation. Carlos, a corporate trainer, felt trapped in his job with a major home and garden chain store. He felt he had potential to do much more than his current job allowed, but was uncertain how to take control of the situation and create a career path for himself. As a result, he continued to do the same job, day after day, for three years.

In hopes of moving his career forward, he decided to perform an analysis of his strengths and weaknesses. Carlos dealt the following seven cards from the *Universal Tarot* (in the following illustration).

Refer to the illustration above—or, if you prefer, pull these same cards from your personal deck and arrange them into the Strengths and Opportunities spread. What ideas do these cards give you? If you were Carlos' brainstorming partner, what would you tell him? Some possible answers:

Card One: Key Strength—Five of Cups. At first, Carlos thought this was an odd card to find in his Key Strength position: a grieving man, staring down at spilled cups. "I'm good at crying?" he asked. Then, on further inspection, the emphasis of the card shifted. "Three cups are overturned, and two are standing. The problem is, this guy's staring at the spill. He doesn't know how to turn around and see what he's got left. Now that's something I can do—find the rainbow in the cloud. When things go wrong, I don't sit around whining about it . . . I look for ways to move on. There's no use blaming people—just fix it."

Cards Two and Three: Supporting Strengths—Nine of Coins and Six of Swords. Carlos puzzled over these cards longer than any others. "A woman in a garden. In a vineyard. She's got a bird. What kind of bird is that? A pigeon? A falcon?" Eventually, Carlos decided this card related to training: "She's taking time, training the bird. Training takes time. It's like letting a vineyard ripen. You don't get results overnight."

Carlos went on to consider Card Three. "That man is rowing people someplace they don't want to go. But they've made a hard decision, and now, it's his job to get them there."

In the end, Carlos decided the spread indicated a wide range of potential strengths: "The ability to see opportunities, my talents as a trainer, and my ability to make difficult decisions under pressure—to move ahead when things get tough."

Only after making this list did Carlos decide these strengths might be exactly the ones a good manager would need. "As a manager, I could focus on people's strengths, train them, and be able to make the tough decisions when the time came. Maybe I'm better prepared to be a manager than I thought."

Card Four: Primary Opportunity—Death. Carlos reacted strongly to the Death card, and even joked, "This card is telling me to just give up! My primary opportunity is Death! What kind of future is that?"

Once Carlos' brainstorming moved beyond physical death to incorporate the idea of endings and conclusions, the card made more sense to him: "I don't like endings. Or even changes. I like things to stay just the way they are. When things change, you run the risk of losing something. I'd rather have what I know is good for me right now than risk it for something better and take a chance on losing it all."

Carlos decided learning to accept change—or even pursue it—could be a meaningful challenge for him. "I've stayed in the same job for four years. I've been afraid that they might notice me if I spoke up, and that I could lose my good job if they knew I wanted something else."

Cards Five and Six: Additional Opportunities—Four of Wands and The Lovers. "Is this Lovers card saying I need to become a gigolo?" Carlos joked.

"The Four is like a wedding, and the Lovers is also like a wedding. Weddings are ceremonies. They bring people together. Now that's something I could work on—bringing people together. No one at work can do that. They give orders, and we do the marching. If someone were to come on the scene and unite everybody, make everyone feel good about what they were doing, that'd be powerful. I'd like to be that person . . . and a good manager would be able to do that, but I can't do that now."

Card Seven: Balancing Strategy—The World. "She's dancing," Carlos noticed. "Maybe this is telling me to stop sitting still and start dancing a little. Have some fun with the whole situation. I looked at a book that said this card was about having it all. Maybe I should be thinking about how I need to make some changes in myself so I can have it all—get everything I'd like to get."

After the brainstorming session, Carlos decided he was interested in a management position and possessed good potential management skills. He also recognized that he lacked experience in managing large projects or groups of people. Further, he said, "I need to get over my fear of change. It's holding me back."

Carlos resolved to approach his manager and ask for assignments that would teach him better management skills. He also decided to focus on "the World"—reaching his goal of having more money and happiness—as a way of getting over his fear of changes. After brainstorming, Carlos realized embracing change would bring his dreams closer.

Your Turn. Again, Carlos' story represents possibilities—not absolute correct answers. Carlos came up with answers that worked for him. (Interestingly, many people find that the answers they brainstormed "for Carlos" also apply to them!)

Before moving to the next section, try the Strengths and Opportunities spread for yourself. It's a brainstorming session that gives you a radical new perspective on your own skills and needs.

The Goal-Setting Spread

As a manager, one of my greatest challenges—and greatest failures—involved Jeffrey.

Jeffrey had a lot going for him. He learned new skills quickly. He had a rapport with computers and design software. Given direction, he enthusiastically jumped on a project and made valuable contributions.

Jeffrey's persistent sense of dissatisfaction, however, tainted his good work. No reward or recognition ever excited him. No completed project stirred his sense of pride. Instead, he became more and more morose with each success. He earned a promotion and an unusually large raise—yet remained restless. He complained constantly and openly searched for new job opportunities despite his success.

In a meeting, I asked Jeffrey a simple question: "What do you want?"

"I don't know what you mean," he said, looking frightened.

"What do you want?" I asked him. "What are your goals? What do you want to get done this year, personally and professionally? How can this company help you reach those goals?"

He shook his head and shrugged his shoulders. "I don't know. I guess I'll just do what I'm doing."

I pointed out the impossibility of rewarding or providing direction for someone without goals. "If you don't know where you're going, chances are good that you won't get there." I suggested we start with short-term goals—what Jeffrey wanted to accomplish in the next three to six months.

Jeffrey half-heartedly agreed, but warned me, "I don't do this kind of thing." In our follow-up meeting, this proved true: Jeffrey refused to outline goals for himself. "I like to keep my options open," he explained. "I don't do limits."

The result? Jeffrey's dissatisfaction with his job grew. He left our company for another, and then left that position after a matter of weeks. Jeffrey lacks direction—primarily because he doesn't know how to set goals for himself, and wouldn't learn to do so.

Goal setting requires us to ask powerful and important questions: What do I want out of life? Where am I going? Is my current job a step on the right path . . . or a detour? What do I value, personally? What's most important to me? How can I use my career to draw these things to me?

Whatever your strengths or growth opportunities, setting goals—having a direction and taking time to evaluate your progress in getting there—is critical to your success. For me, using the Tarot to clarify and set goals—or ponder why I'm having trouble reaching them—proves profitable again and again.

What to Do. This spread is designed to help you:

- Establish what you value—what kinds of things you want and need.

- Define your ideal path—where you want to wind up in five years.

- Define where you are now in relation to that goal.

- Envision short-term steps for getting there.

- Envision long-term milestones for getting there.

The spread consists of six cards (shown on the following page).

The shape of this spread reflects the "crossroads moment" faced when defining personal and professional goals. Which way will you turn? What journey will you set out on? How do you know which way to go?

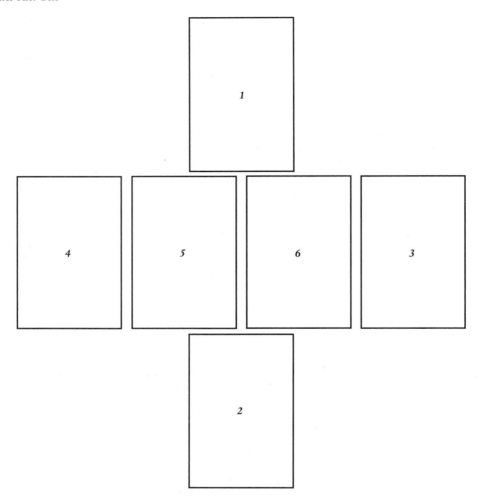

Fortunately, each card in this layout serves as a signpost. Instead of spelling out your future, these cards support exploration of your destination.

Note: Some people prefer taking a different approach with this spread. Instead of dealing random cards into each position, they prefer to choose the cards they feel belong in each position. If randomly dealing the cards doesn't work for you, you might give this a try.

Card One: What Really Matters? The people, symbols, and images on this card prompt you to consider what really matters to you. Your family? Your faith? Your job? Your money? Record whatever ideas occur.

The idea here is to establish a sense of your values. What principles guide you? What ideas, values, possessions, or concepts have powerful meaning and value to you?

As you brainstorm with this card, ask questions like these:

- What do you value most? Make a list of the people, things, and feelings that are most important to you. How do those things connect with this card?

- If you asked the person on this card what he or she believed in or valued most, what would he or she say? How might this relate to your personal values?

- To what degree do the objects on this card remind you of possessions you value?

- To what degree do the people on this card remind you of people you value?

- When you come to the end of your life, what approaches, attitudes, or values would you like others to say you stood for and represented? How might these be related to this card?

Card Two: What Do You Need? What we want or value may be very different from what we need. Use this card to generate ideas about those needs you possess which, for whatever reason, aren't being met. Contemplating this card may reveal motivations, repressed desires, or ignored feelings with bearing on your goals and values.

As you brainstorm with this card, ask:

- What activities does this card suggest? How might these activities represent something you need to do, but have neglected?

- What kind of environment, family situation, or employment opportunity might this card represent? How might this situation connect with something you need, but have neglected or ignored?

- What attitudes or opinions or prejudices are associated with this card? How comfortable are you with these attitudes and opinions? If these attitudes and opinions were expressed about your work, how would you feel? Have you had these attitudes or opinions expressed about your work in the past? How has that affected or influenced your career path?

Card Three: Your Ideal Destination. Use this card to come up with ideas about where you want to be . . . or, in the case of cards you consider negative, a destination you want to avoid!

As you consider the meaning of this card, ask yourself questions like these:

- Where do you want to be in five years? What are things that absolutely won't be a part of your work or world in five years? What would be your ideal future? How might this card relate to or suggest that future?

- How might this card characterize a situation, a way of thinking, or an action that will be important to you five years from now?

- How does this goal or destination tie in with your values? With what you really need? Note: if you have difficulty connecting your ideal future with what you value and need . . . you might reconsider the appropriateness of that destination!

Card Four: Where Are You Now? Use this card to explore where you are in relation to your ideal destination. Compare this card to the Ideal Destination card, noting the differences between your current situation and your goal. As you brainstorm, ask yourself questions like these:

- How might this card represent the situation you're in now? To what extent does the environment portrayed on this card mirror your current environment?

- How might this card characterize actions you're now taking? What actions would this card suggest?

- What ways of thinking are characterized by this card? What prejudices or assumptions?

- To what degree does your current situation differ from your Ideal Destination?

- What about your current situation would have to change in order to transform it into your Ideal Destination?

Establishing your own direction involves identifying your wants, needs, and ideals. Now that you've defined where you are, it's time to establish how you'll get from Point A (where you are) to Point B (where you want to be). Short-term and long-term goals are stepping stones that help you close the gap between your current and ideal worlds.

Card Five: Short-Term Goals. Instead of suggesting a single step, you may find that this card suggests a range of changes you can make to actions, ways of thinking, your environment, or your assumptions. List them all—but remember: the key word here is "short term." What would need to change within the next ninety days in order for you to move closer to your ideal situation?

For each short-term goal you list, ask these questions:

- How does this short-term goal tie in with your values? Is it true to them? Does it support them? Is it an expression of them?

- How does this short-term goal move you closer to your Ideal Destination?

- To what degree is this short-term goal appropriate—something you can accomplish within ninety days?

- To what degree is this short-term goal realistic—something you can really expect to achieve with your current skills and talents?

- To what degree is this short-term goal an objective goal—that is, will you be able to measure your progress toward it and know the precise moment you achieve it?

Card 6: Long-Term Goals. Once your short-term goals are in place, you'll be better positioned to pursue your long-term goals. Think of your long-term goals as targets for change you hope to reach within one to three years.

Like the short-term card before it, this card will likely suggest a range of changes to your actions, ways of thinking, environment, or assumptions. Again, list any and all ideas you have—you can always focus and revise the list later.

For each long-term goal you list, ask questions like these:

- How does this long-term goal tie in with your values? Is it true to them? Does it support them? Is it an expression of them?

- To what degree are these long-term goals supported by your short-term goals? Do the short-term goals look like steps leading you toward the long-term goals? How are the two related?

- To what degree is this long-term goal appropriate—something you can achieve within one-to-three years?

- To what degree is this long-term goal an objective goal—that is, will you be able to measure your progress toward it and know the precise moment you achieve it?

Practicing the Goal-Setting Spread

The Situation. Christine characterized herself as a "frustrated artist." She enjoyed her corporate position, but admitted she was there more for the money and the safety of the extensive health coverage than she was out of any sense of job satisfaction. Her work over the last five years had resulted in a number of promotions and bonuses, but, despite her success, Christine felt she was neglecting her true gifts, and had wandered away from what she was "meant to do."

Hoping to clarify her direction, Christine dealt herself the following cards from the Universal Tarot (see following illustration).

Refer to the illustration above—or, as before, pull these same cards from a personal deck. If you were Christine's brainstorming partner, what would you tell her? Some possible answers might be . . .

Card One: What Really Matters—Nine of Coins. Christine looked at this card for several seconds before speaking. "There's so much in this card. For some reason, I see this woman as a mother. She's standing in her own vineyard—one she owns and built all by herself—and it's profitable for her. She's got to be busy, but she still has time for the little things—like training her pets to do tricks."

But how did these observations relate to Christine's values? "If I made a list of my values without looking at this card, the list wouldn't include motherhood. I admired my own mother for raising a family on her own, and I've always wanted to be a mother myself. I also admire people who do their own thing and make out well—I'd like to be like that, too. I guess my list of values includes being brave enough to step out and do my own thing." After some additional thought, she finally added "making the most of the resources and talents you've been given" to her list of brainstormed answers.

Card Two: What Do You Need?—Page of Swords. Christine studied the figure on this card for some time before noting, "He's all dressed up to fight, and has a sword, but doesn't look very convincing to me. In fact, he looks afraid of a fight, like he likes the idea of fighting more than the fight itself."

To Christine, this card pointed to a feeling she had avoided for many months. "I'm successful at work, but I feel like I'm a pretender. Everyone thinks I'm so together and so focused—but I don't really like what I'm doing, and feel like I'm just going through the motions because I have to.

"I need to feel more certain that I'm doing what's right for me—that I'm doing what I'm supposed to do or meant to do. Also, this guy is a Page, which I associate with beginners, and from the suit of Swords, which is about decisions. Maybe he represents me, because I need to stop merely existing and start making some decisions!"

Card Three: Ideal Destination—Two of Swords. Christine expressed some surprise and dismay that "such a negative card" was in her Ideal Destination position. When brainstorming, though, she hit upon the idea of seeing this card as a representation of something to avoid.

"This person doesn't know what she wants. She's got two swords—she could do a lot of fighting—but she's blindfolded and uncertain." Christine gazed at the card more closely. "She's in a nice place, really. The beach is pretty, and the water looks inviting. The sky is even blue. But she can't enjoy it, because she's pulled in two directions at once."

Christine struggled to relate the image to her Ideal Destination. "I want to be able to enjoy what life has to offer. To be able to take time off and go the beach when I want to. I don't want to be conflicted and confused, or to be blindfolded and not be able to see or know where I'm going. I want to be confident and focused, and know I'm on the right track."

At this point, Christine remarked: "Every one of these cards has something to do with doing what you really want to do—being certain about yourself because you know you're doing what you're made to do."

She went on to say: "You know, I planned on being a writer. I always dreamed of it. I've got two degrees in creative writing that I never use. When I was younger, I always said I would be a writer. Now . . . here I am. I'm paying the bills, but I feel like I've sacrificed what I really wanted to do in the process."

She admitted that, for the last two years, she had wanted to find some way to pursue writing—but that fears about being able to maintain her lifestyle had prevented it. Christine decided that her Ideal Destination included getting rid of her indecision. In her Ideal Destination, she would no longer be conflicted because she would be writing for a living.

Card Four: Where Are You Now?—Seven of Wands. Christine laughed out loud. "That's me. I should be on top of the world, but instead, I feel like I'm constantly at war with myself." Christine determined she wanted to move from this state of constant struggle to an Ideal Destination where she felt confident, focused, and headed toward her dream of writing for a living.

Card Five: Short-Term Goals—The Devil. Once Christine understood that the Devil card had to do with feeling enslaved or "chained to something," she responded positively to the card.

"Within the next ninety days, I should look for ways to break my chains. Not quit my job, or anything drastic like that . . . but look for ways to make use of my writing. Maybe I could make time every day to write—or start thinking about magazine articles I might sell."

Minutes later, Christine had a list of short-term goals, including: make time to write every day, make a list of subjects I'm knowledgeable about, find magazines that might be interested in articles on those subjects, create a space in my home where I feel comfortable writing, and share with my husband my desire to make writing a part of my life again.

Christine expressed real surprise over this list. "It's in line with my values and needs—as a writer, I'll have more independence and freedom. I'll also feel like I'm using my talents to do what I was meant to do."

Card Six: Long-Term Goals—Five of Coins. With these short-term goals in place, Christine confronted her need for Long-Term Goals. "I don't like that picture at all," she said. "Two people starving in the snow. Maybe this is telling me that following my heart will put me out on the streets!"

A few minutes later, though, Christine's perceptions of this card changed. "The people on this card were unprepared for some kind of reversal of fortune. As a writer, I know that I probably won't make the same kind of money I do at the company. My husband and I should start preparing for that now. We can look at the kind of house we could afford on his salary alone, or we can start looking for ways to cut back."

She also realized "working as a writer also means working from home. If I work from home, I'm a lot better positioned to be a mother. I don't want my kids to be raised by a stranger at a day care. If I'm writing, I can take care of them, and work for myself."

Christine left the session excited and focused. "I had put writing completely out of my mind. I never thought how my dreams could point to things I really needed and wanted. Now I feel like I've got a plan that can help me live my dream!"

Your Turn. You may see Christine's cards very differently . . . and again, that's okay. The goal is to become comfortable generating as many ideas as rapidly as possible. Comparing your own brainstorm to hers may give you additional insight into the brainstorming process—but, ultimately, you need to start *Putting the Tarot to Work* for yourself.

When you've completed the three brainstorming exercises in this chapter, you'll have generated a set of insights and ideas you can use to transform your career in ways you never imagined possible.

More Ideas for Generating Change in Your Career

Whatever your career goals, you improve your odds of achieving them if you keep them in front of you. Expressing your goals in physical form—something you can see or touch on a regular basis—further reinforces your intentions. The more you see those goals, the more you think about them. The more you think about your goals, the more they become a part of your consciousness. The more conscious you are of your goals, the more likely you are to notice and take advantage of opportunities for achieving them.

Many of the exercises in this book use spreads—cards explored by placing them in well-defined positions. But there are other ways to use the cards, too, because cards are primarily visual—little photographs or paintings, loaded with meaning.

Memory specialists use images—especially strange or bizarre images—to remember complex lists. The images on a Tarot card can be very effective here: if you associate a particular card with your goal and keep that card where you can see it, the card becomes a daily reminder of your intentions.

Goal Cards

First, spread out the deck on a table or the floor. Scan the images with your goal in mind. Find a card with images, themes, moods, symbols, or people who connect with your goal in some way—the more vivid this connection, the better. When you look at this card, you should be able to say, "There I am," or "That's my goal in a nutshell."

If you're working with more than one goal, you may choose more than one card. You might also consider multiple cards if you want to pursue several different kinds of goals at once: a Cups card for emotional or spiritual goals, a Wands card for career goals, a Coins card for financial or practical goals, or a Swords card when facing a decision.

Once you've selected these cards, it's important to keep them where you can see them. You might consider getting a second deck specifically for goal cards, so you won't have to scramble your goals when you need the cards for other purposes. Some ideas:

- Instead of packing your cards away, leave your goal card—or a layout in which the card appears—on a coffee table or shelf. Let the spread stand for several days. Pause during the day to consider the meaning of your goal card, to envision the goal it brings to mind, or to look for additional connections it makes with other cards in the spread.

- Especially if your card has artistic or aesthetic appeal, consider framing it. Keep the card in the frame on the wall, where you'll see it every day. Deliberately pause when you pass the card to think briefly about your goal and picture it.

- Scan your Goal Card into your computer, making it your wallpaper or using it as a screensaver. When I was dreaming of moving from one city to another and longing for a new home, I scanned in my goal card: the Ten of Cups. Every day, I started and ended my day by gazing on the Ten of Cups, its rainbow of colors, and its happy family, dancing with joy. Perhaps because I kept this goal close at hand and on my mind, I completed a move to a new job in a new city and a new house in less than thirty days!

- Cards are portable—take advantage of that fact. Use your Goal Card as a bookmark. Keep a Goal Card in the car, and gaze at it when you stop for red lights. Let each red light become a reminder of your progress toward your goals!

Your Network of Friends and Contacts

With changes to your career in mind, consider drawing a few cards to help you identify friends, associates, acquaintances, folks at church, coworkers, relatives, and family members who could connect you to a new job. Make the most of these contacts—and use the Tarot to give you ideas. How could these people assist you in finding work?

Summary: Chapter Six in a Nutshell

RATHER THAN LEAVE YOUR career plan to chance, invest a little time in brainstorming a plan designed to take you where you want to go. When you use Tarot cards to brainstorm ideas for enhancing your job satisfaction, the deck becomes seventy-eight steps toward a more rewarding career, enabling you to move confidently from dissatisfaction to action.

Use the Self-Portrait Spread to explore where you are today, the Strengths & Opportunities Spread to become better acquainted with your potentials, and the Goal Setting spread to clarify and author step-by-step plans for achieving your goals. Used together, these three spreads have tremendous power to help you visualize and attain a better future.

In addition to brainstorming with these three spreads, don't forget that Tarot cards can also be used as memorable, visual reminders of your goals. Pick cards that represent your hopes and dreams, and let the card remind you of people and opportunities that figure in your efforts to improve your job satisfaction.

CHAPTER

Reviews Worth Raving Over

Preview: What to Expect in Chapter Seven

This chapter provides Tarot-based brainstorming strategies that:

☞ Prompt more accurate recollection of the past year's achievements

☞ Support a more objective review of performance

☞ Produce specific, positive feedback for both employers and employees

☞ Make the review process faster, easier, and more profitable for everyone involved

An Overview of Reviews

I SAT IN MY office, perplexed.

For the past year, every member of my small team had given one-hundred and ten percent. We created a corporate university on a shoestring budget. We worked nights and weekends to produce training programs that should have taken months to design. We assembled a comprehensive sales management training program from scratch, complete with A/V materials, classroom guides, and instructor's manuals. On top of all this, we wrote and produced eight high-energy training videos on a variety of subjects.

My team wanted to make a difference. We took pride in our work. Our enthusiasm and focus united us . . . and all of us excelled!

Why was I perplexed?

I lifted a corporate memo from my desk and read it again. The first paragraph explained that, as always, salary increases would be tied to an employee's performance rating. Unfortunately, beginning this year, employees rated excellent would receive a maximum four percent raise. Good employees would receive three percent. Proficient employees would receive one percent.

Employees with unacceptable performance would receive nothing.

By these rules, everyone in my group deserved four percent. But the memo also outlined a catch: the company insisted managers rate their employees on a curve. In my group of six employees, only one could be rated excellent. Two could be good, and two could be proficient.

Thanks to the curve, the hard work of one of my employees would be rated unacceptable. Someone, despite outstanding performance, would receive a low rating and, to rub salt in the wound, no raise.

I went to another manager and asked his advice. He sympathized, then confided his secret: "You pick the quietest, least confident person in the group. Look for the introvert. That's usually the one who will take the news with the least amount of protest."

"You do that?" I asked.

He winked. "This past week, in fact. The guy took the news without a word."

Finding this approach distasteful, I locked myself in my office, pulled out a Tarot deck, and started brainstorming. I drew three cards from the Universal Tarot, exploring three strategies for dealing with the unpleasant reality of the situation:

High Priestess   *Six of Coins*   *Six of Wands*

As the only trump, the High Priestess caught my eye. The Priestess connects with silence, secrets, and hidden knowledge. The company directed us not to share its curve-based review system with our employees; the reversal of the Priestess prompted me to consider what might happen if I discussed the constraint openly with my team. The more I thought about the option of honesty, the more I liked it.

The Six of Coins suggests collaboration and cooperation in practical matters. On the card, beneath a huge pair of scales, a wealthy man doles out coins to needy persons. I decided the scales emphasized my need to find some means of weighing my employees' efforts—some objective measurement capable of putting six excellent performers in some kind of order.

But what measurement would I use? In search of a clue, I moved on to the third card. The Six of Wands depicts a victory celebration. Each member of my team had been, in some way or another, celebrated by his or her clients. Each had experienced a victory or two over the year. Counting victories hardly seemed to be a fair way of deciding who would win the "excellent" rating—and didn't make assigning the "unacceptable" rating any easier, either!

The Priestess attracted my eye again. *Secrets,* I thought. *What information is being hidden from me?* Out of nowhere, an idea popped into my head: What exceptions might be allowed for the "rate on a curve" rule?

I called my own boss. With some prodding, he revealed the system *did* allow some flexibility. My team works as part of a much larger organization, and the company only planned to enforce the curve at the organizational level. As a result, I could get around assigning the "unacceptable" rating within my own team! ("But don't spread that around," my boss said. "They're keeping that a secret.")

Pausing to brainstorm prompted me to discover the loophole in the rating system. With that information in hand, I could afford to give my employees the high ratings they deserved, allowing lower performance levels in other parts of our organization to balance the curve. By collaborating with my boss (Six of Coins), I discovered a big secret (The High Priestess), and won a small victory (Six of Wands) for my team!

Pick a Card, Any Card!

When people hear talk of Tarot and job reviews, they imagine their boss facing a line of employees. He walks up and down the line, like an army sergeant reviewing the troops, shuffling a deck of cards as he walks. He stops in front of one employee, who stares straight ahead despite persistent trembling.

"McMurtry?" the boss asks.

"Yes sir?"

The boss whips out a card. "Ah ha! Ten of Coins! That means a ten percent raise for you!"

McMurtry visibly relaxes. "Thank you, sir!"

The boss moves to the next employee. "Now it's your turn, Burtram."

Bertram says nothing, but his bulging eyes never leave the cards.

The boss grins, holding out the Tarot pack. "Burtram, you choose."

Burtram objects, but has no choice. He touches the deck, hesitates, swallows hard, and finally pulls a single card. Holding his breath, he turns it over.

"*Death!*" the boss crows. "I knew it, you slacker! Get out! Get out! You're fired!"

Frankly? Even the system above would improve on the convoluted systems some companies employ. But this chapter isn't about reviewing people based on a "pick a card, any card" strategy . . . and it isn't about using the deck to foretell which employee will be next year's top performer. It is, however, about using the cards as a tool for sharpening recollection of past performance, clarifying dialogue between employer and employee, and focusing thought on improvement and action.

Nobody Loves 'Em, Everybody Hates 'Em

I don't need to consult the Tarot to discover how people feel about annual performance reviews!

Companies hate annual reviews. As one HR officer noted, "Disgruntled employees and downsized workers carry copies of their performance reviews straight to court. Last month's praise becomes this month's evidence of wrongful termination."

Bosses hate annual reviews. One manager told me, "I hate writing them. I hate delivering them. If the verdict is bad, the employee makes me the bad guy for not handling the issue earlier. If the verdict is good, the employee makes me the bad guy for not offering a bigger raise. It's a no-win situation."

Employees hate annual reviews. One of my coworkers noted, "What's the point? You lay out all these professional goals for the year . . . but everyone knows that three months later the department could be headed in a different direction. Reviews amount to meetings where your boss explains that, once again, you're not getting a raise."

She's not alone in her opinion. One nationwide survey found forty-five percent of employees report dissatisfaction with their company's annual review process. So why bother?

Without goals to guide us or feedback to reassure us, jobs become drudgery. Without direction, we lurch from assignment to assignment. Reviewing performance allows us to see our work in the larger context of our personal and professional lives. What do we want to do? Where do we want to go? How much harder do we have to work to get there?

Benefits: Pre-review Brainstorming with the Tarot

Brainstorming with the Tarot prior to a performance review can bring sanity, clarity, and objectivity to the performance review process. The step-by-step exercises in this chapter reveal how managers and employees can use the cards to pinpoint direction, improve performance, and enhance job satisfaction.

Once you integrate Tarot-based brainstorming into your performance review process, you'll enjoy the following benefits:

- *You'll achieve a more balanced perspective on performance.* Managers and employees alike can use the techniques in this chapter to see the past year's achievements and challenges in a more objective light.

- *You'll communicate about performance, including goals and objectives, more clearly.* You'll learn how to isolate—and discuss in a positive, profitable way—the key issues that need to be addressed in a review. The result? Instead of drifting into side issues or swapping vague observations, you'll focus the review process on what really impacts performance.

- *You'll see both achievements and challenges for the opportunities they represent.* You'll learn to take a strategic approach to your best work, positioning it as a stepping stone toward better recognition and higher pay. Better yet, you'll understand how to channel the challenges of the past into future growth and success.

- *You'll deliver and anticipate specific feedback on performance.* Instead of an awkward, generic commentary on the past year's work, you can prompt a focus on actions, attitudes, approaches, and the atmosphere in your organization.

The Spreads

This chapter provides three spreads to aid you in the pre-review brainstorming process. Working with these spreads will refresh your memory of the year's past events and aid you in recalling the specific events you need to remember when completing evaluations (or when preparing to be evaluated!).

The *Fundamental Factors Spread* is short and sweet, using just two cards to launch an exploration of the factors which contribute to an employee's overall performance.

The *Manager's Great Expectations Spread* encourages objectivity by prompting managers to brainstorm about their own assumptions and prejudices prior to beginning the performance review process.

The *Employee's Great Expectations Spread* approaches the review equation from the other point of view. Brainstorming with this spread prior to a review clarifies perspective on past contributions and encourages pre-session planning on the part of the employee.

The Fundamental Factors Spread

Hectic corporate schedules offer little time for reflection. Designed to make the most of limited planning time, the Fundamental Factors spread "cuts to the chase," focusing your brainstorming on two basic elements. These fundamental factors interact with each other to create, contribute to, change, or enhance an employee's performance.

For managers, this spread prompts consideration of the most critical elements influencing on-the-job performance. What really needs to be discussed? What message must this review communicate? What am I overlooking? What's the employee's challenge . . . and what's a way to help the employee meet that challenge?

Employees can use this simple spread to explore their own performance from a more objective viewpoint . . . or to speculate about the perspective of their employers.

What to Do. This spread involves only two cards, each of which represents a fundamental factor in the performance equation. To emphasize this interaction, the cards are arranged one atop the other, creating what looks like a crossroads:

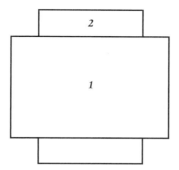

Exact positional meanings are not assigned for this spread. Instead, the two cards prompt consideration of this question: "How do these two factors combine to influence my (or my employee's) performance?"

Based on the cards you receive, you define the positional meanings "on the fly," taking your perception of the meaning of each card into account. The most frequently observed positional meanings for Fundamental Factor cards include:

Card One	Card Two
A symptom	A cause
An obstacle	A strategy
A question	An answer
The employee's expectations	The boss' expectations
A problem	The solution
What you know	What you don't know
Impact of review now	Impact of review later
A needed message	Reception of message
Best effort	Biggest challenge
Biggest achievement	Biggest challenge
Something to celebrate	Something to work on
Performance at present	The performance goal
A strength	A way to maximize it
Commentary on actions	Commentary on attitudes
The past year	The coming year

In most cases, people spot the relationship between the cards right away. In some cases, a glance at the cards and the list above immediately clarifies the relationship captured by the spread. When the relationship escapes you, invest a few minutes describing each card aloud. You might also explore the cards with another person—your boss, or another employee.

A Manager Practices the Fundamental Factors Spread

The Situation. Focused on meeting her team's latest "fire drill" assignment, Gloria forgot completely about pending employee reviews. Up against the company's mandatory submission deadline, Gloria found herself with just three hours to jot notes for use in tomorrow's performance review meetings.

Closing her office door and transferring her phone to voice mail, she shuffled the cards and dealt two for each of her four employees. She began with the cards for Martin, her highest-ranking manager. Gloria depended heavily on Martin; he was consistently her best worker. His excellent performance continued, but, over the past several weeks, she noted a decline in his trademark "can do" attitude. Until this point, Gloria attributed this change to the stress everyone in the department felt as deadlines tightened and resources shrank. Curious about options beyond these assumptions, she began her brainstorming session.

She briefly considered reshuffling the cards and drawing again when she saw Trump 15 (The Devil) and The Ten of Swords.

The Devil

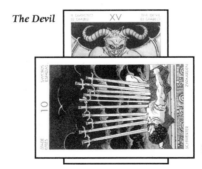

Ten of Swords

Refer to the illustration above—or, if you prefer, pull these same cards from your personal deck and arrange them into the fundamental factors spread. What ideas do these cards give you? If you were Gloria's brainstorming partner, what ideas would you toss out with regard to changes in Martin's performance?

Some Possible Answers. On the Devil card, two people stood chained to a black pedestal, controlled by a horned demon with a fiery club. On the Ten of Swords, a prone figure lay beneath a dark sky, pinned to the earth by ten sharp blades. The darkness of the cards took her breath away.

But what did these cards represent? She knew the Devil usually corresponded to feelings of oppression—being "tied down" to an unpleasant reality. The figures in chains appeared to be slaves of the demon on the pedestal . . . but either of them could shrug off the chains if they wanted to do so. Was Martin debating "breaking the chains" and leaving the department?

Gloria also knew Swords were associated with logic and decision-making, and that ten symbolized completion and finality. In the past, she had always focused on the darkness of the card; today, she noticed what she took to be a sunrise in the background. The image seemed to reinforce the idea that Martin had made a difficult decision that she would be too late to influence or reverse.

Pressed for time, she made a note to herself: "Remember to ask Martin about his satisfaction with his work now, and what you can do to increase that satisfaction. (Is he leaving?)" She decided the cards indicated "How Martin feels" and "What he's decided to do about it."

In her session with Martin the next day, Gloria said, "Martin, as always, your performance sets the standard for everyone in our department. I get the impression, though, that you may be making some difficult decisions. How can I help?"

Martin looked surprised. "What about my work would make you ask that?"

Gloria shook her head. "Your work is as creative and effective as ever. But, while I can't put a finger on it, I sense there's something not quite right. Does the work we're doing now satisfy you? Is there anything I can do to increase that satisfaction? Your contributions are valuable to me, and I want you around for as long as possible."

Martin swallowed hard. "Actually, I've made a decision to take a job somewhere else."

As it turned out, Martin appreciated Gloria's management. A long series of start-and-stop projects, though, resulted in a loss of faith in senior management. No longer able to make a meaningful contribution, Martin felt chained to a job he no longer enjoyed. After much deliberation, he decided to apply for other positions.

Had Gloria not completed the Fundamental Factors spread the day before Martin's review session, news of his pending departure would have completely bowled her over. "I would have spent the whole review trying to work out ways to change his mind—even though, by this time, Martin had made his final decision!"

Instead, she expressed her understanding of Martin's feelings, reinforced her personal appreciation for his work, and spent the remainder of their time together sketching out a transition plan. Gloria's work with the cards didn't help her to be happy about Martin's decision . . . but it did make responding to his departure less emotional and more productive.

Your Turn. Did seeing the Devil card prompt you to consider why Martin might feel chained down by the company? Did the Ten of Swords suggest a finalized decision . . . or a new beginning?

Even if your brainstorm led you to completely different ideas . . . that's okay! The goal is to practice generating the broadest possible variety of ideas—not guess exactly what this book will say. As you practice the Fundamental Factors Spread, you'll become more and more adept at using it to gain perspective on employee performance.

An Employee Practices the Fundamental Factors Spread

Especially when brainstorming alone, compensating for your own natural biases and assumptions becomes critical. To expand the range of ideas that occur to you, take your first impressions and turn them on their ear, forcing yourself to see your insights in a dramatically different light. Keep this in mind as you read Donald's story—it's a lesson in the value of brainstorming beyond the first ideas that come to you.

The Situation. With the next day's review in mind, Donald, a multimedia programmer, sketched out his needs. He and his wife had a new baby on the way. Bills were mounting. Donald knew he needed a raise, and he decided asking for a promotion from supervisor to manager would be the fastest way to get that raise.

Almost as an afterthought, he decided to use the Fundamental Factors spread to see what it might suggest. With his situation in mind, Donald shuffled the deck and drew two cards from the Robin Wood Tarot: the Knight of Wands and the Nine of Cups.

Knight of Wands

Nine of Cups

Refer to the illustration above—or, if you prefer, pull these same cards from your personal deck and arrange them into the fundamental factors spread. What ideas do these cards give you? If you were Donald's brainstorming partner . . . what ideas might you suggest? Remember to be alert—avoid limiting your advice to the messages Donald wants to hear!

Some Possible Answers. Donald knew court cards often represented people. He immediately wondered whether the Knight of Wands represented him. Looking over the card, he noticed the wildly rearing horse with a fiery mane and his rider's troubled, apprehensive look.

This imagery bothered Donald, so he turned his attention to the nature of the card. He knew knights tended to embody the extremes of their suits—in this case, Wands, the suit of intention. Donald decided the Knight meant, "Charge ahead with your plan!"

Seeking confirmation of what he took to be a positive message, Donald looked at the second card, the Nine of Cups. Here, a satisfied merchant sat, arms folded, in front of a display of nine golden goblets. Donald locked onto the satisfaction he saw in the merchant's face, and decided the card meant, "Getting everything you want." In Donald's opinion, the first card pointed to a strategy, and the second card, an outcome.

The next day, he walked into his manager's office and asked for the promotion and raise.

"I understand the need for more money," his boss told him. "I'd like a raise, too. But, especially in light of our falling stock price, the company isn't positioned to give raises this year."

"I understand that," Donald said, brimming with confidence. "But I've got a new baby on the way, bills to pay, and the fastest way to take care of that would be to get a promotion to manager. That's what I need."

"You've explained your needs very clearly," his boss said. "But raises aren't based on need—they're based on performance. This year, as a company, we haven't performed as well as we promised. Even if we had, I don't have a manager's position open."

Recalling his brainstorming session, Donald pressed harder. "I'm afraid that I need that raise and promotion in order to stay with the company. I expect you, as my manager, to go to bat for me and get a position opened up."

His boss shrugged. "Right now, there's not a department for you to manage—and, even if there were, I couldn't point to a level of performance that would justify moving you to management."

Donald's face turned red. "You're saying I don't deserve to be a manager?"

"This meeting isn't about what you deserve . . . it's about what I can justify, based on performance." Donald's boss pulled out a folder. "Your work on the Avery account—was it on time?"

Donald froze. "We were under a lot of pressure. I had a lot going on!"

"But the work was late. Worse, you neglected to give your team members a heads-up about the delay, leaving them high and dry. Just last month—what happened with the research summary your team produced for marketing?"

"Don't lay that on me! That was Brenda's fault."

Donald's boss shook his head. "But you're her supervisor—it's up to you to monitor her work and see it gets completed on time . . . or to alert me if it won't be, so we can make plans accordingly. In that sense, her failure is your failure. I know the raise and promotion would satisfy your financial needs, but I don't see the kind of performance from you that would support a promotion."

Donald left the office furious. What went wrong? Hadn't the cards indicated he should charge ahead and get what he needed to be satisfied?

Back home, he looked again at the two cards. This time, he saw them differently. Now, the Knight appeared to be charging wildly ahead, barely able to stay atop the horse. And where was he charging, out in the middle of the desert like that? The Knight of Wands kicked up a lot of dust, but lacked a plan.

The merchant on the Nine of Cups still looked satisfied, but Donald noticed a new detail: what was holding up that display of cups? Suddenly, the man's self-satisfied expression struck Donald as deceptive, and it occurred to him that maybe, beneath that display, the merchant was hiding something.

Only in hindsight did Donald consider alternatives to his initial brainstorming results. Instead of reaching for objectivity, he focused his creativity on making the cards tell him what he wanted to hear.

"I refused to consider that I might be the Knight of Wands, rushing ahead with my intentions for all the wrong reasons," Donald said. "I was so bent on my own satisfaction, I didn't stop to think whether or not I could support what I was asking for. If I had stopped to think about the meaning of those cards, I would have approached the whole meeting differently!"

Your Turn. How did your brainstorming results differ from Donald's? Did your list of ideas exclude negative possibilities and embrace only the most positive ones? Did you think to associate the Knight, as a court card, with Donald . . . or to speculate about what actions or activities the Knight might represent? Were you distracted by the overtly positive illustration on the Nine of Cups? Did you pause to consider how it might suggest a lack of satisfaction?

Of course, the most important thing is to use the cards to come up with ideas of your own. If you came up with meanings that surprised or engaged you, then this exercise was a success.

At this point, why not pause to explore your own performance, using the Essential Elements spread? What you discover may surprise you!

The Manager's Great Expectations Spread

Employees don't perform in a vacuum. The environment managers create—the expectations expressed, the conscious or unconscious prejudices, and the nature of our interaction with our employees—influences performance. Understanding how assumptions and expectations influence performance often prompts dramatic changes in a perceptive individual's management style.

The Manager's Great Expectations spread explores:

- The assumptions you make about your employees

- How these assumptions shape your interaction with your employees

- How those assumptions impact their performance

What to Do. To get the most out of the Great Expectations spread, complete it once a quarter or so, well in advance of annual performance reviews. If, like most managers, you wait until the last minute to complete reviews, the spread can be used to enhance your objectivity under pressure.

This spread consists of three cards:

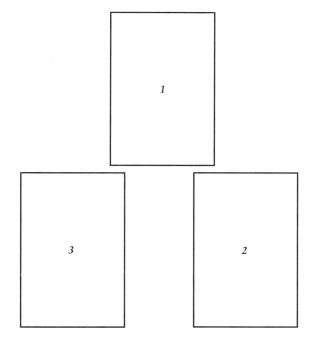

Individual Cards

Card One: Your Expectations. The image on this card amounts to a Polaroid snapshot of the assumptions you make about a particular employee. To help you connect with the personal message this card has for you, ask questions like these:

- What might this card suggest about the expectations you have of this employee?

- How does this card represent opinions or prejudices concerning this employee's actions and overall performance? What assumptions do you make about this employee's capabilities?

- To what extent might this card be a snapshot of the environment your expectations create for this employee—the way your assumptions make his work experience "feel"?

- How likely is it that this card captures what your employee thinks your expectations are? How would his or her perceptions of your expectations differ from your real expectations?

- What does this card suggest about the difference in the expectations you set for this employee and the expectations you set for other employees in your department? The difference between the expectations you have for this employee and yourself?

Card Two: Your Interaction. The image on this card defines how your expectations color your interaction with this employee—the impact your assumptions make on your own speech, behavior, and management style. To connect with the message this card has for you, ask questions like these:

- How does this card characterize your interactions with this employee?

- To what extent might this card describe how your interaction with this employee changed over time? What incidents prompted that change?

- How often do you provide this employee with positive feedback? With negative feedback? What might this card suggest about the nature, frequency, or quality of the feedback you're supplying?

- Interaction is a two-way street. How would this card suggest a kind of interaction your employee needs, but isn't receiving? Could it be a critique of your interaction, and the degree to which that interaction is only one-way?

- Finish this sentence: If my interaction with this employee is like the [Name of Card Goes Here], then this means my interaction with this employee is characterized by _____.

Card Three: Your Impact. This card summarizes the impact your expectations and interactions make on your employee's performance. To connect with the message this card has for you, ask yourself questions like these:

- What might this card suggest about the impact of your expectations and interactions on the quality of this employee's work? The quantity?

- How are your assumptions impacting the way this employee feels about his or her job?

- To what degree might this card represent how your employee feels as a result of your actions? How might these feelings influence productivity? The quality of the work?

- How are your expectations challenging this employee, inspiring a desire to grow or branch out? To what extent are your expectations stifling this employee's performance?

- To what extent might this card represent a goal—a representation of how your expectations and interactions should influence this employee's performance?

Other Considerations. As you look at these three cards, consider, too, what each *type* of card suggests:

A trump in any position invites you to become aware of the special role the associated factor plays in a given employee's performance.

A court card may suggest another person—a previous manager, co-worker, mentor, friend, parent, or sibling, from either your employee's past or your own—plays an important role in the performance equation.

A pip card indicates the factor under consideration expresses itself most often in the small, mundane activities that make up the average business day.

You might also take a moment to look at where the beings, creatures, or people in the cards are looking. Do their eyes draw attention to any one card? Are they all facing in the same direction? If so, what might this suggest?

Practicing the Manager's Great Expectations Spread

The Situation. Evan first interviewed for a position on my team years ago, striking all of us as not quite ready for a corporate career. We called him back for an interview a few years later, and hired him on as a production assistant. Initially, things went well.

With time, however, Evan's performance puzzled me. While others scrambled enthusiastically to complete assignments, Evan slouched. When other teammates requested Evan's help with a project, he always cited his own workload as his reason for not helping. Even so, each time I approached his cube unannounced, I found him surfing the web or composing email to friends. In my opinion, Evan represented our team's weakest link.

On the verge of "managing Evan into a position with another company," I paused to complete a Great Expectations spread using the *World Spirit Tarot*. What I found there caused me to see my relationship with Evan in an entirely different light (see illustration below).

Before reading how I interpreted these cards, write down an interpretation of your own. Rather than make general observations, remember to think in terms of what these cards might have to say about the biases and expectations that might have influenced my evaluation of Evan's

performance. How does the first card indicate my expectations about Evan's performance? What does the second card suggest about the way I interact with Evan? How might the third card describe the impact my expectations are having on Evan's actions? Some possible answers may be:

Card One: My Expectations—The Fool. The title of this card got my attention right away. I expected Evan to play the fool . . . to resist work, dancing carefree while the others of us worked harder to carry his load.

Looking at the Fool, I experienced a sudden flash of insight. Had my expectation that Evan would be goofing off altered the way I dealt with him? Thinking back, I realized I took every opportunity to catch Evan surfing the web or authoring personal email. I also realized I would never monitor the activities of my other employees so closely. Did Evan seem to be goofing off more simply because I watched him more closely?

The Fool also prompted me to think about the difference in Evan's attitude and the attitudes of the other members of my team. I expect my team to give one hundred and ten percent, to embrace challenges with all the vitality associated with the World Spirit Tarot's Fool. Evan's personal style, however, tends toward the somber, with his sense of humor anchored in sarcasm and fatalism. For the first time, it occurred to me that my expectations of Evan might run counter to his nature. Not everyone responds to the world with enthusiasm. To what extent was it fair for me to expect that in Evan?

Card Two: My Interactions—Eight of Swords. Here, a woman, blindfolded and loosely bound, wanders through a dark forest of dangers, stumbling over the sharp swords in her path. In other decks, she appears surrounded by a fence of swords.

Looking at this card, I came to understand how my interactions with Evan no longer offered him an opportunity to succeed. Expecting failure, I stopped entrusting Evan with high-profile projects.

Also, I noticed the degree of isolation and loneliness I associated with this card. Were my expectations leading me to isolate Evan? I had to admit they were. Reviewing the last several days, I estimated I spent several hours a day with other members of the team . . . but my time with Evan could be measured in minutes per week.

I noted, too, the threatening atmosphere of the card . . . and the swords strewn in the blindfolded figure's path. I recalled my interaction with Evan over the last few weeks: approaching him with sudden demands (often presented out of context, with no sense of how his work fit in to the larger picture) and snatching away assignments gone awry and giving them to other members of the team.

Expecting foolishness from Evan, I avoided him, blinded him by not supplying a perspective on how his work contributed to the team's overall efforts, cut him off from maturing influences, and littered his path with opportunities for failure.

As a result, I also limited his assignment list to low-priority work that we often, in the rush to meet deadlines, discarded or heavily revised. Someone in Evan's position had to feel constricted and deprived of vision!

Card Three: My Impact on Performance—The Sun. This card stunned me. I connect the Sun with success, with transformation, with growth. Here, the baby on the pedestal tosses flowers into the morning air. How in the world could this card describe my impact on Evan's performance?

After puzzling over the meaning for several minutes, a message hit me: growth requires sunshine. Evan wasn't growing. Could this be because I had failed to supply a medium for that growth?

Since joining the group, Evan received little direction, training, mentoring, or attention. As a manager, my job includes looking for opportunities to position my people for success—for their own good, and the good of the company. Unfortunately, when confronted with Evan's attitudes, I withdrew, leaving him to flounder without direction, close supervision, adequate feedback, or an opportunity for his own "moment in the sun."

Evan did face challenges—time management, giving his employer his best effort during work hours, and delivering assignments to specs by the deadline. I also realized, however, the role I played in Evan's downward spiral. Expecting him to fail, I actually began contributing to his failure.

I decided to do two things. First, I would invest more time with Evan, stopping by his cube, asking questions about his work, and equalizing the time I spent with him and my other employees.

Second, I would see that Evan had more opportunities to interact with the group as a whole. Instead of inserting myself between Evan and other team members, I decided to encourage them to return unsuitable output, explain how his output differed from what they expected, and request adjustments. Meanwhile, I asked him how I could support his work and what challenges he faced in fulfilling requests. I would also model how I would like him to respond to those requests.

Over the next three weeks, by the way, the results amazed even me. Given additional attention and guidance, Evan thrived. He produced several beautiful graphics and a complex animation for a training video. The quality of his work improved. For the first time, he began approaching me with works in progress, asking what I thought and accepting direction.

At the time of this writing, Evan and I still have work to do in terms of stabilizing our relationship, managing his work flow, and maintaining the quality of his output . . . but I'm far more aware of how my expectations and approach influence his performance. Instead of expecting Evan to play the Fool, I'm expecting him to deliver . . . and my interaction with him has changed dramatically as a result.

Your Turn. Mostly because of my experience with Evan, I suggest spending some time with the Great Expectations spread, analyzing how your own expectations influence your employees' behavior.

Create one Great Expectations spread for each employee, one employee at a time. After completing the spread for one employee, return his three cards to the deck, shuffle well, and choose three more cards for the next employee.

Interested in efficiency, managers always ask, "Why not just deal three cards at once for each of my four employees?" The simple answer: returning one employee's cards to the deck allows those cards to re-appear in spreads created for other employees. These recurring cards suggest valuable insights into how your expectations and interaction with one employee influences the performance of another.

The Employee's Great Expectations Spread

The Manager's Great Expectations spread assists managers in their exploration of how their assumptions impact employee performance. Because this version of the spread focuses on the employee, I present the descriptions of this spread, the exploration questions, and the sample reading from the employee's point of view. Even so, this spread can be used by employers and employees alike to explore the degree to which an employee met the organization's expectations.

What to Do. As an employee, you can use the spread to review the best of your performance over the past year, gain perspective on obstacles to peak performance, and define a direction for yourself and your career.

Managers can use the spread to capture the essence of an employee's best practices, biggest challenges, and opportunities for improvement and growth.

To maximize its impact, complete the Employee's Great Expectations spread in the weeks or days before a performance review.

This spread consists of three cards (see illustration on following page).

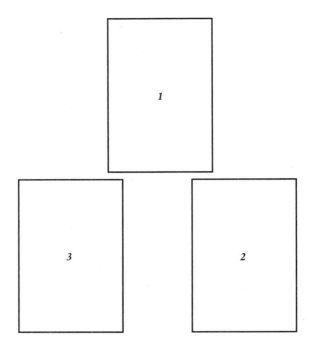

Individual Cards

Card One: Peak Performance. The image on this card characterizes the best of your performance during this past year. To explore the meaning of this card, ask yourself questions like these:

- To what extent might this card represent your "finest hour" this year? Do the images on this card seem to describe a moment or situation from the past year which you see as one of your best? What was that moment? Was it generated by something you said? Something you did? A way you interacted with other people? Was it something you learned? Was it a moment when your mind changed in some way?

- Could any of these elements represent the way you work? The way your work impacts the office environment? The outcome of your efforts? The benefits gained as a result of your efforts? An action you took on the company's behalf?

- To what extent might this card represent a quality or trait of yours which serves your department well? When have you saved the company time or money by putting that trait to work?

- How might this card capture a feeling you experienced upon the completion of a difficult assignment? To what extent did your best work satisfy you? What influenced your feelings at the conclusion of the work?

- To what extent might this card point to what others would characterize as your best work? Which of your accomplishments might you dismiss . . . but others value?

Card Two: Your Challenge. The images on this card connect with the largest obstacle on your path to success. In most cases, you're already aware of this obstacle and its influence. Think of your challenge as an inhibitor: something holding you back. If removed, new growth becomes possible.

To connect with the meaning of this card, ask yourself questions like these:

- To what extent is your biggest obstacle internal? How do you contribute to your own difficulties and challenges? How might you be holding back? Does the image on this card illustrate some attitude, decision, or prejudice that could be adversely impacting your performance?

- How might this card represent an external obstacle—something or someone you don't control that inhibits your best efforts? How does this sabotage your success? How do you participate in and allow that sabotage, supporting it and giving it energy? How might you transform this obstacle into a stepping stone?

- To what extent might the image on this card represent a kind of work you are unable to do—but need to do? How might it point to a skill, talent, or craft needed in order to move forward in your job? What would be the impact on your work if you could perform the activity illustrated by the card? How might your performance change? What roadblocks would be removed?

- Is it possible that this card points, not to the challenge, but the way around it? If so, what strategy does this card suggest?

- How might this card be a snapshot of a moment when you didn't meet your highest standards of performance? What led to that moment? What contributed to the failure? How does that moment impact performance now?

Card Three: Your Growth Opportunities. This card points to future directions capable of helping you achieve goals you may not yet have imagined. Growth Opportunities fly below your professional radar, waiting to be recognized. Think of a Growth Opportunity as a potential, waiting to be recognized and activated.

To help explore this card, consider the following questions:

- What actions do you need to take in order to insure you have the opportunity to grow?

- To what extent might this card represent a task or chore you could take on? A new direction to try? How might it embody an assignment outside of your realm of responsibility with potential to open new doors?

- What hidden talents do you possess? To what extent might this card point to an aptitude untapped in your current position? How can you find ways to put that talent to work? What abilities do you have that aren't being exercised or stretched by your current work?

- How might this card point to a dream job? A new job? A new position? A way to change your current job so that it allows you to do work that would delight you?

- How might this card represent a situation you avoid, but with potential to teach you important lessons? A person with a great deal to teach you? A technology you need to master? A technique you need to learn? A book you should read? A course you must take? A promise to yourself you need to keep

Other Considerations. A trump in any position indicates vital information for you. Spend extra time pondering the meaning of this card! Very likely, it points to realizations that strike to the core of who you are, the kind of work you do, or the path that lies ahead of you.

A court card in any position describes a person (or a personality) with a great deal of influence over the qualities portrayed. Explore court cards by asking yourself, "Who holds influence over this dimension of my performance?" (Remember, a male court card can refer to a female, and vice versa . . . don't let the gender of the card keep you from considering anyone who embodies the card's perspective.)

If you cannot connect the court card to a specific person, consider the qualities represented by the court card. How do these personality traits and approaches influence your work? Do you possess them? If not, how might your work change if you did? If so, how are they impacting your work?

Finally, pip cards invite you to consider how the quality of the card expresses itself in the hum-drum cycle of everyday work. When confronting a pip card in any position, ask yourself how your daily routine and your interaction with others embodies the meaning of the card. Don't overlook the power of the everyday! Habits hold great sway over what we do and who we become.

You might also determine where the beings, creatures, or people in the cards are looking. Do their eyes draw attention to any one card? Are they all facing in the same direction? If so, what might this suggest?

Practicing the Employee's Great Expectations Spread

The Situation. When the time came to prepare for her job interview, Trina felt distraught. The past year—filled with upheaval, layoffs, and multiple changes in leadership and management—hadn't given her many opportunities to shine. Now, with reviews pending in less than a week, she would find herself sitting opposite a new manager placed over the department just six weeks earlier.

Months of seeing one day's bright new direction become the next day's abandoned strategy left Trina feeling unfocused and unprepared. She found herself becoming less of a team player. Worse, her review, instead of offering a stepping stone to greater things, seemed more of an opportunity to do little more than say, "I'm still here."

As a last-ditch effort to focus her thoughts, Trina selected the Employee's Great Expectations spread. She dealt three cards from the *Universal Tarot*:

1

3

2

If you were Trina's brainstorming partner, what ideas would these cards generate for you? Write down your recommendations before moving on. Remember to consider as many interpretations for each card as possible. After doing so, look for a common thread or theme among some of your interpretations as a way of deciding which meanings deserve more emphasis than the others.

Some Possible Answers. All those swords caught Trina's eye. She decided her reading would have a great deal to do with decisions and choices she had made, or ways her actions had conveyed and communicated those decisions to others.

Card One: Peak Performance—The Four of Swords. Trina studied this card, which she felt depicted a young knight asleep in a church. She knew that, traditionally, the Four of Swords connected with peacefulness, stability, and serenity . . . but didn't understand how that connected with her peak performance.

At first, especialy in light of the past year's upheavals, the card prompted Trina to debate whether her best work had simply been maintaining some degree of sernity in the face of sweeping changes. She considered this, but decided against it. As each wave of layoffs and restructuring approached, she had been as panicked and upset as everyone else. Serenity was the farthest thing from her mind.

She was also aware of several assignments where her state of mind interfered with her work. On a regular basis, her work now fell short of her own expectations. So . . . she really couldn't say she possessed serenity or the ability to "take things in stride." What could the card represent?

Her next insight hit like a lightning bolt: the knight on the card wasn't just meditating—he was asleep on the job! His trusty sword remained at the ready . . . but if the situation demanded it, would he really be able to make the sudden transition from deep sleep to clear-eyed action? Trina felt it was far more likely that, no matter what took place, the knight would continue dozing—perhaps even while others crept in to steal the swords hanging above his head.

Now the message of the card became clearer: over the past year, as she put forth less and less effort for a company she no longer loved, she had metaphorically fallen asleep on the job. She still possessed a sharp wit and a keen mind for business, but now her personal "swords" were under-utilized and neglected—making it easier for others to sneak in and outperform her.

Trina decided she would be frank with her new employer: this past year, with all its turmoil, offered her few opportunities to perform to her usual standards. As a result, she would be unable to point to her best work. Having recognized this, she felt a new hunger for challenging assignments that would "wake her up" and get her career back on the right track.

Card Two: Biggest Challenge—The Ten of Swords. Trina took one look at the pierced, bleeding figure on the Ten of Swords and empathized right away. "How many times over the past year have I decided it was up to me to make a difference? I'd read some book about positive attitudes, then go to work determined to make the best of every opportunity. By noon, though, they would have laid somebody off or canceled some project I loved. I'd be right back on bottom again. Finally, I just got tired of trying."

Trina realized the biggest obstacle to improved performance was her attitude. In addition to being in a rut, she doubted her job could change for the better. Tired of picking herself up again and again, she essentially quit her job . . . without leaving the premises.

"I can't control what happens to the company, but I can control the way I respond to it," Trina said. "I'm sick and tired of having a bad attitude. I want an assignment that gives me a chance to be proud of myself and my work again. Pick a direction, give me marching orders, and let me get something done that makes a difference!"

Card Three: Growth Opportunity—Six of Swords. Trina knew that Swords concerned decisions, logic, and ways of thinking. She also knew that Sixes connected with collaboration, sharing, and cooperation. "At first, I focused on the person in the hood. She looks defeated. I wondered if the card was suggesting that I should make a decision to give up and move on. But then I focused on the man steering the boat. And that's when it hit me: this upcoming review was an opportunity in disguise—a chance to bring my new manager around to seeing me as I see myself. Rather than focus on what had or hadn't been done this past year, it would be a chance to say, 'This is who I am, and this is what I can do for you. Put me to work.'"

Despite this optimistic take on the meaning of the card, Trina found herself drifting back to her initial impression. "Here's someone who's been asleep. He's been beaten down. And now he's in a boat, having made a decision to leave. I like the more positive reading best, but I want to stay open to all the possibilities."

At the review, Trina decided to be as honest as possible. She described how the past year hadn't afforded many opportunities to exhibit her best qualities. She mentioned being weary of working that way. She expressed a desire to make a change—and told her new manager, point blank, that she needed his cooperation to make that change. "I said I wanted him to give me some new assignments, new direction, and give me an opportunity to prove to myself."

Her manager's response disappointed her. "He hemmed and hawed. He said he applauded my good attitude and would remember it. But more than anything, he seemed threatened. Over the next two weeks, I reminded him I was ready for new assignments, but he never passed me any."

Ultimately, Trina decided to look for new work. "I remembered the Six of Swords. I was tired of being asleep, tired of feeling beaten down. Once I decided my new manager wasn't different from the last few, I realized making a change was up to me. So I moved on. Without the reading, I would probably have just kept waiting for the axe to fall."

Your Turn. So how did you do? Did you emphasize meanings related to numbers and suits—or did you focus on the images used to illustrate each card? Did you think exclusively about positive meanings . . . or did some potentially negative or unpleasant meanings appear in your reading?

Remember—the point is to practice the process . . . not to guess the meanings Trina might assign. The important thing is to begin using this spread to explore your own "great expectations"! (In fact, some people who complete this exercise with Trina's cards find they've actually generated good advice for themselves. Did you?)

Summary: Chapter Seven in a Nutshell

NO ONE LIKES REVIEWS, but without the opportunity for reflection and direction reviews provide, work becomes drudgery. Using the Tarot in pre-review brainstorms brings sanity, clarity, and greater objectivity to the performance review process.

The Fundamental Factors Spread cuts to the chase, isolating the two basic elements with the greatest influence on employee performance. The Manager's Great Expectations Spread explores how a manager's expectations shape and influence the actions of employees. And the Employee's Great Expectations Spread encourages employees, prior to a review, to explore their own peak performance, biggest challenges, and growth opportunities.

CHAPTER

Building Better Business Relationships

Preview: What to Expect in Chapter Eight

This chapter provides Tarot-based brainstorming strategies that:

☞ Explore the image you present to others

☞ Map and analyze your personal network of contacts

☞ Capitalize on the success of your mutually beneficial contacts

☞ Analyze and improve unhealthy business relationships

The Importance of Healthy Business Relationships

DESPITE OUR URGENT NEED, we were on the verge of giving up.

Again and again, our department requested development and hosting of a training web site from Information Services. Again and again, I.S. pushed our request down its list of priorities. Like clockwork, our request dropped off the development group's radar screen. When we resubmitted our request, the cycle started again.

I shared our dilemma with other departments. "That's odd," one manager said. "We requested space for an intranet site, and had it the following week. We didn't even have to go through the development request process. The guy from I.S. just did the work on the side."

Frustrated, I made an appointment to meet with the head of the I.S. development team. At the meeting, Toby, a red-faced man with receding hair, sat across from me, folded his arms, and asked, "What's this about? I'm pretty busy."

"Our department needs space for an intranet site," I began.

Toby pushed a stack of forms across his desk to me. "Then do what everyone else does. Fill these out, and we'll prioritize your request."

I handed him photocopies. "We've filled those forms out several times. We've been prioritized several times. Then, for reasons I don't quite understand, our project just drops off your project plan."

Toby's face turned even redder. "You can't just come in here and demand an intranet site be developed. We have a process. Everyone has to go by the process. You'll have to fill out those forms."

I shook my head. "Toby, everyone *doesn't* have to go through the process. I spoke with at least two department managers who made their requests after ours. Without ever filling out forms or appearing on the priorities schedule, they got their sites."

Toby's forehead, cheeks, and ears turned scarlet. He rose to his feet and pointed to the door. "You want a site? Then fill out the forms. This meeting is over. I've got work to do."

I took a deep breath. "Toby, your group exists just for the purpose of fulfilling requests like ours. I've made it clear we've filled out the forms and played by the rules. As your customer, I'm telling you your process is broken. Now, what do we have to do to get action on our request?"

Toby shook. "Now you know how it feels, don't you?"

I blinked. "What?"

Toby's mouth widened into an ugly smile. "Our group came to you a while back, asking your department for some software training. Your boss took one look at our request and said your group just didn't do that kind of training."

I shook my head. "I don't remember that specific request. But that's true—we don't develop or deliver software training."

He folded his arms and looked smug. "What goes around comes around," he said. "You don't develop software training for us, we don't develop web sites for you."

"Toby, when did all this happen?"

He paused. "Three years ago."

His reply stunned me. "Three years ago? Toby, I wasn't even here then!"

He pointed to the door again. "Your boss was. Maybe this will teach him a lesson."

So much wasted time, energy, and money . . . all because the parties involved allowed one incident to ruin a critical business relationship!

Healthy . . . or Unhealthy?

Success in business depends on the achievement of balanced, mutually-beneficial relationships.

In return for a customer's money, a company supplies the products or services the customer needs. In return for an employee's efforts, an employer supplies benefits and paychecks. Coworkers and colleagues lend access to their insights and skills in order to gain access to each other's expertise and experience. Everyone involved in the relationship profits from it.

Many people confuse pursuing profitable business relationships with becoming a "user." Having been manipulated in the past, they worry about becoming someone who forges relationships as a way of manipulating others for personal gain.

What's the difference between a dishonest effort to manipulate others and an honest effort to make the most of your personal network? Your intentions.

Manipulators, in an effort to inflate their apparent value, enhance their image with boastful deceits. Manipulators bribe others with offers of assistance, thinking only of what they will get in return. Manipulators grant favors in an effort to engineer indebtedness in those they aid. Manipulators give very little and demand a great deal, always providing only what's necessary in order to reach their selfish goals.

On the other hand, people focused on healthy business relationships conduct a frank, honest assessment of the scope of their abilities. Doing so positions them to identify their best opportunities for making valued contributions. They assist others because they realize a unified team—to everyone's benefit—works harder, faster, and smarter. They take great pride in contributing to and supporting their own success . . . and the success of those around them.

When business relationships become unbalanced—when services cost too much, when the paycheck pales in comparison to the work we do, when a coworker demands much but offers little—our degree of satisfaction declines . . . along with our success! On the other hand, healthy relationships provide successful business people with an unparalleled degree of support . . . and a broad range of professional options.

The Benefits of Exploring Business Relationships Through Tarot

Mention consulting the Tarot about business and relationships, and most people will think you've been phoning your Psychic Phone Pal about a tryst with your boss. This chapter doesn't focus on those kinds of relationships!

Every employer, every customer, every vendor, and every coworker you've ever encountered becomes a node in your personal network. With an eye toward your future success, this chapter shows you how to use Tarot to explore your personal network, enhance the quality of your relationships, and understand how your connections to others can be the key to a more satisfying career. Applying these techniques allows you to:

- *See yourself as others see you.* Understand your impact and influence. Using the Tarot, you'll develop a more objective view of the role you play in your own network . . . and the opportunities you have to aid and support others.

- *Align your words with intentions and actions.* Clear communication plays a key role in supporting healthy business relationships. The chapter includes an exercise designed to help you express your goals and communicate your intentions more clearly. As you speak with more confidence and insight, others will respond by strengthening their relationships with you.

- *Handle conflicts.* Defuse issues before they escalate. Your network offers you multiple points of view on any situation. While nothing can replace wise advice from people you trust and admire, this chapter includes a spread designed to simulate that process and generate new solutions.

- *Analyze your relationships.* Build healthier relationships based on strengths and successes. You'll examine your existing network with an eye toward its strengths and weaknesses. You'll arm yourself with an action plan for expanding the network with new connections . . . and for repairing problematic relationships.

Spreads and Exercises

This chapter includes both spreads and exercises, all designed to help you explore your personal network and the relationships supporting it.

Exploring your personal network begins with an examination of your own contribution to that network. What do you have to offer? How are your contributions perceived by others? The *Mirror, Mirror Spread* provides a sobering glimpse of yourself as others see you. Completing this spread helps you grasp the differences between the image you intend to project and the image others perceive.

Mapping Your Network transforms your invisible business connections into a visual model of your relationships with others. Using Tarot cards to construct a map of your interaction with others helps you identify the scope, content, and structure of your personal network. Mapping the network also enables you to poll the network for advice and insight into business challenges and opportunities.

The *Working Relationship Spread* provides an opportunity to learn from your own successes, encouraging you to understand why your best relationships work as well as they do. In the process, you'll gain greater appreciation for these partnerships . . . and learn how to replicate that success again and again.

On the other hand, the *Problematic Relationship Spread* examines those one-sided relationships limited by neglect or lost of trust. Most people ignore or avoid unhealthy aspects of their networks! This spread offers an alternative to ignoring unhealthy nodes in your business network, encouraging you to consider strategies for improving or repairing them.

Mirror, Mirror Spread

The Mirror, Mirror Spread provides a glimpse of how others see you. Think of it as a portrait from the perspective of your coworkers and customers. Because of the degree of objectivity and self-examination required by this spread, people rank Mirror, Mirror among the most difficult spreads in this book.

A tip: If the meaning of a given card fails to be readily apparent, make a note and struggle with it for a while. When unable to understand how a particular card applies to you, ask your boss, customer, or coworker. You'll find they see an application right away!

What to Do. While working with this spread, people tend to make one of two mistakes:

They believe this spread paints them "as they really are." By design, this spread helps you step outside your personal biases and explore how others see you. Others may see you very differently than you see yourself . . . but their viewpoint is just another perspective, and not necessarily more accurate than your own.

Rather than get caught up in an emotional response to the information in this spread, put the information to work! If the perceptions of others differ dramatically from the "you" that you intend to project, don't fret. Instead, consider how changes in your approaches, actions, words, or habits could help others see "the real you." Always ask, "What do I want to do about this perception?"

As a reminder that this spread reflects the perspective of others, I designed this spread to resemble the shape of an oval mirror. The spread consists of six cards (shown on the following page).

Card One: Attitude. Your overall attitude amounts to the emotional tone you project. Remember, the attitude depicted here isn't the attitude you want to project or you feel you project. Instead, this card reflects how others perceive your attitude—how they interpret your general approach to life and work.

To further explore the meaning of this card, ask yourself questions like these:

- How might the actions taking place on this card represent an action or habit of yours used by others to define your overall attitude?

- To what extent is this card a snapshot of an incident or situation which formed other's opinions about your attitude or outlook?

- What words would you use to characterize your own attitude? How many of those words are reinforced by this card? How many of those words would be contradicted by this card?

- What attitude do you feel this card suggests? Recall a time when you projected this attitude.

- To what extent might this card identify a particular person whose attitude you recognize? How do your own attitudes compare to the attitudes of this person?

```
        ┌───────┐
        │       │
        │   1   │
        │       │
        └───────┘
┌───────┐         ┌───────┐
│       │         │       │
│   6   │         │   2   │
│       │         │       │
└───────┘         └───────┘
┌───────┐         ┌───────┐
│       │         │       │
│   5   │         │   3   │
│       │         │       │
└───────┘         └───────┘
        ┌───────┐
        │       │
        │   4   │
        │       │
        └───────┘
```

Remember: this card invites you to explore how others see your attitude at work. How would you feel if others saw your attitude in a way described by this card? If you feel the attitude depicted here is a positive one, what might you do to further reinforce this perception of your attitudes? If negative, what might you do to alter their perceptions in the future?

What attitude do you want to project? What actions can you take or changes can you make to project that attitude? How might this card suggest strategies for doing so?

Card Two: Your Communications Style. Because of its dramatic impact on how others respond to you, the way you communicate—your tone, your manner, your choice of words, and even your body language—can influence others far more than the words you actually say. Rather than critique how well you communicate with others, this card captures the overall tone and nature of your communication as perceived by employers, coworkers, and/or employees. Do you tend to be blunt or tactful? Direct or general? Focused or rambling? All business or too personal? This card prompts an exploration of how others perceive what you attempt to share.

Imagine how the people on this card would communicate in a crisis. Imagine how they would deliver praise. Imagine how they would explain a problem. What aspects of this image prompt you to think these things? Now, consider how you communicate in a crisis, how you deliver praise, and how you explain complex problems or assignments to others. How do your styles differ from the styles depicted here?

To further explore the meaning of this card, ask yourself the following questions:

- What actions appear on this card? What people? To what extent might the images on this card represent something you do—a gesture you make or a posture you assume—when communicating with coworkers, employers, or customers?

- How would you define the emotional tone of the card? How do you communicate that emotional tone when talking to others? Imagine that others believe this emotional tone dominates the way you communicate. What might you be doing that would communicate this particular tone?

- How might this card bring to mind someone else—perhaps someone whose communications style you imitate or emulate? If the card reminds you of another person, how does your style differ from that person's style? Why might others think that you and this person communicate in the same way?

- To what extent does this card bring to mind a past event? To what extent does the card represent a time when you communicated clearly (or poorly) with those around you? To what extent might this moment have been one that shaped your communication style? What impact did this moment have on your life in general?

- How might the images and symbols on this card point to certain elements of your communications style? How might they draw attention to your speed of speech, your word choice, or the degree to which your voice rises and falls as you speak? Do you think they describe your mannerisms . . . or ask you to consider discarding, revising, continuing, or improving them?

Card Three: Your Work. In the world of work, what you contribute—or what you are perceived to contribute—is all-important. I've worked with individuals who imagine themselves hard-working, valuable members of the team . . . but whose coworkers and employers see them as unfocused, distracted, and reluctantly productive. I've also worked with modest people who feel they contribute very little . . . but whose teams perceive them as the most valuable players. This card describes how others value your contribution—their overall perception of the quality of the work you do.

To further explore the meaning of this card, ask yourself questions like these:

- How might this card be a commentary on the quality of your work?

- If the number on the card represented a score of your work, what would such a score indicate about the value others place on your work?

- To what extent does the situation or environment on the card remind you of a situation or environment in your past? How did you feel about your work back then? How did others characterize your work back then? How has the quality of your work or your attitude changed since then? How have your actions reflected that change?

- How might a person depicted on this card be a symbol for someone whose opinion of your work is very important right now? What kind of value does that person place on your work today? How would he or she critique your performance?

- To what extent might this card represent how you want others to feel about your work? How can you change or alter your working habits so that others are more likely to perceive your work this way?

Card Four: An Opportunity for Growth. Ask others what you could do to grow or change, and they frequently soften what they have to say for fear of hurting your feelings. Not this card! The card in this position spells out what others would identify as your most promising opportunity for change . . . what you could do, in their eyes, to become a more valued player.

Remember that this information may or may not take you in a direction you want to go! Directions or changes desired by others are not always in our best interest, but are certainly worth considering.

To further explore the meaning of this card, ask questions like these:

- What are the characters on this card doing? How might these actions represent a new direction for you to take? How do you feel about that action? What are the possible outcomes of that action?

- How might this card represent some change in your attitude? In your work habits? In your communication style? In your overall approach to life? How would you feel about making the change suggested here? Why?

- Consider the number of the card. Find the two cards in the deck that come just before and just after this card. (For example: if the card is the Three of Wands, find the Two and the Four.) Imagine that the card from the spread captures some aspect of who you are right now, and that the other two cards show alternative directions or approaches. How do you feel about these alternatives? What would be the value of going backward (to the Two, in our example) or forward (to the Four)? What would be the impact on your work?

- What's the best possible meaning for this card? What's the worst possible meaning for this card? How might these extremes suggest options for change or growth?

- If the person on this card were a career counselor, what growth opportunity might he or she say you possessed? To what extent are you now positioned to work on this deficit, gaining skills or insights? What perpetuates this weakness? How can you grow beyond it?

Card Five: Your Greatest Strength. This card represents a frank, honest answer to the question, "In your opinion, what is my most valued quality?" The Greatest Strength card will depict some aspect of how you think, what you say, or what you do that others find valuable on a regular basis. It may also point to a situation in which others' perceptions of your greatest strength were formed.

To better understand the meaning of this card, ask yourself questions like these:

- What qualities do the figures on the card represent? How might these qualities be considered strengths in the workplace? What actions or achievements of yours might prompt others to believe you possess this strength?

- What are the figures on the card doing? What strength would be required in order to perform this activity? Why might others think you possess this strength?

- To what extent might this card point to a moment or incident which revealed your true strength?

- What could the suit of the card suggest about your greatest strength? To what extent does it hint that your greatest strength could be physical or financial (Coins), mental or intellectual (Swords), spiritual or emotional (Cups), or inspirational or professional (Wands)?

- To what extent might this card be a portrait of someone who possesses a similar strength? To what extent might the person on this card be someone who lacks your greatest strength and, therefore, needs your support?

Card Six: Your Reputation. Your reputation amounts to the shorthand an employer, coworker, or employee might use when describing you to a stranger—a capsule that tends to summarize your best (or your most challenging) features. Your reputation sets expectations before you ever appear on the scene. Arriving with a firm understanding of those expectations empowers you, allowing you to decide whether to perpetuate or challenge them.

To further explore the meaning of this card, ask yourself questions like these:

- Imagine asking someone else to pick a card from the deck that best describes you. Imagine that person hands you this card. What message would that person be trying to send? If this card served as a "shorthand description" of you, what qualities, approaches, abilities, or perspectives would such a card suggest?

- To what extent might this card capture a phase you're going through? For example, if the card were the Five of Wands, you might say, "I've been going through a Five-of-Wands phase lately," meaning you've experienced instability, conflicts of interest, arguments, or confrontations. How might this phase influence your reputation with others?

- Now imagine someone uses the same card to describe you to someone else. In the example above, your boss, coworkers, or employees might say, "This person is a real Five-of-Wands-type person." How might this card provide insights into how others see you? What have you said or done recently that might reinforce this reputation?

- To what extent might this card represent your reputation as a worker? As a leader? As a customer? As a team member? As a representative of your company? As a member of your profession? As a person?

- If the reputation represented by this card displeases you, what actions could you take to change it? If this card reflects a reputation you like, how can you further reinforce it?

Practicing the Mirror, Mirror Spread

The Situation. When Wanda landed her first job—working for minimum wage in a retail store—her mother gave her advice: "To get ahead, be everyone's best friend."

Based on this, she determined she would treat everyone at work as though they had been her friends for years. She laughed, joked, and took every opportunity to get to know her coworkers personally. She took interest in their personal lives, and dedicated herself to getting to know and understand their feelings and motives.

Complicating this was the fact that everyone at work seemed to hold her at arm's length. She decided this had to be because she was new . . . or because they were uptight. In Wanda's opinion, people at the store needed to loosen up, to learn to enjoy their life, and not be so serious all the time. She redoubled her efforts to get laughs, win friendship, and become everyone's confidant.

After her first month on the job, Wanda appeared for her first review. "It totally shocked me. At first, I thought my boss was reading from someone else's review by mistake. He told me other people felt I didn't do my share of the work. He said he had gotten complaints from managers that I interfered with the work of other people. He said many people felt uncomfortable about my jokes."

Wanda explained she was just being friendly. "I told him most of the people working for him needed to loosen up and learn to laugh." The owner's reply stunned her. "He said he wasn't paying people to be my friends . . . he was paying them to work, and that I needed to keep that in mind. He gave me two weeks to be a better performer."

Wanda decided to use the Mirror, Mirror Spread to better understand how her coworkers and employers felt about her work. She dealt herself six cards from the Universal Tarot (as shown in the spread on the following page).

Pause now and imagine that Wanda hires you as her career counselor. Read the cards in this spread, using each one to prompt insights and recommendations. Be sure to write your thoughts down before proceeding! Some possible answers might be . . .

Card One: Attitude—The Fool. At first, this card made Wanda angry. "I thought the card was saying I was a fool." Then she remembered this position explores attitudes—specifically, how others perceived her attitude.

1—Attitude

6—Reputation

*2—Communications
Style*

*5—Greatest
Strength*

3—Your Work

*4—Growth
Opportunity*

"This guy looks happy and carefree. He's on a walk, he's carrying a flower, and he's got his dog with him. It's a sunny day. I work hard to project that carefree attitude, so at first, I figured other people were actually seeing the attitude I wanted them to see."

"Then I read a little about the Fool, and found out this card is associated with beginnings and beginners. I also noticed this card was the only trump in the spread, meaning that its message was the most important one for me to figure out. So I spent a little more time with the card, and decided it meant that other people saw me as the Fool—a total beginner, without any experience at all. That hurt . . . but, with me just getting started, what else could I be?"

Remembering to consider how she might change this perception of her attitude, Wanda said, "I suppose I could try to act more professional. Be more serious. But that would mean acting more like them and less like me!"

Card Two: Communications Style—Page of Cups. Wanda took one look at the Universal Tarot's Page of Cups, with his pink, puffy knickers, huge hat, and cup full of fish, and laughed out loud. "That's how they see the nature of my communications? I need a communications makeover, then!"

Wanda saw the Page as silly, even clownish. "I've been trying to make everything a joke, because I figured everyone loves to laugh. I laugh about everything, even things people think are serious, as a way of trying to help them see what's funny about even the worst situations. Maybe this card is saying I'm taking that too far."

Wanda decided to look for opportunities to change her communications style. "I want to be seen as someone who has a good time, but I don't want to be mistaken for a clown. Maybe I'll back off on the jokes a little."

Card Three: Work—Five of Coins. Wanda spent more time with this card than with any other. "It shows beggars. But I'm not a beggar . . . I don't go around asking for anything."

Wanda decided to work with the number and suit of the card. "Five is all about conflict. When I think of conflict, I think of people fighting. And coins are the practical suit." She studied the picture for several seconds. "I wonder why these people are out of work? Maybe they got into a fight with their boss!"

The card prompted Wanda to review her job performance. She recalled several incidents, including a number of times when the owner had asked her to get back to work. "I was just talking to someone—trying to make a connection with them. He seemed to think we were wasting time. So maybe he thinks I spend more time talking than I do working. Maybe I need to focus more on the work, and get it done first."

Card Four: Growth Opportunity—Eight of Coins. Wanda felt this card served as a commentary on the previous card, the Five of Coins. "See? This man is busy working. He's off alone in his shop, focused on the work. He's one of the people I would probably tell to lighten up and live a little."

Despite her initial reaction, Wanda invested several minutes debating how the card translated into a growth opportunity. "I'm sure this means the people around me think I need to work harder. I never thought of how my joking and talking might make me seem lazy . . . I just thought I was being friendly."

Card Five: Greatest Strength—Ace of Cups. Wanda expressed excitement over the Ace of Cups. "I associate Aces with opportunity," she said. "But why would other people be thinking my greatest strength has to do with emotions and feelings?"

An earlier card gave Wanda a new inspiration. "When people think of how I communicate, they see me as the Page of Cups—an emotional beginner. So how can I take my eagerness and make it into something people at work will value? Maybe, instead of chatting up other employees, I should turn my attention to the customers. I could start asking them about their day, for example, or talking with them about whether they're finding what they're looking for."

Card Six: Reputation—Eight of Cups. Put simply: Wanda didn't like this card or its implications at all.

"This person is walking away from eight cups. He looks hunched over and tired. From the way the cups are stacked, it looks as though one cup is missing." She frowned. "Does this mean people think I'm about to quit?"

Wanda reluctantly wrote down a few additional ideas: "Cups are about emotion and feeling. I think eight has to do with work." She looked up from her list. "Maybe this is saying other people expect me to be someone who has some work to do in terms of managing my emotions. Until I do, I'll have a reputation as someone that drives people away."

With the entire spread on the table before her, Wanda shook her head in amazement. "This gives me so much to think about. I actually was thinking of quitting, because my boss and I saw things so differently. Now, while I don't necessarily agree with everything other people may think about me, I at least have an idea of how I can change what I'm doing in order to change their opinions."

Wanda went to work the next week with a new attitude. She continued to be friendly to everyone, but she focused on getting her assigned work done first. When she finished early, instead of offering to chat, she asked if she could assist others with their duties. When this proved impractical, she took it on herself to walk the store floor, introducing herself to customers and asking how she might help.

Two weeks later, the store owner commented on her rapid improvement. "He still thinks I talk too much, but he's a lot happier with my work . . . and the customers love me. I'm convinced that, if I hadn't taken the time to see myself as other people were seeing me, I wouldn't be working here now."

Your Turn. How did your advice to Wanda compare with her own conclusions? Even if your insights differed greatly from hers, congratulations are in order. The point is to improve your own brainstorming ability—not to predict what someone else would say!

After practicing the Mirror, Mirror Spread, using Wanda as an example, complete the spread for yourself. Be prepared, though, to work with certain cards for some time before grasping their message for you . . . especially if the cards seem to suggest you might not be the "fairest of them all" under some conditions!

Mapping Your Personal Network

Understanding how you are perceived and what you have to offer positions you to plan for growth . . . and to better understand how you relate to others.

Having established a portrait of yourself from the perspective of others, now it's time to map your own network—to create a model of your professional relationships and analyze the scope, content, and structure of that network. In this exercise, you'll build a map of your own network of professional relationships using Tarot cards.

What to Do. Instead of dealing cards randomly, you'll:

- Select a card to represent yourself, placing it at the center of your network.

- Select a card for each of the professional contacts in your network—customers, coworkers, or bosses.

When mapping your network, be sure to include your boss, contractors, coworkers, contacts in other departments or in other companies, and customers with whom you deal on a regular basis.

In each case, you should select a card which, in your opinion, represents a quality that person brings to your network. Some examples:

- A stern department head who emphasizes rules, order, and organization above all might be represented by The Emperor.

- A coworker who is always willing to lend a hand might be represented by the Six of Coins.

- A customer with whom you have a mutual, cooperative relationship with might be represented by the Three of Coins.

- A customer with a demanding, negative approach might be associated with the Five of Wands.

- A boss whose insight you admire and value might be represented by the King of Wands or even the King of Cups.

Don't fret over your choices—go with your gut. Remember, too, that you can represent unhealthy relationships with reversed, or upside-down, cards. You can always choose a card that represents how a relationship should be working, then use the reversed card to describe the relationship as it actually is.

You may find it helpful to map out your network on a piece of paper first, drawing lines and circles to identify relationships between you and members of your network. Once you create a diagram that satisfies you, select cards for each person in the diagram, re-creating your diagram in cards.

Analyzing Your Network

Take a look at the network you've built. Begin your analysis of the network by answering the questions below:

- What is the ratio of reversed to upright cards? Of "negative" to "positive" cards? What might this say about trends in your professional relationships?

- What suit, if any, dominates your network layout? What might the dominance of this suit suggest about the kinds of contacts you value? What might it say about the kinds of contacts you neglect or overlook?

- Imagine that the goal is to "balance" your network by including an equal number of Cups, Coins, Swords, and Wands contacts. How many of each kind of contact would you need to add? What might this suggest in terms of plans to expand and enhance your network?

- How many contacts in your network are represented by trumps? Why did you select trumps for these contacts? What does this suggest about the role this person plays in your professional life? What is the ratio of trumps to suit cards? What does that ratio suggest about the level of influence these people hold in your life?

- Look at the overall shape of your network. Where did you place yourself? Are you centered? Is the network around you symmetrical? Lopsided? Skewed? What does the shape of your network suggest to you? If you were to rearrange the network in a more pleasing shape, what shape would it take? What might that shape (or the difference between the current shape and the edited one) suggest about your relationships?

- Try removing cards from your network, one at a time. Each time you remove a card, ask how your professional life and career would be impacted if contact with that person were lost. When you have the answer, replace that card and remove another.

- Think back to one year ago. How many of these people would still be a part of your network? Would last year's network diagram be larger? Smaller? How many cards would be reversed?

- Project your network forward in time by one year. How would you like for that network to expand? What "missing pieces" would you like to integrate? What reversed or problematic relationships would you like to repair or enhance?

Finally, for each contact in your network, ask, "How does this person support my goals?" Force yourself to find a positive answer, even for reversed contacts. When done, consider each card again, asking, "How does this person inhibit my goals?" Force yourself to find a limiting response, even for upright contacts.

Be sure to write down and preserve a description or diagram of your network. Date this diagram so you can monitor changes in your network over time. At a minimum, indicate the name of each contact, the card you selected to represent that contact, and whether or not that card was upright or reversed.

The Network as a Source of Solutions

Your network model becomes a powerful problem-solving tool, bringing the collective wisdom of your network to bear on any issue you face. In the best of all possible worlds, you would be able to telephone valued contacts and discuss ideas; occasionally, time and distance make this impossible. When this is the case, you can simulate a session with your contacts, using cards from your network diagram.

Simple Network Polls. Polling your network generates solutions and ideas that differ surprisingly from those you might generate on your own. Use the two methods below to generate quick insights, using cards from your network diagram as problem-solving tools.

Single Card Draw. Formulate your question. For this exercise, use only cards from your network diagram. From this subset of the deck, draw a single card. Once this card is selected, ask yourself the following questions:

- What answer would this person give me in this situation? Why? Would I take that advice? Why or why not?

- Was this the card you hoped to receive . . . or that you would have preferred to receive? Why or why not? What does this reveal about your bias in this situation?

- What would this person do if he or she were facing the same situation? How appropriate would that action be?

- Imagine this card, instead of representing a contact in your network, represents an action to be taken. What action should you take?

- Imagine this card, instead of representing a contact in your network, describes a belief or assumption you've made that complicates your ability to solve your problem. What would that belief or assumption be? How can you move beyond it?

Advice from the Network. While focusing on your question, pull the cards from the deck that represent your network contacts. Place these cards in a semi-circle before you, as though your entire network had been assembled to offer you advice. Include positive and problematic contacts—you want the benefit of a variety of perspectives.

With the network assembled, shuffle the remainder of the deck. Working from left to right, deal one card to each of your contacts. Place the card so that it can be associated with the contact without obscuring it. (Some people deal these cards into a second semi-circle beneath the first, while others prefer to place the new cards over, but slightly shifted away from, the contact cards.)

Imagine that you've brought your situation, issue, question, or problem before your network. Each contact now offers you a single card of advice—an approach, solution, or answer from his or her unique perspective. Imagine each contact wants to assist you, but can only pass you advice in the form of a single Tarot card. As you study the advice cards, keep in mind the unique personality and qualities of the person who offers it, allowing that information to enhance the meaning of the advice card.

For example, imagine receiving the Five of Coins, associated with financial or physical instability, as your advice card. If this card is offered by the fiery, passionate Knight of Wands, the blended message might become, "Before charging ahead as I would do, ask yourself what's at risk. What could you lose if you act before thinking more carefully about this issue?"

Offered by the nurturing Queen of Coins, the blended message might become, "Remember to weigh the costs of your actions against their ability to help you meet your physical and financial goals. So you give something up . . . how does this loss help you reach your best financial or physical potential in the long run?

The same card in the hands of the Page of Swords might suggest, "Your current course of action suffers from a poverty of logical, rational thought. Back up. Question assumptions. Review your reasoning. You're new at this, so make sure your arguments and ideas are in order before proceeding."

If you have multiple decks, this exercise affords a good opportunity to pull contact cards from one deck, while using another complete deck to deal the advice cards. This method allows contact cards to also turn up as answer cards, allowing members of your network to refer to each other and reveal additional insights through their interaction.

For example, perhaps you select the King of Cups to represent your morale-boosting boss and the King of Coins to represent the all-business, all-profit, "nothing matters but money" vice-president to whom your boss answers. You pull these from one deck, placing them in the semi-circle to offer advice.

Then, from a second full deck, you deal advice cards. This method makes it possible for the King of Coins to offer his advice in the form of a picture of himself, saying, in essence, "Consider doing what I would do in this situation." He might also offer up the King of Cups, directing extra attention to the card offered by that advisor: "Consider how integrating your boss' morale-boosting approach in this matter might also boost profits—and pay special attention to his advice, considering how it might help us financially and emotionally."

The Working Relationship Spread

In most corporate and business settings, the rapid pace and hectic environment force us into a "fire drill" mentality. We focus on the emergency of the hour, throwing our creative energy into surviving the storm. As a result, we frequently forget to evaluate the healthy aspects of our business. We fail to stop and ask, "What's going right . . . and why?"

The same mentality pervades our business relationships. We obsess on the boss we can't please or the coworker who intimidates us. We worry about the upset client or struggle to acquire the information we need from a recalcitrant product manager. We rarely focus on our successful business relationships: those day-to-day allies who support our success and share our small victories.

The Working Relationship Spread provides an opportunity to learn from your own successes. Instead of troubleshooting a relationship gone awry, it invites you to lavish attention on the business relationship you feel is the most mutual and the most beneficial. Understanding why a certain relationship works well will heighten your appreciation for that partnership . . . and aid you in replicating that success with others.

Use the Working Relationship Spread anytime you want insights into why a partnership with a specific coworker, employee, boss, group, vendor, or company works well.

What to Do. This spread consists of seven cards. Unlike other spreads in this book, not all cards in the Working Relationship Spread are chosen randomly.

Before you shuffle and deal cards one, four, five, six, and seven, deliberately select two cards: one to represent you, and another to represent the person or group with whom you have a healthy, working relationship. The court cards, with their portraits of individuals, are especially well-suited for this use, though you should feel free to select any card you feel captures the essence of yourself and the other person(s) involved in this relationship.

Place these cards in positions two and three in the diagram on page 154, then randomly select the remaining cards.

Card One: Foundation. This card represents the quality, shared experience, skill, or perspective binding together the two people in this relationship. While you may be very different people, this foundation represents a common element supporting your ability to work well together. Your mutual foundation creates your rapport, enabling clear communication and shared vision. In simple terms, this card captures "what makes you click."

To fully explore the meaning of this card, ask yourself questions like these:

- To what extent might this card recall a past event that united the two of you, or showcased your complementary talents and skills?

- How might this card describe a point of view, a philosophy, a value, or an approach the two of you share? How might it illustrate a difference of opinion, taste, or mindset?

- Examine the people, if any, on this card. What emotions do their expressions and actions illustrate? How do these emotions play into your relationship?

- What actions or activities do the characters on your card perform? To what extent might these activities be associated with the successful work you share with your working partner?

- If this card comes from the Minor Arcana, what qualities are suggested or represented by its suit? If this card is a court card, how might the card represent some person the two of you assisted, served, or confronted successfully? If this card is a numbered card, what qualities are suggested by the number of the card?

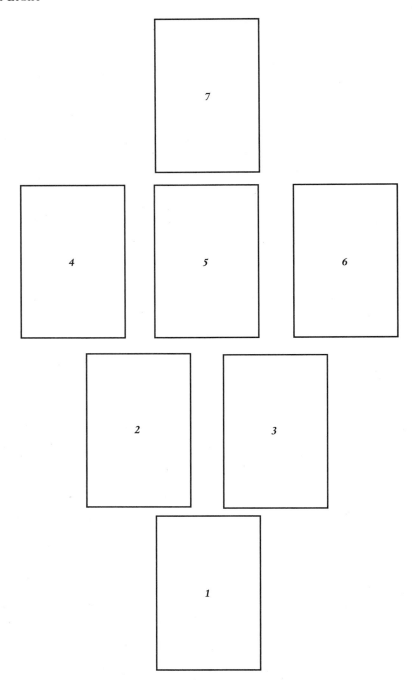

Card Two: You. This is one of two cards in the spread you select deliberately, removing it from the deck before dealing the others. Many people select a court card for this position. If you feel led in this direction, which card would further emphasize the qualities you bring to this relationship? Your enthusiasm, excitement, or status as a beginner (Pages)? Your emphasis on action and solutions (Knights)? Your ability to empathize, provide insight, or nurture others (Queens)? Your take-charge attitude, leadership ability, or maturity (Kings)?

When selecting a card to represent yourself, keep questions like these in mind:

- Which qualities or traits of mine make this partnership stronger?

- What card in the deck best reflects the way I feel about this relationship?

- How might a card from the deck illustrate a moment from your mutual past in which you took the lead or made a significant contribution? How does this card describe that situation? How might it represent your own actions, attitudes, feelings, or way of thinking about that situation?

- Which card best reflects qualities the other person values about me?

Don't struggle too long over the selection of this card. In my experience, you'll know it when you see it!

Card Three: The Other. Like Card Two, you select this card deliberately prior to shuffling and dealing the deck. If you select a court card for this position, choose one that emphasizes qualities you value in your partner. Enthusiasm, excitement, or status as a beginner (Pages)? Emphasis on action and solutions (Knights)? An ability to empathize, provide insight, or nurture others (Queens)? A take-charge attitude, leadership ability, or maturity (Kings)?

When selecting a card to represent the other person (or group) in this business relationship, ask questions like these:

- Which of my partner's qualities do I value most?

- Which of my partner's qualities or traits make this relationship stronger?

- Which card in the deck best reflects how my partner feels about this relationship?

- Which card from the deck might illustrate a moment from our mutual past when my partner took the lead or made a significant contribution? How does this card represent that situation? How might it represent my partner's attitudes, feelings, actions, or way of thinking about the situation?

- Which card best reflects the qualities you value in your partner?

As with Card Two, don't struggle over this choice. Look through the cards with your partner in mind. Focus on your partner's best qualities, and a card will present itself.

Cards Four, Five, and Six: Keys to Success. Unlike cards in most spreads in this book, these three cards are not assigned an exact positional meaning. Think of them as a picture puzzle illustrating the story of your mutual success. The commentary provided by these cards explains why your relationship with this person works so well. Watch for cards representing:

- Moments in time or situations
- Actions taken, responsibilities, or capabilities
- Attitudes, beliefs, or understandings
- Judgments, prejudices, or conclusions
- Approaches, insights, or opportunities
- Problems, issues, or challenges
- Solutions, victories, or achievements

As you examine individual cards, ask yourself, "How does this card illustrate a reason why our relationship works so well?"

In addition to understanding the meaning of each card, you must also discover how the individual cards relate to each other. Relationships commonly noted among these cards include:

- Distant past, recent past, the present
- Past, present, future
- A trait of yours, a trait of your partner's, a mutual trait
- A problem, a solution, a success
- A mutual, three-step approach to communication or problem-solving
- Issue, decision, action
- Strength, weakness, balance
- A way of acting, a way of thinking, and a way of feeling
- Three situations you faced well together
- Three reasons why the two of you work so well together

Feel free to rearrange the order of the cards to better represent the story. Some times, rearranging the position of these cards—swapping Card Four for Card Six, for example—immediately clarifies their meaning and relationship. The goal is to find an arrangement of the cards that makes sense to you and illuminates the relationship in a way that pleases or surprises you.

Card Seven: Plans for Growth. Because people change constantly over time, relationships wax and wane over the years. Some leave the direction of their relationships to chance. Others, fearing change, stagnate their relationships rather than "mess with success."

An alternative to these extreme approaches involves deliberately charting a course for your relationship: pausing to reflect on the question, "How can I grow this relationship, enhancing the mutual benefit and making it stronger and more profitable?"

Card Seven, then, suggests plans for that growth. As you explore the meaning of this card, keep questions like these in mind:

- How might this card suggest an existing activity or approach the two of you share? How does this activity or approach influence the future of your relationship? What would be the effect of continuing or discontinuing that activity or approach? How might the activity or approach be modified or refined, resulting in the growth of your relationship?

- How might this card point to a situation you should create . . . or avoid? To what extent might the situation represented on this card point to a situation in the past which holds the key to further growth? How might the situation on this card become a goal—something to work toward?

- How might this card represent a change or shift in the roles you play in this relationship? For example, if you frequently benefit from the guidance or direction of your business partner, this card could suggest possible benefits associated with finding areas where you could play the mentor.

- To what extent might this card point to an inhibitor to future growth?

- Imagine the people or beings on this card are answering the question, "What can I do to improve this business relationship?" What would these people or beings say if they could speak? Imagine, too, that they are unable to speak, but respond to your question by "acting out" their answer. What do their movements, actions, or expressions suggest?

Practicing the Spread

The Situation. In my role as senior manager of a training development team, I depend heavily on Michelle, my manager of training design. I focus on intention and result; Michelle possesses an eye for detail. These qualities balance and compliment each other, enabling us to crank out highly effective training despite grueling deadlines and inadequate resources.

In the interest of understanding how I might move toward such balance and mutuality in all my business relationships, I decided to use the Working Relationship Spread to achieve a clearer understanding of how our partnership works.

Before shuffling and dealing, I selected cards to represent both me and Michelle. I began by choosing Card Two—a card to represent me. While thumbing through the Robin Wood deck, I asked myself, "What qualities do I bring to my business relationship with Michelle?"

I decided my most valued traits would include my vision for the department and our roles within it, my desire to be a dependable leader, my intention that our work be both creative and effective, and my ability to provide direction without seizing control. Ultimately, I chose the King of Wands as my self-portrait: a creative individual, intent on making visions into realities, positioned as a leader.

Then, I asked myself, "What qualities do I value most in Michelle?" I made a list including these factors: her analytical ability, her eye for detail, her ability to cut through fluff and isolate meaningful content, her skill in organizing and ordering information, and her overriding concern for the quality of the participant's experience.

With this list in mind, I selected Card Three: the Queen of Swords. Again and again, Michelle blends rational analysis with an unwavering awareness of the needs of the training participants. She thinks and feels with equal intensity, allowing both faculties to influence her creative and professional decisions. Using the principles of good training design as a guide, she organizes raw information into modules that engage, inform, and entertain. Given the association of Swords with communication and logic and the Queen's association with nurturing and sensitivity, I couldn't imagine a better card to represent Michelle.

I placed these cards in the spread, then shuffled and dealt the rest of the deck, producing the layout shown on the following page. Look over the cards in this spread. Make notes about the qualities you feel these cards might represent, then read my commentary on each one. Some possible answers . . .

Card One: Foundation—The Magician. The Magician is Trump One, a number associated with unity of purpose and intention. The Magician card connects to creative power, productivity, and the channeling of energy to make things happen. When a magician says, "Abra-

7—Plans for Growth

4—Keys to Success

5—Keys to Success
(Center)

6—Keys to Success

2—You

3—The Other

1—Foundation

cadabra," he uses the power of words to conjure something out of nothing. His work usually involves a set of skills unknown to and unrecognized by those who come to enjoy the show. His high degree of skill makes his work appear effortless.

The Robin Wood Tarot depicts the Magician as master of all four suits: emotional Cups, analytical Swords, energetic Wands, and practical Coins. His headdress connects him with the natural world, while his robe connects with the internal, metaphysical, or spiritual world. A lemniscate, the symbol of infinity, hovers above his right hand, the hand of order. The Magician exudes confidence and control.

I suppressed a smile when I saw this card. Again and again, the vice president to whom we report brags that Michelle and I "pull rabbits out of hats"—his way of praising our ability to produce high-quality training against impossible deadlines. Our round-the-clock efforts often go unseen by others, concealing our effort and making our work magically appear out of nowhere. We both enjoy the look of shock, surprise, and pride this prompts from our superiors!

As the Foundation card, the Magician also suggested shared skills, vision, intention, and direction served as the base of my working relationship with Michelle. As creative individuals, I focus on movement and inspiration, while she focuses on detail. We both love how our work brings order to chaos, creating well-organized material out of disorganized ideas.

I spent some time focusing on the four implements on the Magician's table—what did these symbols suggest about our partnership? Then it hit me: by mastering these four implements, the Magician embodies qualities represented by all four suits. This represents well the holistic, four-dimensional approach to design and management Michelle and I share.

Every program we design appeals to the participants in four ways. We insist our courses incorporate accurate, clearly organized information (Swords), emotionally engaging activities and exercises (Cups), and practical applications of their classroom experience (Coins) designed to help the participants reach their goals (Wands).

By the time I finished my meditation on the Magician as the foundation of our relationship, I had far more appreciation for all the traits Michelle and I had in common—and a deeper understanding of why we work so well together.

Cards Two and Three: You and the Other—King of Wands and Queen of Swords. The analysis of these cards occurred before I dealt the spread, as the process of selecting them requires consideration of our valued qualities.

Cards Four, Five, and Six: Keys to Success. While the foundation card represented what Michelle and I have in common, the Keys to Success cards told an unstructured story about the factors contributing to our success.

I decided the first of these, Justice, referred to the role of balance and good decision-making in our relationship. I felt the scales of Justice represented to our ability to evaluate a situation, while the sword in her hand pointed to our ability to make quick, incisive decisions under pressure. The fact a trump represented this quality felt right to me, because I agreed these qualities play a huge role in our success.

At her most positive, the Queen of Cups becomes a nurturing, sensitive leader who makes decisions guided by emotional and spiritual insights. At her worst, she is a leader who makes decisions based only on emotional data, without consideration for logic, reason, or practicality. Looking at the Queen, I immediately thought of Tina, a former member of my team.

Despite formal training and a degree in instructional design, Tina's emotional issues frequently eclipsed her ability to lead others, as her teammates were often unwilling to follow someone they saw as unbalanced, reactionary, and unprofessional. At first, Michelle (who lacked formal design training) felt intimated by Tina's degree. Ultimately, however, Michelle saw how her own nine years of business experience and natural grace gave her the advantage over Tina. That realization greatly boosted Michelle's self-confidence.

For me, Tina drove home a difficult lesson. As her manager, I found myself addressing inappropriate behavior for the first time in my career. Worse, I received calls from clients who refused to work alone with Tina because her flirtatiously-worded emails and phone calls made them uncomfortable. Despite the fact I spelled out specific guidelines, Tina's inability to control her emotions brought me grief again and again.

Our exposure to someone like Tina increased our appreciation for clear-headed, game-free interaction between equals, and reinforced how rare a mutual relationship built on respect could be in the corporate environment. Meditating on the Queen of Swords helped me realize what a turning point Tina had been in my relationship with Michelle.

At first, the Seven of Swords struck me as out of place in a set of cards about success. The image of a man, apparently a thief, sneaking over a wall with swords bundled under his cloak doesn't exactly inspire visions of partnership.

And then, it hit me. Over the years, Michelle and I have learned we can trust each other. Our relationship works well because neither of us worries about the other "sneaking out" to tell others about our professional decisions and plans.

Card Seven: Growth—Three of Swords. In many decks, the art on this card suggests heartbreak. Swords, however, are the suit of logic, reason, and intellect; three is the number of creation and expression. The Three of Swords, then, concerns itself with going from idea to execution, from planning to production. In a Three of Swords moment, we confront, for the first time, the actual product of our plans. While sometimes we produce exactly what we intended, many of us have experienced the "heartbreak" associated with projects that fall short of our high expectations.

Michelle and I shared many successes, but we also shared a frustration: a growing list of great training products that the company, for various reasons, never deployed. One project in particular—a comprehensive sales training program—demanded many hours of hard work, which we gladly volunteered. Looking at this card brought that program to mind, and I realized that the sight of it gathering dust on a shelf in our office was, in fact, heartbreaking.

I spoke with my own boss about the importance of properly implementing and evaluating training programs. With time, he agreed our department could do a better job at this, and began to allow us to contact old clients to see how our work was being used. For the first time, we dedicated people on our team to surveying impact, and we were able to see how our work affected others.

When we spoke about it later, Michelle and I discovered we had both been thinking of leaving the company, mostly due to dissatisfaction over never seeing our favorite programs implemented. In retrospect, we discovered that working together to increase our job satisfaction had enhanced our already-productive business relationship!

The Problematic Relationship Spread

Positive, healthy relationships expand and strengthen your network of professional contacts. But what about one-sided relationships, relationships limited by neglect or loss of trust, or relationships with individuals whose perceptions of you are distorted by prejudice or bad first impressions?

The boss you never satisfy. The department head who blames everyone else for his own failures. The coworker who hogs all the glory and shares none of the credit. The woman who takes your work and claims it as her own. The employee who misses deadlines without apology. The team member who always wants help, but never offers it. A customer who consumes time and effort, but has no apparent intention of making a purchase.

You know—the sort of people you think of when you see Trump Fifteen!

An unhealthy relationship is any business connection that fails to provide mutual, beneficial support. The strategy you choose when dealing with them has long-term ramifications for your career.

What to Do. This spread consists of five cards (see following illustration).

Cards One and Two: The Conflict. Cards One and Two represent the factors that put you at odds with The Other. The two factors—opposing points of view, clashing values, incompatible approaches, or disparate goals—make up the heart of your conflict. These cards represent the source of the unhealthiness and dysfunction in your relationship.

To fully explore the meaning of Cards One and Two, ask yourself how these cards might represent:

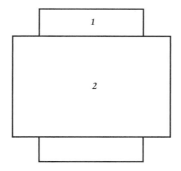

The Conflict

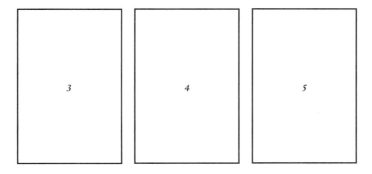

The Bridge

- *Two different perspectives on the same problem.* Most people easily assign one of the two cards to their own point of view, but frequently experience difficultly understanding the other card (just as they struggle to understand the other person!).

- *Two conflicting goals.* Especially if one card captures what you want or what you are working toward, ask yourself what goal the other card in the pair might represent. How would two people working toward these two very different goals react to each other?

- *Two opposing opinions.* Strongly held opinions—conclusions, prejudices, or beliefs—frequently lie at the heart of conflict. Frequently, these cards depict two vastly different assumptions about life or work.

- *Two incompatible value systems.* One may value harmony, while the other profits by chaos. One may be guided by a strong work ethic while the other feels inclined to stop and smell the roses. If these cards represent values, what would those values be?

- *Two motivations.* What drives you? What rewards you? How might these cards point to opposing motivations which fuel conflict again and again?

- *Two passions.* What do each of you feel strongly about? What do you care most about? To what extent does this other person share those feelings? How might these cards represent those passions?

- *Two sides of the same story.* To what extent might these cards be a picture of the same idea, action, or situation . . . from two very different points of view?

- *Two extremes.* When two people are as different as night and day, they may find themselves fighting like cats and dogs. To what extent might these cards represent opposite extremes of the same spectrum?

- *Two shared qualities.* The heart of your conflict might not be a matter of opposition—fact is, the two of you might be so much alike, you amplify each other's worst qualities. How might these cards represent an approach, a belief, an opinion, or a tendency the two of you share?

A word of caution: often, one card represents what seems to be a positive trait (strength, for example) and the other, a more negative one (the Seven of Swords, for example, which often depicts a thief). Especially in this spread, people often automatically assign the more negative card to the other person! To guard against this prejudice, try articulating the most positive and negative possible meanings for each card—and apply both to yourself. The one that "fits" may surprise you!

Cards Three through Five: The Bridge. The Bridge suggests three steps you can take to improve the health of the relationship. Taking these steps may not mean the two of you start fan clubs for each other. In fact, The Bridge may take you in the opposite direction, inspiring you to stay out of each other's way, agree to disagree, or even find other work. Sometimes, the only healthy option requires embracing difference . . . or gaining distance!

As you explore The Bridge, keep these questions in mind:

- *Which cards suggest actions?* With an eye toward improving your relationship, what actions are called for? Should something start . . . or stop? How do these actions influence the health, wealth, status, or well-being of the people involved?

- *Which cards relate to the process of making decisions?* How might these cards represent influences which alter or affect your decisions? To what extent might these cards represent decisions that need to be reviewed or reversed?

- *Which cards relate to other people?* What influence might these people have on your relationship? To what extent is that influence beneficial? To what extent is it problematic? What roles do these people play?

- *Which cards relate to situations?* How have those situations impacted your relationship? What decisions or actions created, supported, perpetuated, or ended those situations?

- *Which cards relate to feelings and emotions?* Are these emotions someone needs to confront? To admit to? To move past? What actions must be taken to alter these emotions? To enhance them? To acknowledge them?

Practicing the Problematic Relationship Spread

The Situation. Moving into a new position, Diane inherited a group of eight employees. Within just two weeks, she felt she connected with all of them—but one.

Randall presented himself well. He dressed sharply, he spoke professionally, and he received new assignments eagerly. All seemed to be going well until Diane needed one of Randall's latest reports . . . and could locate neither Randall nor the report.

Other members of the team met her inquiries with embarrassment. "Randall sets his own hours," they said. "He started coming and going as he pleased a few months back."

When Randall turned up the next day, Diane explained why his behavior was inappropriate. "I need to know how to reach you, and your team members need to know when you'll be in the office."

To her shock, Randall met these observations with a shrug. "I'm always coming in early and staying late. To get that kind of flexibility from me, I expect some flexibility from you. But if you want me to be an eight-to-fiver, I can be."

Diane paid closer attention to Randall's schedule over the next several weeks. Randall frequently arrived two hours late without any explanation. He took leisurely lunches, leaving at 11:30 and returning as late as 1:45. Claiming that he would sign on to the company's intranet and work late at night to make up the difference, he often left by three or four "to beat the traffic."

After three weeks of observation, Diane addressed the attendance problem in no uncertain terms, specifying the hours she expected Randall to keep. But for each incident she cited, Randall offered a series of circular explanations and excuses. His skill in defusing her observations left her feeling confused and unfocused.

Over the next several days, Randall's performance deteriorated further, and his disregard for departmental policy became more flagrant. In an effort to develop an effective strategy for dealing with Randall, Diane turned to the cards.

(You may be thinking, "Forget cards—Diane should be shuffling her pack of pink slips!" Nothing would have pleased her more—but her company policy demanded managers collect months of documentation before firing anyone. In short, her best option was to find a way to get Randall to perform to her standards.)

Using the *World Spirit Tarot,* she drew the following five cards (see illustration on page 167).

If you were brainstorming with Diane, how would you read these cards? Write down your answers before reading her conclusions. Some possible answers might be . . .

Cards One and Two—The Conflict: Ten of Wands vs. Five of Swords. When Diane saw these cards, she laughed with recognition.

"I spotted myself immediately in the Ten of Wands. The figure in the illustration cowers in the corner of the card, threatened by a cascade of tumbling wands. In my mind, the wands became straws, literally breaking my back. I also liked this card's agricultural setting, too: as a manager, I'm charged with direction, growth, and results. Avoiding a confrontation amounted to cowering in the corner instead of working to make our partnership more fruitful."

She felt the other card pictured Randall's situation. In this version of the Five of Swords, a wounded soldier limps painfully through a desolate, storm-tossed landscape. Low gray clouds blot out the sky, and a torrential downpour sweeps in from the west. Surrounded by broken

1—Bottom

2—Top

The Conflict

3   TWO OF SWORDS

4   16 THE TOWER

5   20 JUDGEMENT

The Bridge

swords, the poor fellow on the card brandishes his last weapon—which is also broken. The only intact sword on the card? The one held by the figure's shadow!

Diane nodded. "Randall needs to stop being controlled by his shadow, decide what he wants to do, and move from the chaos of the Five of Swords toward the collaboration of the Six of Swords!"

Cards Three, Four, and Five: The Bridge—Two of Swords, The Tower, Judgement. In the World Spirit Two of Swords, a lone fighter stands astride a gap in the earth. In the dark of night, this man works, blindfolded, with two gleaming swords. The scene provokes a feeling of practice— that this is a solitary warrior who is working on his craft.

Diane decided this card represented her Present situation at work—avoiding conflict and straddling the gap. She had to adopt one way of thinking about work: hers or his.

Card Four, the Tower, will never win a "Most Subtle Tarot Card Award." In the World Spirit Tarot, we look down from heaven as lightning strikes the Tower below. A figure with blazing, radiant hands falls into a whirling, chaotic abyss. Dizzying and disorienting, the card points to sudden, unexpected, transformation arising from a decisive incident.

Randall had built himself quite a Tower: assumptions that he could do as he pleased, assumptions that his work was beyond criticism or improvement, assumptions that he merited special treatment. In addition, he dealt with confrontation—especially the polite confrontation so typical of timid, corporate job reviews—in ways that rattled and confused others. The result? He focused more on avoiding input than understanding it.

Diane brainstormed a bit longer, then said, "The time's come for what a manager friend of mine calls a 'Come to Jesus meeting.' I need to get Randall's attention in a dramatic, direct, and undeniable way. But how?"

That question led her to Card Three: Judgement. Here, Maat, the Egyptian god of the afterlife, kneels in the swirling desert sand. On his ceremonial collar, he bears an all-seeing eye, an unblinking focus on words and deeds. In one hand, Maat holds a feather; in the other, a human soul.

Diane laughed. "I'm certainly not in a position to judge Randall's soul! I am a judge of his work, though, weighing it against our departmental standards."

Putting the message of the three cards together, Diane came up with a plan of action. Rather than continue to feel oppressed and burdened by Randall's attitude, she would create a Tower moment: a dramatic, undeniable confrontation comparing Randall's work to a clear, objective standard of performance.

Randall came to the meeting wary and on edge. Diane greeted him and went straight to the point. "Randall, your performance isn't where we need it to be."

Randall launched into a now-familiar litany of excuses and justifications, quickly changing subjects, and steering the conversation expertly toward a discussion of her capabilities as a manager.

She interrupted him. "We're not here to talk about me, Randall. We're not really even here to talk about you."

He narrowed his eyes. "What?"

"We're here to talk about your work." Diane pulled out copies of Randall's last three reports. "Our department's standards of performance are simple: reports must be on time, accurate, and conform to our standards for structure and content. We're going to review your last three reports in an effort to discover the extent to which they meet those standards."

"No one's ever talked with me about those standards!" Randall said. "Where are they published? Where are the details? I know my rights, and asking people to conform to standards they aren't told about is illegal!"

She fixed Randall with a patient, but firm, gaze. "Do you really mean to argue that you didn't know your work had to be on time? This report was due on Friday, August 16. You turned it in on the following Tuesday. Was this report on time?"

"I had a doctor's appointment!" Randall said. "I told you that—"

"Was it on time?" Diane asked, interrupting.

Randall squirmed. "That one wasn't."

"Thank you," she replied. "Now, let's talk about the next report."

Slowly, methodically, they worked their way through samples of Randall's work. He finally admitted that each report had been late, inaccurate, sloppily edited, or poorly organized. The impact of this methodical exploration of his work had a dramatic impact. Randall looked at her. "So you're firing me?"

"No," Diane said, allowing her surprise to show. "In fact, I'm giving you your next assignment. I'm also clarifying my expectations with regard to that assignment: it must be on time. It must be accurate. It must be well-edited and organized."

Randall looked suspicious, but accepted his next assignment. Each time he passed in a report, they met to determine the extent to which the work met the departmental standards. The following report was on time, but inaccurate. The next was on time and more accurate . . . but badly in need of proofreading.

"I didn't have time for that," Randall said. "I was trying to meet your deadline."

"Someone in your position must be able to provide an accurate, well-edited document by the deadline," Diane said, not budging an inch.

By creating a meeting designed to shake Randall out of his sense of complacency—and by insisting on reviewing his work according to an objective standard—Diane slowly engineered improvement in Randall's work. Soon, he was regularly submitting reports that were on time, accurate, well-organized, and edited.

Your Turn. Everyone has at least one problematic business relationship—or at least a business relationship marred by some unhealthy patterns or unfortunate history. Use the Problematic Relationship spread to explore that relationship—what you discover could turn a perceived enemy into a confirmed ally.

Summary: Chapter Eight in a Nutshell

HEALTHY CONNECTIONS BETWEEN COWORKERS, employers, customers, and vendors make up a critical network of support. The Tarot builds a visual model of these relationships, making it easier to evaluate their strength and integrity.

The Mirror, Mirror Spread provides a glimpse of how others see you in terms of your attitude, your communications style, your work, your opportunities for growth, your greatest strength, and your reputation. Using this spread, you can achieve a more objective view of your own efforts and contributions, and better understand the role you play in the relationships of others.

Mapping Your Network facilitates an analysis of the scope, content, and structure of your personal network. These cards can be used to generate solutions and ideas surprisingly different from those you might generate alone.

The Working Relationship Spread provides an opportunity to learn from your own successes. Focusing on your most mutual and beneficial relationships enhances your appreciation of them and aids in replicating that success.

The Problematic Relationship Spread examines your unhealthy relationships. By analyzing the dynamics driving these relationships, you build an understanding of how they work against your success.

CHAPTER

Planning Perfect Presentations

Preview: What to Expect in Chapter Nine

This chapter provides Tarot-based brainstorming strategies that:

☞ Provide quick feedback on the potential effectiveness of your presentation

☞ Aid you in identifying your skills and opportunities as a speaker

☞ Clarify the needs and expectations of your audience

☞ Make your message as memorable as possible!

Solving the Presentation Puzzle: *In the Spotlight*

RESPONDING TO FIELD MANAGERS' reluctance to "do training," senior management created Spotlight Meetings. My bosses wanted the Spotlight Meetings—a combination of news updates and skills training sessions—held once every two weeks.

Because of my reputation as an engaging trainer, senior management selected me to deliver the "train the trainer sessions" over Internet-enhanced conference calls. Following the call, field managers would then schedule and deliver the same content to their sales reps.

With our department's guidelines for on-line presentations in mind (use humor, change slides frequently, and incorporate interaction), I created the deck for the first Spotlight Meeting. I came up with jokes appropriate for the material. I expanded the slide deck, adding relevant graphics and visual gags. I created a series of competitive games to use as reviews. By our broadcast date, I felt thoroughly positioned for success.

The call, however, was a complete and total disaster.

I started the session with an overview of the project, peppered with humor. No one laughed. I stepped through the slide deck, using visuals to reinforce my points. The audience responded with boredom that bordered on annoyance. When forced to do so, the managers participated in the competitive quizzes . . . but offered terse, reluctant answers and refused to enter the spirit of the event.

Later, mystified by the failure, I locked my office door, took out the *The Robin Wood Tarot,* and drew three cards, brainstorming answers to these three questions:

- How did my audience feel about today's sessions?

- Why did they respond as they did?

- What can I do to make the next sessions more successful?

I received these three cards in response to my questions:

Five of Swords   *The Emperor*   *Eight of Coins*

How did the audience feel about today's sessions? Swords concern themselves with mathematics, logic, critical thought, and decision-making. The number five suggests instability and chaos. The artwork on the Five of Swords depicts a laughing young man with a sword in hand. He looks back over his shoulder at two other men. They turn away from him, apparently angry or upset. The card suggests that the younger man's delight comes at the others' expense.

I studied this card for several minutes. The young man in the foreground drew my attention most—maybe because he looks a bit like me! (We're both redheads.) In the end, I couldn't escape the feeling that the audience felt disconnected and turned off as a result of some unbalanced decision I had made. But what decisions? And how had they been unbalanced?

Why did the audience respond as they did? The Emperor, the fourth trump, suggests order and stability achieved through control. One glance at the Emperor, and his air of authority and self-confidence become apparent.

While studying the Emperor card, an idea popped into my head. The field managers saw themselves as Emperors, in control of their own kingdoms. Especially in light of sagging sales figures, they would be feeling the pressure to perform . . . to be seen by their own managers as skilled and effective leaders.

The on-line training approach I selected for this session emphasized humor, exploratory learning, and competition—designed specifically to appeal to sales reps. Managers, on the other hand, might feel that the humor "talked down" to them. They might also be uncomfortable with a learning strategy that included the pressure to perform on the spot (since failure in the game might be taken as a commentary on their management ability).

With the image of the Emperor in place, the message of the Five of Swords became clear:

by deploying the on-line training strategy developed for use with sales reps, I failed to take into account the differences making managers unique. As a result, the call alienated the audience and cast me as someone having fun at the learner's expense.

Which led me to my final question: What could I do to make the next calls more successful? I spent several minutes looking over the Eight of Coins. Coins are the suit of physicality and practicality; eight is the number of productivity. The young man on the card is an apprentice, learning to produce coins by carefully imitating a model the master provides.

For the managers, delivering training in the form of Spotlight Meetings represented a new—and intimidating—responsibility. As a result, they needed me to model exactly what they should do in front of their reps. Instead of throwing a multimedia extravaganza, I needed to focus on what an Emperor required in order to direct his troops with confidence and authority!

Again, the message seemed clear: focus future sessions on practical, step-by-step processes.

With that in mind, I revised my approach for the next call. Instead of humor, I emphasized a "no nonsense information for busy people" approach. I stepped the managers through the exact slide deck they would use with their own reps, pausing for questions along the way. Instead of competitive games, I scheduled time for them to ask their questions directly to experts I invited to the call. In essence, the revised call taught the information—and modeled how the managers should present it to their reps.

When the time came, managers participated wholeheartedly. They appreciated the no-nonsense approach, and, at the conclusion of the session, expressed astonishment that an hour-long session could deliver so much useful information!

The Benefits of Planning Presentations with the Tarot

The success of that second call more than justified the fifteen minutes I spent brainstorming and problem solving with Tarot cards. Believe me—I wish I had invested that time up front, before delivering the disastrous first session!

The exercises and spreads in this chapter will make your presentations as effective as possible. Use them! Once you start *Putting the Tarot to Work,* as a creative tool while preparing your presentations, you'll:

- Gain a deeper understanding of your audience's motivations and needs
- Focus on the change your session should engender
- Clarify your message
- Enhance the audience's recall of your message

- Approach the topic as holistically as possible

- Improve your effectiveness as a speaker

- Critique your presentations—before making them!

- Gain a more objective perspective on your own performance

The Presentation Pyramid

I jokingly call this the "If You Do Nothing Else" spread for presenters! The Presentation Pyramid spread takes us back to Mrs. Weathersby's ninth-grade speech class. (See, Mrs. Weathersby? I was listening!) Over and over, Mrs. Weathersby stressed that any communication involves the communications triangle: the presenter, the audience, and the message. If a speaker lacks awareness of how any point in the triangle impacts the others, communication suffers. And finally, with all the talk of aliens and Egyptians associated with the Tarot, referring to that triangle as a pyramid just adds to the fun.

What to Do. The Presentation Pyramid spread designates one card for each of Mrs. Weathersby's three communications concepts, arranging them in the shape of a pyramid (shown below).

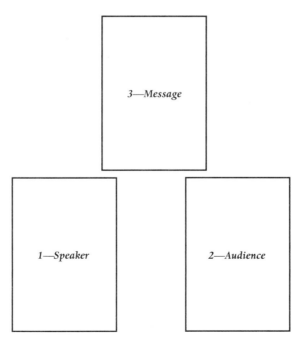

Notice that the Message card lies at the top of the pyramid, reminding you that communicating your message effectively is the number one goal of any presentation. At the base of the pyramid, the efforts of the speaker (or facilitator) and the responses of the audience determine the degree of success with which that message is transmitted.

Individual Cards

Card One: The Speaker. As the author or presenter of the presentation, you bear the responsibility for communicating the message in a way the audience will understand and appreciate. This card represents the answer to the question: "In order to make my presentation as effective as possible, what do I need to keep in mind about myself?"

When exploring the meaning of this card, ask yourself questions like these:

- How might this card point to information your audience would value, but which, because of your expertise, you've left out or taken for granted?

- Could this card be a snapshot of some aspect of your own experience: your feelings, your progress, or your insights? Has your experience with the subject given you material you could offer in the form of stories that would help your audience connect with your points? Might this card point to a presentation you've made in the past . . . reminding you of some important lesson learned?

- How might this card be a commentary on your level of preparedness—especially if you're delivering information compiled by others? If time prevents you from becoming an expert, to what extent have you defined a strategy for answering in-depth questions beyond the scope of your grasp of the material?

- To what extent might this card point to some aspect of your methods—your speech patterns, your presentation style, your use of exercises, and your approach to presentations in general—that deserves special consideration?

- What activity is depicted on this card? What does that activity imply about you as a presenter? Might it be something you should practice? Something you should avoid? Something you could do to keep the audience more engaged?

Card Two: The Audience. An intimate knowledge of your audience helps you edit and organize your material. This card represents the answer to the question, "What do I need to keep in mind about my audience?"

When exploring the meaning of this card, consider questions like these:

- Identify any people, figures, or beings on the card. What are their expressions? What are they feeling? What has happened to make them feel that way? How might this card capture your audience's current attitude toward your topic? Toward having to come to your presentation? The response you hope to achieve (or avoid!) at the end of your presentation?

- What activity or action does this card represent? How might this activity make your session more participatory and engaging?

- Could the activity depicted on the card point to the work done by your audience? The work they need to do? The action they need to take upon hearing your message? How would knowing the answers to these questions influence what you have to say?

- People respond most strongly to presentations which state, right up front, the WIFM: "What's in it for me?" How might the image on the card point to a need you should fill for this audience? A motivation to which you could appeal? A benefit your session could offer? Does your current approach incorporate an appeal to the audience's needs, motivations, or benefits in the first sixty seconds?

- Might this card represent some activity or exercise you could incorporate in your presentation that would help the message "come alive" for this particular audience?

Card Three: The Message. Neither the skill of the speaker nor the enthusiasm of the audience can compensate for a muddled message! This card explores the question, "What do I need to keep in mind about my message?"

When exploring the meaning of this card, ask yourself questions like these:

- To what extent might this card represent a simple, visual summary of your message "in a nutshell?" For that matter, is there a card in the deck that could? If not, you may want to think about what the point of your message really is—the one thing you want the audience to remember—and then find a card that captures or represents that idea in some way.

- Imagine a presentation coach sent this card to you as a reminder of a way to enhance the communication of your message. The card might hint at a way to set up the room for this presentation. It might point to an exercise, game, or icebreaker that would reinforce the message. It could suggest a hand-out or "take-away" to keep your message fresh in the audience's minds. It might describe certain assumptions your audience makes about your topic . . . and a way to take advantage of those assumptions. What reminder did your coach send you?

- Why are you delivering this message in the first place? Is your presentation primarily designed to inform the audience? Move them to take a certain action? Point out an assumption and change that assumption? Convince them of the value of a new way of thinking about or approaching the issue? Inform them of critical information that changes how they perform their work? Enhance their motivation? How might this card remind you of the purpose behind the message you will deliver?

- How might this card characterize a strategy for presenting your message? Might it suggest an alternative means of presenting the message that could be more effective? Might it suggest an activity, a discussion, a panel, or some other presentation method that could be more effective than a straightforward presentation? Might it recommend a simple presentation in lieu of something more complex or involved?

Other Considerations

- Before proceeding, note the type of card in each position. Which aspect of your presentation needs the most attention right now: the speaker, the audience, or the message itself?

- A trump card in any position indicates the need for special focus on that dimension of your presentation. Which positions are held by trumps? Why might this aspect of your presentation merit special attention right now?

- A court card in any position indicates a person or influence with special relevance to some aspect of your presentation. Which positions are held by court cards? To what extent might this card suggest someone with whom you should consult before proceeding? An expert you could invite to reinforce your message? A trusted friend or coach who might tell you something important to keep in mind?

- Note the numerical value of both pips and trumps. Imagine a coach assigned these scored to the various dimensions of your message—the higher the score, the greater the need for attention. Which aspects of your message has your personal coach indicated need the most attention?

Practicing the Spread

The Situation. Kenneth works as a product manager for a large corporation. A large part of his job involves introducing new products to internal corporate officers, executives, trainers, and sales reps. As products develop, Kenneth creates a single, comprehensive PowerPoint slide deck including all product details. When called on to present to any audience, Kenneth uses the same deck again and again.

Increasingly, Kenneth finds his presentations met with impatience, indifference, and, occasionally, hostility! He takes his position very seriously, and the strong negative responses he receives when presenting concern him. At his last presentation, many sales reps in attendance left the room for coffee the minute he approached the podium. Just last week, the company's CFO dismissed Kenneth's presentation after just five minutes, waving his hand and saying, "You got three minutes. Get to the point."

Kenneth started brainstorming by writing the question, "How can I make other people recognize the value of knowing all the details about my product?" He eventually decided that making others do anything could prove difficult, so he rephrased his question to be: "What can I do to help others get what they need out of my presentations?"

Kenneth pulled these three cards from the *Robin Wood Tarot:*

3—Message

1—Speaker

2—Audience

If you were brainstorming with Kenneth to identify recommendations for improvement, what ideas might you suggest? Write yours down before reading the commentary below. Remember—the goal is to generate as many ideas as possible . . . not to match, exactly, the interpretations in this book! Some possible answers . . .

Card One: The Presenter—The Emperor. At first, Kenneth mistook the message of this card to be an endorsement of his current approach. "When I'm presenting," he said, "I *should* be in control. People *should* listen. After all, when it comes to my subject, I'm the Emperor!"

A good friend reminded Kenneth to see the card as a suggestion for improving his performance as a presenter. Kenneth struggled with the idea, but eventually decided, "The Emperor might have trouble understanding the language of the common people. Maybe I should try harder to put my presentation into words everyday people can understand."

Card Two: The Audience—Wheel of Fortune. In the Robin Wood deck, the Wheel of Fortune depicts one woman moving through various emotional states, from joy to despair. Kenneth worked hard to apply this image to the audience. "Pay attention to how the audience is feeling?" he guessed. "Try to make bored people more engaged?"

Ken's friend asked, "Based on this card, what can you do to make the bored people more engaged?"

Kenneth thought about the question. "This card is about change and timing. Maybe I can change what I'm doing based on how the audience is responding?"

He wrote that down, too.

Card Three: The Message—Ten of Wands. Kenneth didn't like this card at all. He took one look at the man carrying the bundle of wands and said, "This is saying my message is a burden. But they have to know it! And it's my job to tell them!"

This led to a discussion of burdens—and how they vary, based on each person's strength. Combining this message with those of the other cards gave Kenneth an idea: "Maybe this could mean I need to find out how much each person in the audience can carry, and give them just that much and no more."

At the end of his session, Kenneth revised his initial impressions into a prescription for action. He would change what he had to say (the length of the presentation, the level of detail, and the words he used) based on the nature of his audience in an effort to "speak the audience's language." He would observe the audience closely, and edit out selected portions of his presentation if they didn't apply directly to what the audience needed to know. Finally, he would limit the level of detail in his presentations, telling audience members how they could get more information if and when they needed it.

Several weeks later, Kenneth reported an improvement in the success of his presentations. "I've started using just five slides with executives. They love that. I give the engineers all the details, and that seems to work. I asked a sales rep what he needed to know, and he said reps just want features and benefits . . . what to say to a customer. So now, when I speak to reps, that's what I say."

Kenneth also noted that his interpretation of the Emperor had changed. "In some ways, I was being the Emperor—laying down the rules about what people needed to know." He laughed. "Things are better now that I'm trying to understand what the audience needs me to deliver."

Your Turn. Did your brainstorm prompt you to consider ways in which Kenneth's attitude as a speaker bordered on the imperial? Did the Wheel suggest ideas about timing, repetitive cycles, or changing patterns of response? And how about the Ten of Wands—did it suggest to you that Kenneth's "all or nothing" response might generate messages the audience found burdensome?

Remember: gauge your success by the number of ideas generated as a part of this exercise . . . not by how closely you guessed Kenneth's own interpretations! And before undertaking your next presentation, try brainstorming with the Presentation Pyramid as a way of refining and focusing your material. Your audience will thank you for it!

You may also discover you need more detail than this simple spread provides. For example, you might want to explore more completely each point on the Presentation Pyramid—the speaker, the audience, and the message—in an effort to make your presentations as powerful as they can be.

The remaining spreads in this chapter examine those three factors in much greater detail. When time allows, I urge you to complete them. If you do, you'll begin to see your presentations in an entirely new light . . . and your audience will respond to your message in ways you never thought possible!

Speaker's Insight Spread

The Speaker's Insight spread provides an in-depth look at . . . you!

When planning a presentation, most of us obsess on our message. What to say? How to say it? In fact, we spend so much time thinking about the message, we tend to ignore our audience . . . and, to an even greater extent, ourselves. As a result, we're likely to ask, "Should I cover third quarter profits first?" At the same time, we avoid asking, "What can I do to become an even more effective presenter?"

Sound, objective criticism, offered in positive ways, is very hard to come by. The Speaker's Insight Spread, however, allows you to consult the Tarot as you might a trusted mentor—someone you trust to tell you plainly what others might avoid saying.

Even the most capable presenter can improve some aspect of his or her skills. The Speaker's Insight Spread will help you do exactly that.

What to Do. After pausing to clear your mind, ask, "How can I become the most effective presenter I can be?" With that done, deal four cards, arranging them in a vertical line:

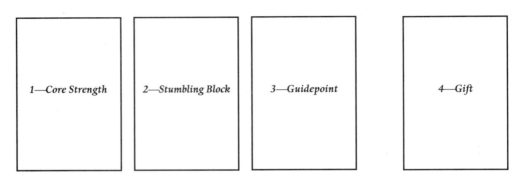

1—Core Strength   2—Stumbling Block   3—Guidepoint   4—Gift

Individual Cards

Card One: Core Strength. At the center of this spread lies your core strength: an aspect of personality, expertise, or experience that makes you especially well qualified for this presentation.

Card Two: Stumbling Block. Just ahead of you lies the stumbling block: an aspect of your personality, expertise, or experience with potential to interfere with your ability to deliver the message.

Card Three: Guidepoint. Your Guidepoint amounts to a valuable lesson, gleaned from past experience, with potential to improve the effectiveness of this presentation. This card may point to an experience, an insight, a method, or even a person who taught you a valuable lesson.

Card Four: Gift. Think of the Gift card as a note from a professional presentations coach. This note, in the form of a picture, addresses some aspect of your performance as a presenter. Follow this advice to improve your presentation remarkably!

Other Considerations

As always, look to see where trumps appear. Trumps indicate a powerful insight or message with important personal relevance. Spend extra time brainstorming meanings for any trump card in your spread.

Remember, too, that court cards often represent people:

- A court card in your Core Strength may prompt you to consider the degree to which you possess the qualities or skills you associate with other speakers. Alternatively, the court card may embody a quality of yours which you can put to good use when making presentations.

- The same court card in the Stumbling Block position may remind you of someone whose example you wish to avoid. It might also suggest a person whose criticism (or praise!), while offered in the past, wields subtle influence over your presentation style today.

- A court card as Guidepoint may remind you of someone from your past who gave you good advice. It might also prompt you to consider the extent to which a given quality, approach, or skill was present in speakers you admired or enjoyed.

- A court card as Gift may point to a speaker you could emulate. It might also suggest someone capable of giving good objective feedback for your current presentation.

Of Special Note

When working with this spread, it's always tempting to externalize the messages. You may want to relate the Stumbling Block, for example, to a member of the audience. ("Whenever the Director of Marketing sits in, all she does is pick my presentation apart!")

Remember: these cards speak to you. Their messages are about you. Deflecting their message by focusing it on others defeats the purpose of the spread!

Practicing the Spread

The Situation. When Coral's boss asked her to participate in a presentation on the capabilities of the Knowledge Resources group, she agreed. Her coworkers, nervous about making a presentation to the new vice president over their department, backed out one by one.

Ultimately, Coral found herself developing and delivering the entire presentation—alone! Feeling overwhelmed—but lacking any way out of the situation—Coral resolved to be the best possible presenter of her department's message.

Coral selected four cards from the Sacred Circle Tarot (see illustration, next page).

Imagine that you're Coral's brainstorming partner. What ideas would these images prompt for you? Write down at least three possible observations for each card before reading the suggested answers. Some possible answers might be . . .

Card One: Core Strength—Ten of Discs. For now, Coral ignored the keyword on this card, studying the image instead. To her, the ten discs appeared to block the way into a green and verdant valley. In addition, she noticed three hawks or eagles soaring through the air overhead.

1—Core Strength   *2—Stumbling Block*   *3—Guidepoint*   *4—Gift*

"I suddenly realized that the discs represented barriers only if you traveled by land," Coral said. "If you could take another approach—flying instead of going by horseback, for example—you could easily get into the valley."

In an effort to relate this card to her own strengths as a presenter, Coral reviewed past presentations for what she considered to be their "high points." Again and again, her most successful presentations involved surprising the audience in some way—delivering the message in a way that defied expectations. "Rather than always take the expected road," Coral explained, "I do something unexpected. One time, instead of presenting dry performance figures, I used audience members to act out results. The managers loved it."

Coral then considered the keyword printed on the card: tradition. "My best presentations defy tradition," she said. "My strength as a presenter lies in my ability to go beyond what's expected and really get the audience's attention."

Card Two: Stumbling Block—Nine of Discs. Again, Coral studied the image on the card: nine disks, integrated into a wall of boulders, blocked progress into a valley where storm clouds gathered.

"The keyword—Gain—sounds positive," Coral noted. "But, just looking at this card, I don't get a positive feeling. To me, this is a card about progress being blocked. I can't see a way around the obstacle. Does that mean I have a stumbling block I can't get past?"

Coral studied the card several minutes more before gaining an insight: "I've never had formal presentations training," she said. "When I get up to speak, I do worry about that—maybe I'd gain a sense of confidence if I got some presentation training. Right now, I do what feels right . . . but I'd like to know that what I'm doing is really the right thing to do."

The insight delighted Coral. "With tight deadlines, I always rush ahead and do whatever I'm asked to do. I never stop to think about what I need. On my own, I would never have thought to ask for presentations training. If this is going to be a part of what I do on a regular basis, then I need to be trained to do it."

Card Three: Guidepoint—The Moon. Coral recognized the Moon as a trump card, and invested special time in debating its message.

Coral liked the cool, calming colors of the Moon card, but found the bats, moths, and what she described as "wilting flowers" vaguely disturbing. She spent about ten minutes thinking about what the Moon might mean to her. "The moon goes through cycles," she said. "It changes, going from a crescent up to full and back again. Maybe this card is a reminder that everything changes?" She shook her head. "I just don't understand the message of this card."

Recalling that the card fell in her Guidepoint position, Coral tried to understand the Moon in relation to some lesson from her past. "One thing I have learned, especially at our company, is that the same things happen over and over again. This is the third new vice president to take over our department in as many years." Suddenly, Coral's eyes widened. "Wait! We did a departmental presentation just last year! I can save myself a ton of time by finding that presentation and updating it a little! That way, I won't have to start from scratch!"

Card Four: Gift—The Star. Coral felt a strong, immediate, and positive response to the Star. "When I see the Star, I always think of Christmas and the Star of Bethlehem," Coral said. "It's a message of hope, no matter how dark things seem to be. And I love the feeling of this card: the bright fire in the center of the circle of stones, the wisp of smoke rising into the sky. It's comforting to me."

Coral said, "To me, this card amounts to a message from my coach that says, 'Relax. Take what you know, make the most of the resources you have, and do your best.'"

Coral's investment in brainstorming paid off. When Coral asked her boss about the presentation from the previous year, he seemed shocked. "He said he'd forgotten about that," she laughed. "But he found a copy on his laptop and emailed it to me. Sure enough: it covered our capabilities, our organization, and our mission. I updated the template and changed the slide about our work in progress. Instant presentation!"

After the successful session, Coral asked her manager for presentations training. Delighted with the results of her work, he gave her the go ahead. "What seemed overwhelming at first turned out to be an opportunity for me," Coral said. "I'm glad I stopped to think before plunging ahead!"

Your Turn. What ideas did these cards prompt for you?

The real test, of course, comes when you complete this spread with your own presentation skills in mind. Why not pause now, deal four cards, and experience your own "mini-seminar" on presentation skills? Seventy-eight knowledgeable consultants stand ready to help you become the best presenter you can be!

The Audience Analysis Spread

A good friend and coworker with high hopes for promotion spent months grooming himself for the position of his dreams. He even came up with a good plan for getting it, by outlining a new and valuable service he could offer our company. He prepared an elaborate presentation (complete with animation and sound!), approached senior management, and waited for their response.

It never came.

I knew Robert's qualifications, and shared his frustration with senior management's apparent indifference to his proposal. Eventually, I asked Robert to share his presentation with me. Excited to have an audience at last, he passed me a CD-ROM.

Sixty-three slides later, I understood why senior management dismissed Robert's ideas: he failed to keep in mind the special needs of his audience. Busy senior managers lack the time (or the inclination!) to watch a sixty-three slide presentation—their schedule requires a presenter to get to the point. Worse, in a presentation to an audience obsessed with impact on the bottom line, Robert buried the benefits of his program on slide forty-three.

Robert's presentation was a technological triumph. His idea could have changed the direction of the company. Unfortunately, his proposal never received a reply, because Robert failed to consider the needs of his audience.

When speakers *do* think about the audience, they tend imagine a group of passionate, obsessive learners with only one mission in life: to absorb the presenter's every word. Nothing could be farther from the truth! A thousand-and-one priorities clamor for any audience's attention: *Why am I here? What's in this for me? Why did he wear that bright yellow tie? Who approved the purchase of these uncomfortable chairs? When's lunch?*

To improve your chances of breaking through the noise and indifference, you must author your message with the audience in mind. Acknowledging this fact, the Audience Analysis spread facilitates a focus on the most important people in the room.

What to Do. Simple but powerful, the Audience Analysis spread consists of only four cards (shown at the top of the next page).

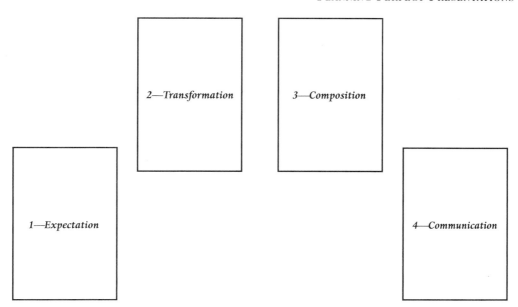

Card One—Expectation. This card suggests what the audience anticipates with regard to your presentation. You can play to this, presenting exactly what people expected. You can also defy expectations, catching your audience off guard. Once you know what the expectations are, that choice is entirely up to you.

Playing to expectations—giving people what they want—tends to please. (Senior managers, for example, prefer information delivered in short, sweet packets filled with "nothing but the facts.") Playing against expectations gains you the advantage of surprise—but runs the risk of alienating the audience.

Time spent exploring what you feel the audience will expect provides valuable insights into the appropriateness of the presentation you've planned.

As you explore the meaning of this card, keep these questions in mind:

- What are characters on this card doing? To what extent might the actions depicted on this card point to an expectation about method you will use? Does the audience expect a lecture? A demonstration? A panel discussion? A hands-on experience? Could the card depict something the audience will expect to be able to do after attending your session?

- What are the characters on this card feeling? Are they excited? Bored? Reluctant? Eager? To what extent might this card suggest how your audience expects to feel about your presentation?

- What are the characters on this card thinking? How do they evaluate what they see or hear? To what extent might this card suggest a way your audience will evaluate the content of your presentation? What value has this audience assigned to your presentation before they arrive? Why would they make that assessment?

- What prejudices or assumptions would characters on a card like yours make? How would these prejudices and assumptions color an audience's reception of your presentation? What would they be eager to hear? Reluctant to hear? Why?

- What do the characters on this card think of you? How would they respond to you? What do they seem to know about your history or your past performance? How might they embody a scene from or opinion about your past performance? To what extent would your actual audience share this opinion of the presenter?

Card Two—Transformation. In every presentation lies an assumption: the audience needs to be changed in some way (otherwise . . . why make the presentation?). Engineering that change is the goal of your session!

How does this audience need to change as a result of your presentation? To explore this question, consider your card from these perspectives:

- How might this card suggest something your audience needs to do? An action they need to take? An activity that needs to start or stop? Some change in the way something is done . . . or the efficiency, speed, or method associated with that activity? (Pay special attention to these questions when this card is a Wands card.)

- How might this card suggest something your audience needs to know or believe? Something they need to be convinced of? A perception or conclusion that needs to be embraced or abandoned? An idea that needs to be considered or evaluated? (Pay special attention to these questions when this card comes from the suit of Swords.)

- How might this card suggest something your audience needs to feel? An emotion they need to experience? A response or reaction they need to acknowledge or challenge? (Pay special attention to these questions when this card comes from the suit of Cups.)

- How might this card suggest the need for your audience to make a change in its value system? On its evaluation of a particular resource? On the emphasis it places on money, rewards, or benefits? To what extent does your audience need to change the criteria used to make its decisions and evaluate options? (Pay special attention to these questions when this card comes from the suit of Coins.)

Card Three—Composition. What kind of people will attend your presentation? As a group, how do they differ? How might they be alike? A firm understanding of your audience—of the types of people who will attend your presentation, the variation within that group, and their nature, etc.—will help you tailor your message accordingly.

When exploring the composition of your audience, ask yourself questions like these:

- If the card is a trump card, to what extent might this card point to an over-riding concern or point of view common among your audience members? A major crossroads or test they face? A force they represent, embody, or interact with on a regular basis?

- If the card is a court card, how might this card identify qualities or characteristics of your audience that you should keep in mind? To what extent might this card be a portrait of someone you've known before whose attitude, approach, or actions correspond to those of your audience?

- If the card is a pip card, how might this card identify the common denominator among members of your audience? Is that common denominator a way of thinking (Swords)? A common prejudice with regard to your subject (Cups)? A tendency toward practicality and the need to understand value (Coins)? An interest in action, change, or creation (Wands)?

- Imagine this card comes to you as a quick description of your audience's degree of familiarity with or skill level in your topic. What skill level would be indicated by this card? What features of the card indicate that skill level to you? Why?

- How might this card help you understand differences among members of your audience—ways individuals within the group vary?

Card Four—Communication. The default mode of communication for most presentations is a lecture: one person talks, and the audience listens. This continues to be the case, despite the fact that the best research shows few people have the ability to learn merely by listening (the majority of us, it turns out, learn best when seeing demonstrations or doing things, step by step, ourselves).

The Communication card hints at methods or approaches you could use to go beyond a lecture. Use this card to spark ideas about alternative ways to communicate your message—or even to sensitize yourself to alternatives you should avoid!

As you ponder the message of this card, ask yourself questions like these:

- What are the characters on this card doing? What activities are taking place? How might these suggest an activity or exercise with potential to enhance or illustrate your message for this audience? Is there a demonstration in progress? A group or panel discussion? A game or competition? A lecture? An activity requiring personal research?

- How might this card point out an activity or exercise that would be inappropriate, given the status, size, or composition of your audience? If you already have an activity or exercise in mind, how might the card suggest the audience's reaction to it?

- How would you describe this scene to an audience that couldn't see the card? How might describing or visualizing a similar scene assist your audience in better understanding your message? To what extent might elements or symbols from this card be useful as "mind pictures" that would help your audience keep your message in mind?

- To what extent might this card suggest take-aways—handouts, small gifts, toys—that could reinforce or remind the audience of your message in days to come?

Also, consider these strategies based on the type of card in the fourth position:

- If Card Four is a Swords card, consider the value of distributing key information in advance of your presentation, then using your time to discuss or engage in dialogue about that information.

- If the card is a Cups card, consider adding to your presentation an opportunity for attendees to react, respond, or share their insights and questions.

- If the card is a Wands card, consider adding an activity—giving the audience something to do that's specifically designed to reinforce some aspect of your message.

- If the card is a Coins card, consider centering your presentation on the value the topic has for your audience, focusing on what's in it for them, the benefits associated with your topic, or the savings that can be realized in practical, objective terms.

- If the card is a trump, consider organizing your message around a single, powerful theme, which you could reinforce with graphics, logos, icons, or repetitive images.

How might this trump suggest an appropriate theme, or graphic elements associated with your theme?

Practicing the Audience Analysis Spread

The Situation. Kristal worked as a Customer Training Rep for a large wireless communications company. Her job included holding training sessions demonstrating the unique functionality and capabilities of the cell phones sold by her company.

Over time, Kristal built up a library of standard functions and features associated with each product, pulling from these to customize a presentation for a given customer. While this worked well for several months, increasingly, her audience failed to find her presentations relevant to their work. On her session reviews, the audience frequently wrote "Presentation should have more to do with my work" or "Focused on what I could learn from the booklet, and should have shown me why these features were important or added value."

Following a sale to a large and important customer, Kristal wanted her training session to be as valuable and supportive as possible. Before running a series of training sessions for the customer's sales executives, Kristal brainstormed with the Audience Analysis spread, hoping to adapt her approach to suit the needs of her audience.

She dealt the following four cards from the *Nigel Jackson Tarot:*

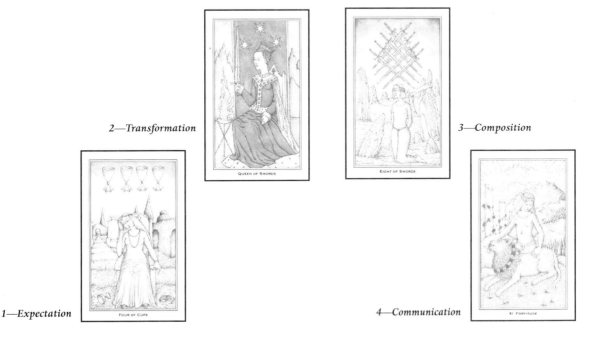

2—Transformation

3—Composition

1—Expectation

4—Communication

Before reading Kristal's ideas about these cards, take a moment to jot down your own brainstorming results. However, some possible answers might be . . .

Card One: Expectation—Four of Cups. "Nothing subtle here!" Kristal exclaimed. In the Four of Cups, a woman sits on an uncomfortable throne, her head in her hand. Kristal took one look at this card, representing what her audience anticipated, and summarized it in one word: "Boring!"

The suggestion that the audience might expect a dull presentation prompted Kristal to consider ways she could defy that expectation. "They think I'm going to just come in and say, 'Press this, and your phone does this.' Instead, I think I might try talking about ways the different features of our phones can save them time and money. Instead of talking about speed dial in terms of the number of entries you can save, I'll start by pointing out how important it could be to have your best customers' numbers in speed dial—especially when they have complaints or requests and you need to get in touch with them quickly."

The card inspired other ideas, too: "I can't stand the way the woman on this card just sits there! I think instead of lecturing, I'll try to integrate things for the audience to do. Maybe I'll introduce a feature, then have a competition—maybe have them enter speed dial numbers against the clock. I could give out little prizes as incentives. That way, instead of just sitting, these sales reps will have some kind of activity that reinforces what I'm teaching them. A game will appeal to their competitive nature, too!"

Card Two: Transformation—Queen of Swords. Kristal stared at the image of the Queen of Swords, who studies intently the sword in her hand. "When I think of Queens, I think of a more collaborative, intuitive management style. I can't see how this relates to a way my audience needs to change. I'm not there to tell them how to be better sales reps and managers. I'm there to show them how the phones work!"

After studying the picture several minutes and describing its elements out loud ("There is a queen seated in a chair. She studies her sword. She is considering how to use the sword."), an exciting new idea occurred to Kristal.

"These reps haven't had cell phones before. In fact, email—which is usually slow—has been their primary way of keeping in touch with each other. They may not have considered how the availability of these phones increases their availability to each other. They could meet on the go, for example, without having to come in to the office. If they spend a part of the session entering each other's contact info into the speed dialer, they would leave the session with a powerful conferencing tool in hand."

With the Queen of Swords in mind, Kristal decided she would focus her entire presentation on the new technology's potential to change the way the sales team worked and collaborated together. She even considered inviting each participant to outline ways the technology could make the team more efficient as part of the program. That sounded more interesting than lecturing about "what button to press to make a call!"

Card Three: Composition—Eight of Swords. What kind of people would be in Kristal's audience? She studied the Eight of Swords as a way of exploring the composition of her audience.

Kristal began by describing aloud exactly what she saw in the picture. "I see a woman on her knees, her hands behind her back. She looks like a prisoner. The swords above her head look complicated and threatening, even though the colors in the picture are calming."

Kristal studied the picture further. "Eight is the number of work. Swords are the suit of logic and evaluation." She laughed out loud. "The audience of this session is made up entirely of sales reps and managers. They only make money when they're out selling . . . and so this training, from their point of view, is a total waste of their time. They're being forced to attend, so they feel like prisoners!"

With this aspect of her audience in mind, Kristal again adjusted her agenda for the course. "The session needs to be as short as possible . . . and they need to know that up front. In addition, to help them feel the time we do invest is valuable, I'm going to skip the basics—most people can figure out how to send and receive a call—and go right to the advanced features with the most potential to have an impact on a sales rep's work. I may even give them a list of features, and ask them to rank them in order of importance. That way, they feel more control over the presentation and feel less like prisoners!"

Card Four: Communication—Fortitude. Kristal knew this card was called Strength in most decks. After studying the image of the slender woman stroking the submissive lion, Kristal concluded, "Sales reps are an audience that respects strength. They respect people who produce results—other reps who prove their strength by making the big sales."

At first, this insight left Kristal at a loss—while she supported sales, she wasn't in sales herself, and couldn't position herself as a successful sales rep. Then she had a new idea. "I could get a sales rep to come with me and talk about how our phones played a role in her success."

The presentation Kristal delivered a week later differed dramatically from previous cut-and-dried training sessions. She started the session with a statement from her guest: a successful sales rep who explained how the features of the phone he carried boosted his sales by twenty-two percent over three months.

As Kristal covered the top five unique features of the phone, she stressed the benefits of each feature again and again. She tested the audience's mastery of the features with a series of lively games and quick competitions that had the audience entering information into their phones at a frantic pace. She closed the session by asking audience members to list three ways their phones would change the way they worked.

Her session review sheets came back more positive than ever. "People actually had fun in the session. I defied their expectations, delivered my material in a way that engaged them, and made the whole session fun. Some folks came back to later sessions just to see how their friends did in the competitions!"

Your Turn. So how did you do? Remember—sparking your own ideas is far more important than coming up with the exact ideas Kristal generated in her brainstorm.

Before moving on, try the Audience Analysis spread yourself! If you have no pending presentation, you can always practice the spread by analyzing an audience you know well—your department, or a group of coworkers—just to reinforce your brainstorming ability.

Message Analysis: The Visual Outline

The message you deliver comprises the meat of your session—the information the audience needs to know. A firm grasp of your message helps you appear more confident as a presenter, and increases the chance your audience will value what you present.

Achieving that level of familiarity with your message results from exploring your subject matter as completely as possible. A good presenter considers her subject from every possible angle, anticipating questions and isolating "holes" in the information.

With this practice in mind, the Visual Outline Spread translates your message into simple, easy-to-remember visual metaphors. Instead of focusing on the words of your message, you condense your message into a series of "memory pictures." This time-honored memory trick offers a number of benefits to presenters:

The visual layout of your message is easier to recall than an outline. Ever watched a speaker who constantly referred to notes? You probably felt he hadn't adequately prepared for the session. You can reduce your dependence on outlines and notes by translating the main points of your message into a sequence of Tarot card pictures. These images prove much easier to recall than memorized text!

A visual outline facilitates a critique of the content of your message. When substituting Tarot card images for the main points in your message, you see your message in an entirely new way. You may notice, for example, you message includes "Sword points" (information designed to explore reasons and logic), "Coins points" (information about finances or resources), and "Cups points" (information designed to motivate the audience), but no "Wands points" (information telling the audience what to do next). At the very least, you'll achieve a fresh perspective on what you have to say.

The visual outline increases your overall familiarity with your message. Every minute spent translating your key points into Tarot images amounts to time spent internalizing and studying your material. Studying your outline the conventional way engages the language-based portions of your brain—you see the words on the page and "hear" them in your mind. Converting your outline to visual data provides you with a new angle on the same information, exploring it through pictures and images. The result? A more holistic knowledge of your message.

What to Do. Unlike many other exercises in this book, the structure of this spread varies according to your presentation outline.

Examine your presentation outline—even if you only have a handwritten list of two or three main points for now. Rather than select cards at random, spread the deck face up on a large table. For each major point in your outline, select one card which you feel captures its essence.

Some advanced users enjoy creating more detailed outlines using trumps as main points and cards from the Minor Arcana as sub-points, but this system quickly becomes complicated. I recommend beginners use no more than three to seven cards to represent an entire presentation.

Practicing the Message Analysis Spread

Example One: The Visual Outline. As practice, take the following presentation outline, and select from your personal deck the cards which you feel best illustrate each main point.

1. Profits are good, but not what the company promised investors.
2. As a result, the investors are not happy.
3. The company must now make some tough decisions.
4. Some people will be laid off.
5. We'll all have to work smarter as a result.
6. The result, though, will be greater financial stability.

Select your cards before reading the following suggested answer. The suggested answer is based on cards from *The Robin Wood Tarot,* and is provided only as a guide for comparison.

Since the illustrations on your personal deck may vary, you may choose different cards! There are no right or wrong answers. The important thing is to choose cards which would help you remember the main points of the presentation.

Presentation Point	*Suggested Robin Wood Card*
1) Profits are good, but not what was promised	Seven of Coins
2) As a result, investors are unhappy	Five of Cups or Four of Coins
3) The company must now make difficult decisions	Two of Swords or Seven of Cups
4) Some people will be laid off	Six of Swords or Ten of Swords
5) We'll all have to work smarter as a result	Eight of Coins
6) The result will be greater financial stability	Strength

Example Two: Corporate Moments. For further practice in associating Tarot cards with ideas and information, complete the following chart. For each of the following corporate moments, find an appropriate card. Try to select cards that illustrate the moment itself . . . not the emotional response to the moment.

A new product fails to perform to standards, and the company suffers great loss as a result.

In the effort to meet a new challenge, the company brings together experts from many different disciplines and perspectives.

Auditors arrive to assess how closely the company complies with industry standards.

Unrest among employees causes several personal and professional confrontations.

You earn a promotion and a larger salary, but the reality of the new position is not quite what you had expected.

With profits sagging, the time arrives for the company to take quick action to preserve its financial integrity.

The company forms a partnership or completes a merger with another company.

The company decides to limit losses by discontinuing a product line and starting over.

The company holds a "no holds barred" brainstorming session in search of new ideas.

Listless employees waste time, needing strong direction.

A manager tells you what a great job you're doing, and offers you tips on how to earn even more commissions.

_____
_____

The company elects a new CEO.

_____
_____

The company celebrates an anniversary.

_____
_____

   Suggested answers for this exercise are in the following table. Remember, though, that finding the card that captures the moment for you, personally, is more important than choosing the same card I selected!

A new product fails to perform to standards, and the company suffers great loss as a result.

Five of Cups (if the loss is more of a blow to the ego), *Five of Coins* (if the loss is small and financial in nature), or *The Tower* (if the loss is catastrophic).

In the effort to meet a new challenge, the company brings together experts from many different disciplines and perspectives.

Temperance (if the meeting has major implications for the company's future) or the *Three of Coins.*

Auditors arrive to assess how closely the company complies with industry standards.

Justice captures the idea of conforming to regulation. You might also choose a card illustrating the emotion the company feels in response to the audit.

Unrest among employees causes several personal and professional confrontations.

Five of Wands or *Seven of Wands.*

You earn a promotion and a larger salary, but the reality of the new position is not quite what you had expected.

Eight of Coins.

With profits sagging, the time arrives for the company to take quick action to preserve its financial integrity.

The *Knight of Coins* (Knights suggest action, and Coins reflect the financial implications of the crisis).

The company forms a partnership or completes a merger with another company.

The Lovers or the *Two of Cups*

The company decides to limit losses by discontinuing a product line and starting over.

Death, which suggests a permanent end and the start of a new cycle.

The company holds a "no holds barred" brainstorming session in search of new ideas.

The *Seven of Cups.*

Listless employees waste time, needing strong direction.

Four of Cups, a card frequently associated with boredom or dissatisfaction.

A manager tells you what a great job you're doing, and offers you tips on how to earn even more commissions.

Queen of Coins, combining financial savvy with a nurturing influence, regardless of the gender of the manager.

The company elects a new CEO.

Emperor or *King* of any suit, depending on the reasons why a particular candidate was chosen. Some people focus on the idea of the election instead of the candidate, leading them to choose the *Three of Coins*.

The company celebrates a major victory.

Six of Wands or *The Chariot*.

Example Three: Well-Rounded Presentations. Some people, in an effort to provide a "well-rounded" presentation, use the following outline as a guide when authoring content:

- Choose a trump card to represent the overall theme of the presentation.

- Choose a Cups card to remind yourself of how the audience should feel—an illustration of the emotional response the audience will have toward your presentation.

- Choose a Coins card to represent "What's in it for the audience"—the benefits and advantages associated with your presentation.

- Choose a Swords card to represent the logic behind your thinking—why the audience should accept, adopt, or believe what you say.

- Choose a Wands card to represent your key message—a reflection of what it is you hope to accomplish or change with the presentation. Incorporate this card into a call-to-action issued at the end of the presentation.

Others use this same outline, but feel free to place any card in any position. In other words, if the illustration from a Wands card connects with their "Coins" point, they don't hesitate to place the Wands card in the Cups position.

Summary: Chapter Nine in a Nutshell

WHEN USING TAROT CARDS to prepare your corporate presentations, you gain a deeper understanding of your message, your audience, and yourself.

The Presentation Pyramid spread heightens your awareness of how each factor in the communications triangle—the presenter, the audience, and the message—impacts the others. Use this spread to complete a last-minute test of your presentation's effectiveness. Your audience will thank you for it!

The Speaker's Insights spread provides clear, objective criticism of your performance as a speaker. What are your strengths? What skills need reinforcement? Completing this spread amounts to taking a course on "Becoming a More Effective Speaker," but the spread requires a much smaller investment of time and money!

The Audience Analysis spread focuses your attention on the most important person in the room: your listeners! Use this spread to anticipate expectations, explore the composition of your audience, identify an approach designed to communicate your ideas as powerfully as possible, and define the impact your presentation should have on the audience. Get to know your audience, using cards in this spread to explore their expectations and identify the presentation methods best suited to their learning style.

Finally, building a visual outline of your presentation offers you a wide range of benefits. By representing each point in your outline with a striking visual image, you'll improve your recall of critical ideas. Including "suit points" from each Tarot suit makes your presentation more holistic . . . and therefore more appealing to a broader range of listeners. Invest a few minutes converting your message into a visual outline! In the process, you'll clarify your message and make it much easier for everyone—including you—to remember.

CHAPTER

Seeing the Future

Given the tone and approach of the rest of this book, the title of this chapter may shock some readers. After spending so much time establishing Tarot's practical value as a creativity and brainstorming tool, am I really about to close the book with a chapter on fortune telling?

In a word: No.

Your Personal Crystal Ball

THE EXERCISES AND STRATEGIES in this book won't help you pinpoint the date and time you'll meet your true love or get that big promotion. Even so, *Putting the Tarot to Work* is, in fact, a book about seeing the future.

When you:

- Brainstorm possibilities and outline options

- Envision a path for growth

- Set goals and define a plan for achieving them

- Focus on action and work to create positive change

- Plan ahead for meetings and interviews

- Explore ways to improve your relationships

- Anticipate how others will respond to your messages

. . . you are, for all practical purposes, seeing the future! Best of all, this kind of seeing the future far outranks any kind of fortune telling. Instead of positioning you as a victim of some inescapable fate, this approach empowers you! Rather than watching passively as events unfold, you play an active role in defining and obtaining the future you most desire.

In other words: by planning carefully, anticipating change, envisioning alternatives, making commitments, and taking action, you *make* your future . . . which turns out to be a lot more satisfying than telling it.

What's Next?

As you continue brainstorming with the Tarot, you'll discover all kinds of useful applications for the cards. You'll adapt the ideas in this book to your unique way of working . . . which will, in turn, inspire more ideas and strategies.

Just this week, for example, I've used Tarot cards to:

- Brainstorm ideas for employee appreciation activities

- Identify suitable awards for top performers

- Plan my vacation

- Give clients advice on unexpected ways to expand their business

- Enhance my review of a corporate web site's contents

- Explore new ideas for advertising my own business

- Develop a concept for a retail client's in-store signage

- Come up with the idea for this chapter!

Your personal use of the Tarot as a brainstorming tool is limited only by your imagination . . . and your willingness to give the cards a chance.

The Tarot: The Swiss Army Knife of Creativity

You'll also realize that every process in this book—while offered here in the context of *Putting the Tarot to Work*—can be used in other ways:

- The brainstorming processes generate ideas for any challenge you face—not just business challenges.

- You can go beyond planning for professional growth, adapting those exercises to plan for personal, emotional, spiritual, or financial growth as needed.

- Goal-setting applications, offered here in the context of making a business plan, readily apply to setting personal goals.

- Techniques offered here for planning business meetings lend themselves to preparations for almost any meeting, event, or project.

- The network analysis strategies outlined earlier could easily be used to examine the health and mutuality of personal or family relationships.

- Methods for refining and clarifying presentations can be applied to all kinds of communications, from personal letters to ad campaigns.

To share your ideas, applications, and success, stop by www.tarottools.com! I look forward to hearing from you.

Remember: The seventy-eight cards of the Tarot deck link to an infinite number of ideas and applications. All you have to do is pick a card . . . any card!

Mark McElroy
Summer 2002

Appendix A: Sample Meanings and Associations

ALMOST EVERY TAROT DECK comes with a "little white book" (in some cases, a large and colorful book!) packed with "divinatory meanings" for each card. These meanings differ from deck to deck, based on the designer's whim. Many of the meanings listed for certain cards will not be useful or appropriate in the corporate realm, where connecting the Lovers card to "budding passion" or the Six of Swords to "a journey over water" has little practical value.

For most of the exercises in this book, you should go with the intuitive meanings—associations and ideas you generate simply by looking at a card and letting your mind roam free.

Sometimes, when you're stuck, having a jumping-off point can be useful—that's when you should turn to this appendix. The meanings below are not offered as official or even traditional meanings for the cards. In each case, though, some effort has been made to take traditional meanings and relate them to business.

Some of these meanings will work or make sense. Others won't. Whenever possible, disregard what's here and substitute your own meanings—ideas and associations that make sense to you. If your take on a card is completely different . . . celebrate, and go with what the cards means from your own perspective.

Whatever you do, don't take these suggestions as authoritative or binding. Use them when they are useful, and ignore them the rest of the time. Never, ever let yourself be restricted by the meanings offered here. Consider them to be guidelines or useful starting points . . . nothing more.

The Trumps

0—Fool (Enthusiasm and Inexperience)

The craving for new beginnings and fresh approaches. Learning from mistakes. Taking risks. Thinking out of the box. Sacrificing "sacred cows" or poking fun at revered ideas. Being guided more by instinct and excitement than by experience. Insistence that work should be fun. Baseless optimism. Expressing curiosity. Asking question after question in an effort to understand something better.

I—Magician (Empowerment and Creativity)

The drive to innovate. The need to make something new or valuable. Getting things done. Taking action—any action!—now. Drive. Ambition. Taking raw materials and assembling something new or unexpected. Being given authority. Directing a meeting, group, or organization. Brainstorming. Refusing to be satisfied with a single answer, approach, or strategy.

II—Priestess (Reflection and Reception)

The need to listen, learn, and digest information without taking action. The ability to keep confidences, even in extreme situations. Analysis. Seeing things as they are, or attempting to see them from an entirely different angle. The tendency of employees to work and think like their managers. A "wait and see" approach.

III—Empress (Development and Growth)

Training. Benefits. Finding a mentor. Spending time with employees to observe their work and offer positive feedback. Getting back to nature for inspiration, guidance, or meditation. Coaching and counseling. Surveys. Rendering outstanding customer service. The driving need to find or offer security and assistance. The need to consider how actions impact people.

IV—Emperor (Authorities and Directives)

The CEO. Doing something because senior management orders it, whether it makes sense or not. The pressure to be a team player. The culture of conformity. The importance of having a common goal, vision, or direction. Delegating authority appropriately in order to make the best possible use of resources.

V—Hierophant (Externals and Regulations)

Keeping up appearances. Logos, advertisements, and corporate image. Public and investor relations, and other "official sources." Certifications. Rules and regulations, along with those who enforce them. Testing and administration. Standards. Faith. A reminder to step outside routine and try something new. Refusing to be confined by standards or "the way it's always been done."

VI—Lovers (Affiliations and Partnerships)

Finding just the right team member to complete an organization. Combining departments or teams. Selecting a new vendor or signing a partnership agreement. Bringing wide-ranging experts together. Identifying an unrealistic, emotional attachment to an idea, approach, or concept. Applying ideas or approaches from one discipline to problems in another. Important meetings and events. The need to network.

VI—Chariot (Victories and Triumphs)

Beating the competition "hands down." Scoring a huge contract, making an outstanding sale, or overshooting a goal. Establishing a reputation for excellence. "Striking while the iron is hot." The desire to be recognized as the best. Winning at all costs. Persistence. Adopting strategies from battle or warfare. Learning how to do something by watching those who have done it well before.

VIII—Strength (Resolve and Focus)

Aligning yourself with trends. Positioning yourself to take advantage of a political or financial situation. Overcoming resistance. Making something happen by sheer force—or examining the role of force in your approach. Taking control of a project or team. The need to bear down and deliver against all odds. Dependability. Having the "courage of your convictions." Focusing on your strengths—or identifying weaknesses, flaws, or opportunities with potential to hinder success. Testing an idea by trying to "break it."

IX—Hermit (Solitude and Isolation)

Pinning down a problem. Holding a retreat to focus on skills or issues. Taking a sabbatical. Becoming or contracting with a freelance worker. The need for reflection and planning. Going in search of an unusual or unconventional source of inspiration. A closed-door meeting. Confidential information. Non-disclosure agreements.

X—Wheel of Fortune (Cycles and Fluctuations)

Payback time. Stocks rising and falling over time. What goes around comes around. Adopting a random strategy or approach in order to achieve different results. Exclamations of, "Here we go again!" A sense of déjà vu. Anticipating the future based on past experience. Looking for patterns and cycles. Doing things at the right time. Taking a gamble. Assessing risk.

XI—Justice (Evaluations and Deliberations)

The need to see everyone treated fairly. The motivation to make responsible decisions based on all available information. Making sure reward is scaled to effort. Weighing all options. The role of reason, logic, and objectivity. Considering repercussions. Comparing one thing to another. Identifying your assumptions and prejudices. Seeing things as they really are.

XII—Hanged Man (Trial and Transformation)

Desperate circumstances which give rise to innovation. A reprimanded employee who becomes a leader. The desire to learn from adversity. Looking back to see progress, even in difficult times. Sharing life lessons. Need for vision and awareness. Deliberately trying to see a situation from an unusual or unconventional perspective—or any point of view other than your own.

XIII—Death (Endings and Transitions)

Leaving one job, department, or assignment for another. The end of a quarter, financial year, or sales cycle. Firings and layoffs, but also promotions and options. Reorganizations. Providing or enforcing a deadline. Closing a sale. Relinquishing control of a project. Letting go of old habits or approaches. Final verdicts.

XIV—Temperance (Blending and Mediation)

Understanding how everything connects to everything else. Mergers and acquisitions. Swapping one idea, element, or approach for another, just to see what happens. The need to take the middle path. Arbitration. Dividing resources fairly among different groups. Making a fair profit (instead of fleecing the customer . . . or losing your shirt!).

XV—Devil (Manipulation and Selective Vision)

Refusing to avoid unprofitable or unhealthy activity. Working mindlessly. Making tough decisions with negative impact on others. Falling victim to a "blind spot" in your thinking. The tendency to value profit over people. Bottom-line thinking carried to extremes. Working against your own best interests. Asking the forbidden questions. Exploring unpopular ideas. Playing the "Devil's Advocate."

XVI—Tower (Destruction and Revision)

Taking something apart to see how it works. Rearrangement of basic elements in order to see or create something new. Scrapping a project and starting from scratch. Going back to basics. The urge to start over. A decisive action taken despite the consequences. Starting from square one. Unexpected "right-sizing" of a company. Shattering expectations or discarding old approaches and tried-and-true ways of thinking.

XVII—Star (Hopes and Goals)

Setting goals based on values. Quantifying and defining dreams and best possible futures. Visualizing yourself in your perfect job. A relentlessly positive, "can do" attitude. The power of optimism. Outlining the best possible scenario. Asking what's possible instead of what's practical. Overcoming fears. Tying your efforts to the hopes, dreams, and desires of others.

XVIII—Moon (Illogic and Mystery)

The need to turn things upside down. Fears and concerns. The compulsion to "go a little crazy" from time to time. A walk on the wild side. Risk taking. Trailblazing. Listening to hunches or "gut feelings." Doing the opposite of what others expect. Making decisions without adequate information. Choosing to disregard the bottom line.

XIX—Sun (Sensation and Satisfaction)

The driving, undying desire to do deeply satisfying work. The need to pause and celebrate major achievements. Opening up to new ways of working. Using your senses to explore an idea more fully. Doing what "feels good." Seeing major plans come to fruition. Intense activity. Risk of being too busy to appreciate progress. Becoming so busy, you're dizzy.

XX—Judgment (Decisions and Conclusions)

The need to end deliberation and make a decision. Sending out a call to action. Rendering a decision. A final opportunity for correct action. Finding your true calling. Understanding context. Seeing the "big picture." Valuing a grasp of reality over the need for further research. Exploring the consequences of actions or strategies under consideration.

XXI—The World (Completions and Realizations)

Being richly rewarded for work you'd do for free. Taking an idea to extremes in order to explore it further. Being supported by those around you. Doing everything necessary to get the job done. Understanding you have everything you need to achieve the goal. Becoming aware of differences between what you set out to do and what was actually achieved. Evaluating what's needed in order for a project or plan to be complete.

Cups

Ace of Cups (Motivation)

An opportunity to do fulfilling, meaningful work. Inspiring others to feel good about what they do. Commending or celebrating top performance. Recognition. Exploring the role feelings or emotions play in an issue or challenge.

Two of Cups (Union)

Meetings. Efforts to seek agreement. Contract deliberations. Joint efforts. Professional courtesy. Agreeing to disagree. Two friendly, but differing viewpoints. Mixed emotions. Inspiring a sense of unity. Bringing together all parties concerned.

Three of Cups (Celebration)

An event or party designed for emotional impact. A PR campaign designed to provoke a positive response. A large corporate event. An awards program. The value of play. Reviewing or celebrating what works.

Four of Cups (Distraction)

Boredom. A "ho-hum" response due to repetition or monotony. Mindless, repetitive work. The feeling that you're stuck in a rut. Hoping for a new idea or influence. Changing locations, approaches, or strategies to "shake things up" a bit.

Five of Cups (Loss)

Focusing on failures instead of triumphs. Pessimism. Harsh criticism. Poor job reviews. Inability to deliver. Uncertainty or dread. Plummeting morale. "All uphill from here!" Acknowledging errors or weaknesses in order to move forward. Identifying what doesn't work as a way of finding what does.

Six of Cups (Donation)

Volunteering. Pro bono work. Providing a customer with added value. Delivering more than someone expected or paid for. Causing others to feel obligated or indebted. Outlining how each person contributes to a solution (or a problem!). Finding ways to share the workload.

Seven of Cups (Imagination)

Brainstorming. Extrapolating or projecting. Working with scenarios. Role-playing. Practicing. Speculation. Anticipating customer objections or interest. Analyzing your situation as if it were a dream, looking for meaning in the events and people involved.

Eight of Cups (Dissatisfaction)

Knowing work doesn't meet a standard. An employee who fails to deliver to expectations. Lack of fulfillment. Failing to pay a vendor. Disappointing a mentor. Continuing to look for additional alternatives, even after isolating one good one. Identifying as many new ideas as possible.

Nine of Cups (Satisfaction)

A job well done. Feeling relief or joy over the completion of a well-received product. Being lulled into a sense of complacency by neglecting to consider alternatives. Asking "What works?" as part of developing a new approach or idea.

Ten of Cups (Contentment)

Knowing something is as good as it can be. The down-time between one urgent assignment and the next. An opportunity to pause, reflect, evaluate, and appreciate. Asking, "What could make this better?" or "What could make this even better than it is?"

Knave/Page of Cups (Impression)

Making a first impression. An initial grasp of a plan, situation, or emergency that may or may not be accurate. Keeping up appearances. Balancing enthusiasm with knowledge and experience. A desire to be admired, valued, or understood. Exploring how an initial impression about an approach, strategy, or idea has changed over time. Listing the first things that come to mind.

Knight of Cups (Illumination)

Training others. Helping others see, understand, or become excited by a principle or an idea. Explaining difficult subject matter in simple, engaging ways. Providing context. A desire to make an important contribution, whether recognized or not. Listing the benefits of an idea or approach for a given audience.

Queen of Cups (Intuition)

Sensing the "mood" of employees or management. Attempts to bolster or measure morale. Acknowledging the relationship between morale and productivity. Empathizing with customers or coworkers. Going with a hunch. Leaping to conclusions. Identifying how you feel about an approach, strategy, or solution . . . and why you feel that way.

King of Cups (Expression)

A gesture made to impact morale. A reprimand made in hopes of improving performance. Job reviews. Sales pitches that appeal to emotions and feelings instead of the pocketbook. Earning respect by offering straight talk. Writing benefit statements. Prioritizing opportunities or actions in terms of what will make the situation better as quickly as possible.

Coins

Ace of Coins (Challenge)

A financial, professional, or physical opportunity. A chance to make money or add perceived value. Improvements that require work, commitment, or obligation. Listing the resources needed to launch a project. Identifying costs associated with a project.

Two of Coins (Evaluation)

Weighing two options based on price or added value. Making budgetary choices. Fudging the numbers. Acknowledging financial uncertainty. Requesting a cost analysis. Asking "What's in it for me?" Identifying what you really value or want to achieve before you make a choice.

Three of Coins (Production)

A product or service. A prototype. Initial earnings or customer responses to a new product. The manufacturing process. Deliveries. Plans and processes. Drafts. Making out a project plan. Identifying every step needed to get a job done. Examining your step-by-step process with an eye toward improving or streamlining it.

Four of Coins (Maintenance)

Cost-cutting taken to an extreme. Preserving the status quo. Stinginess. Watching expenses in an effort to predict need. Enforcing budgetary guidelines. The need to break with routine. Outlining the rules and restrictions—and generating ideas for bending, transcending, or breaking them.

Five of Coins (Inadequacy)

A lack or loss of resources. Layoffs or budget cuts. Focusing on obstacles instead of solutions. Refusal to ask for assistance or aid. Being honest about what you need. Calling in consultants or experts. Taking advantage of the opinions and insights of others. Calling a summit.

Six of Coins (Redistribution)

Handing out work assignments. Shipping, provisioning, and fulfillment. Donations to charity. Incentives. Changes made to balance budgets or increase fairness. Swapping jobs to build appreciation for the work others do. Volunteering for a role outside your usual range of experience or authority. Delegating work.

Seven of Coins (Instinct)

Realizing that things "don't add up." Gut feelings. Dread. Handing off inadequate work to satisfy a deadline. Corporate direction that conflicts with your personal values. Speaking up, despite the consequences. Saying what's on your mind. Asking, "What are we doing by habit that we should question?"

Eight of Coins (Productivity)

Completing assignments or meeting deadlines. Isolating yourself to focus on work. Assigning value based on output. Quantity over quality. Identifying what keeps you from getting a job done . . . or what's needed to get the job done. Asking, "How can I boost productivity?"

Nine of Coins (Prosperity)

A wealth of resources. Seeing a project to successful completion. An abundance of training and feedback. Exploring the possible without regard for budget or cost. Asking, "If money wasn't a factor, what would we do?"

Ten of Coins (Attainment)

Profit without satisfaction. The burden of having "too much stuff." The need to feel inspired or satisfied by work. Retirement. Restlessness. Looking for other jobs. Identifying what's needed to put an issue to rest once and for all. Asking, "What do I need to give up in order to improve my performance?"

Page of Coins (Preservation)

Frugality. Cutting costs or saving money by any means. Arresting progress out of fear of change. Treading water. A new company, trying to survive. A stable stock price. Finding unexpected ways to conserve cash or curb expenses. Identifying costs associated with every dimension of your situation. Listing new ways to make money or increase profits.

Knight of Coins (Invention)

Using familiar materials to improve an existing product or make something new. Coming up with unexpected options. Completing a deadline with surprising speed. Identifying a new source of revenue. Making money. Finding budgetary support for new endeavors. Doing what people least expect. Using an existing item in a new or unconventional way.

Queen of Coins (Habituation)

Doing a job made comfortable by familiarity. Using repetition to teach a skill. Showing someone how to do something, step by step. Realizing profit by nurturing employees. Providing for creature comforts. A workplace that feels more like a family. Looking at the habits associated with your issue, and whether they need to be better maintained . . . or broken completely.

King of Coins (Intervention)

A manager "puts things back on track" or forces work to be done to standard. Clarifying and providing direction. Creating or restoring balance. Making assignments based on skill levels, perceived responsibility, or past performance. Good management. Asking, "How have we gotten off course?" Re-evaluating options or actions based on what really matters.

Swords

Ace of Swords (Choice)

An opportunity to employ logic, objectivity, or decision-making skills. Evaluating or prioritizing everyday tasks. Choosing a path or identifying an approach. Outlining what you would choose—and identifying what values or experiences drive those choices. Articulating what you need to know in order to make an informed decision.

Two of Swords (Debate)

Two colliding points of view or value systems. Duality of thought. Inability to make a clear choice. Choosing the lesser of two evils. A competition without a clear winner. Focusing on causes instead of symptoms. Asking, "What differences divide us?" or "What do we have in common?" Making a list of pros and cons.

Three of Swords (Variance)

A product that falls short of or exceeds expectations. A job review that is more negative or positive than expected. A decision that, once made, seems ill-informed. Determining the extent to which you've stuck with your original plans. Asking, "How might changing my plans (or sticking to them) impact this situation?" Accepting that no project ever turns out exactly as planned.

Four of Swords (Suspension)

Choosing not to make a decision. An argument or presentation that stifles all disagreement. A situation or issue that catches everyone "sleeping." Brainstorming. Putting off a decision until you have more information. Taking a break or going for refreshments. Exploring what happens if a specific process quits or gets interrupted, even temporarily.

Five of Swords (Commitment)

Declining some opportunities to make the most of others, even at the cost of disappointing certain people. Priorities, as dictated by values and goals. Establishing the extent to which an opportunity or strategy aligns with what you really want to achieve. Asking, "What keeps us from doing this?"

Six of Swords (Committee)

Collecting points of view. Collaborating on a process for getting work done. Setting aside personal vision for the good of the company. Asking for input to guide a decision. Beating a dead horse. Making sure that everyone impacted by a decision has input into it. Getting approval before moving forward.

Seven of Swords (Agenda)

Choosing to conceal motives or ideas. Strategizing before speaking or acting. Selecting one approach, based on your goals. Justifying theft. Judging others as less important. Pausing to evaluate what you hope to achieve before outlining a plan for getting there. Identifying the real goal, then authoring the steps that must be taken to achieve it.

Eight of Swords (Restriction)

Focusing on why something can't be done. Last-minute obstacles which hinder a product launch, sale, or project completion. A radical approach initially dismissed as impossible. Streamlining or simplifying an idea or approach. Exploring the objections people will raise in an effort to block progress or avoid commitment. Anticipating how people might break the rules or attempt to get around the system.

Nine of Swords (Conclusion)

"No turning back now!" Limiting options. Regretting previous decisions, or recognizing their impact. Relief that a decision is made. Waking up to the impact of your choices. Asking how a program will impact others. Determining whether the ends justify the means. Asking, "What stops us from doing this right now?" Calling for an end to debate.

Ten of Swords (Obsession)

Refusing to move from deliberation to action. Abandoning logic and reason. Tweaking something to death. Destructive criticism. Endless second-guessing. Escapism. Backing off or cooling down. Going in search of "fresh eyes" to take a look at your project. Giving up on logic and letting emotions dictate action. Identifying how you tend to look at things, and deliberately trying to see them in a new or unusual way.

Page of Swords (Information)

Gathering the facts needed to make an informed decision. Not knowing enough to make a good decision. Acknowledging you need to know more. Starting your research. Deciding to have an open mind. Writing a report or an executive brief. Reading the headlines. Asking, "What do we need to know in order to be successful?" Evaluating the quality or freshness of the information you have.

Knight of Swords (Investigation)

Drawing conclusions from research. Asking the difficult questions others avoid. Deciding who must be laid off vs. who remains. HR investigations. "Secret shopping" of a competitor's products to gather competitive information. Holding a Q&A session. Getting time with subject matter experts. Conducting interviews.

Queen of Swords (Inclination)

A predisposition toward a certain point of view. Corporate culture. The company's way of getting things done. Past experience (sales records, successful or failed efforts) which influence future decisions. Encouraging collaborative decision making. Asking, "What do they expect us to do?"

King of Swords (Decision)

Going to senior management for "the last word" on a subject. A corporate officer who ends a debate by making a decision for better or worse. Someone empowered to call the shots. Authority to set limits or give direction. Signature authority. Going with a strategy, despite uncertainty, rather than extending debate. Learning by doing (as opposed to trying to get all the answers before proceeding).

Wands

Ace of Wands (Vision)

A clear picture of the goal. An idea that everyone understands, appreciates, and supports. A chance to take something from inception to execution. Announcing new direction. Articulating a new plan in detail. Anticipating questions and reactions. Positioning a new idea in a way that gathers support and sparks enthusiasm. Asking, "What do I need to do to make my vision a reality?"

Two of Wands (Opinion)

An almost-formed idea or intention. A dissenting viewpoint. Two managers who give conflicting direction. Hearsay vs. facts. Editorial comments and articles. Taking a survey to determine direction. Giving everyone their say. Getting everything out on the table. Inviting criticism of an idea or approach from both supporters and skeptics.

Three of Wands (Mission)

Agreeing on a goal, vision, or direction. Launching a new project. Rallying everyone around a project or plan. Producing what was planned. Seeing work begin. Doing the work that you have a calling to do. Achieving what was intended. Asking, "What do we really need to achieve?"

Four of Wands (Teamwork)

Working together to achieve a common goal. A production by committee. A smooth-running project plan. Good division of labor. A conservative, "tried and true" approach. Consulting with others in your field for advice or input. Looking at how each person contributes to the success or failure of a project. Understanding your personal role in a larger project.

Five of Wands (Dissention)

Disagreement over values, mission, direction, or decisions. Argument. Debate. Meeting opposition. Confronting competitors. Disorganization. "Working against each other." Playing the Devil's Advocate. Pretending you dislike your own idea or approach in order to see it differently. Anticipating objections. Exploring ways to create controversy or shock.

Six of Wands (Victory)

Settling a disagreement. Being recognized as a leader by your peers. Winning a competition. Awards. Being proclaimed a leader, or receiving a promotion. Reviewing a successful effort in order to capture best practices. Sharing best practices. Looking at successful competitors in order to better understand how something is done.

Seven of Wands (Determination)

Pressing on despite the odds. Bearing up under attack. "It's my plan, and I'm sticking with it." Resolving to face overwhelming deadlines without feeling overwhelmed. Regrouping after a setback. Coming up with an alternative plan. Getting around an obstacle—or breaking through it. Calling for a brainstorming session to solve an unexpected problem.

Eight of Wands (Acceleration)

Rapid change, planned or unplanned. A frenzied day. Moving from one chore to another without time to think. Finishing up faster or earlier than expected, for better or for worse. Asking, "How can this be done faster?" Emphasizing the "need to haves" over the "nice to haves" in order to more quickly complete a project.

Nine of Wands (Achievement)

Reaching a goal, but exhausting everyone in the process. Being on the lookout for anything that threatens the fulfillment of your plan. Defending a project or decision. Defining the terms of success to facilitate objective measurement of achievement. Asking, "How will I know whether or not I've reached my goal?"

Ten of Wands (Exhaustion)

Pursing a burdensome course of action. Comprehending the need for a change of direction. Acknowledging that things aren't going as you planned. Giving up. Asking, "Under what conditions should I abandon this approach and try another?" Asking, "What approaches are yet to be tried?" Admitting the need to take a break in order to move forward.

Page of Wands (Submission)

Accepting an assignment. Turning drafts over for review. A manager acting as "just another team member." Allowing yourself to be guided or directed by others. A willingness to disregard rank, roll up your sleeves, and just get the job done. Acknowledging reality, and moving forward based on that reality.

Knight of Wands (Persuasion)

Bringing others around to your point of view. Making a presentation to management. Building grassroots support. Developing or placing advertisements. Making a sales pitch. Pressuring someone to give in or agree. Emphasizing positives, excluding negatives. Asking, "What would make me agree to this?" Articulating benefits or answering the question, "What's in it for my audience?"

Queen of Wands (Collaboration)

Reaching goals by defining "What's in it for me?" for all parties involved. Bringing the group around to a common point of view. Getting "buy-in" by making sure everyone has (and is working on) an assignment they perceive as critical. Rule by committee. Bringing in experts or consultants. Reading the literature associated with a subject.

King of Wands (Dominion)

A manager puts a complex plan into motion to achieve an important goal. "Lighting fires" under people to prompt action. Prodding people to get the job done. A leader who stirs things up, but always with a purpose in mind. "My way or the highway." Defusing objections. Closing a discussion. Micromanaging.

Appendix B: Decks Recommended for Personal and Corporate Use

T HE LIST OF AVAILABLE Tarot decks grows daily—in fact, the sheer variety of decks now available overwhelms most first-time deck buyers. Think of the list below as a starting point when shopping for your own use . . . but please don't consider this a list of decks approved for (or even preferred for!) use in a corporate setting.

As mentioned in chapter 2, almost every Tarot deck on the market contains at least one card depicting a nude human body. Some of these—like the nudes on the *Rider-Waite Tarot*—amount to line drawings with little potential to offend. Other decks—like *The Robin Wood Tarot* and *Alchemical Tarot*—depict bodies more frankly or accurately, but do so in ways that most adults understand to be artistic.

From a corporate perspective, a few decks—the *Cosmic Tribe,* for example, which incorporates full-frontal photographs of nude male and female models—amount to a sexual harassment lawsuit waiting to happen. While fine for personal use, in a business setting, they should be avoided in these litigious times.

If you have any concerns about the imagery on any deck you purchase (or about the maturity or sensitivities of your coworkers), always err on the side of caution. Never hesitate to pull potentially offensive images from a deck prior to a brainstorming session. Better to miss out on a few ideas than have to schedule a brainstorming session on "What I'll Say at My Harassment Trial!"

Suggested "First Decks" for Beginners / Personal Decks

    Connolly Tarot (U.S. Games)

    The Robin Wood Tarot (Llewellyn)

    Universal Tarot (Llewellyn)

    Universal Waite (U.S. Games)

    World Spirit Tarot (Llewellyn)

Suggested Decks for Corporate Use★

    Alchemical Tarot (Thorsons)

    Giant Rider-Waite Tarot (U.S. Games)

    Navigator's Tarot of the Mystic SEA (U.S. Games)

    Osho Zen Tarot (St. Martin's Press)

    Secret Tarot (Fireside / Simon and Schuster)

    Universal Tarot (Llewellyn)

    Universal Waite (U.S. Games)

    Voyager Tarot (Merrill West)

    World Spirit Tarot (Llewellyn)

★ Some cards may need to be removed in certain settings. Review the deck carefully before use.

Further Reading and Resources

Want to know more about Tarot and the broad range of applications for the cards? If so, this list of books and Internet resources will come in handy. And don't forget: the most recently updated version of this list can also be found at the web site specifically designed to support readers of *Putting the Tarot to Work:* www.tarottools.com.

Books

Bunning, Joan. *Learning the Tarot.* York Beach, ME: Samuel Weiser, Inc., 1998. A comprehensive "first book" of Tarot meanings, complete with a series of detailed beginner's exercises. While the book assumes the cards will be used for divination or fortune-telling, the concise summaries of card meanings provide good "hooks" on which new users can hang a wide variety of associations.

Decker, Ronald, Thierry dePaulis, and Michael Dummett. *A Wicked Pack of Cards.* New York: St. Martin's Press, 1996. For those curious as to how Tarot cards became associated with fortune-telling and occult practice, this book provides a well-documented history of the evolution of Tarot from bridge-like trick-taking game to mysterious cards capable of predicting the future.

Greer, Mary K. *The Complete Book of Tarot Reversals*. St. Paul: Llewellyn Publications, 2002. A comprehensive guide to reading "reversed" or inverted cards, providing eleven different strategies for reading reversals.

————. *Tarot for Your Self*. North Hollywood, CA: Newcastle Publishing Company, Inc., 1984. An introductory text designed to get beginners working and interacting with the cards. While admittedly focused on divinatory, meditative, and personal applications, the exercises in the book can be adapted for a variety of uses. This book will be of special interest to readers curious about personal applications of Tarot for self-exploration and discovery.

————. *Tarot Mirrors*. North Hollywood, CA: Newcastle Publishing Company, Inc., 1988. A workbook and textbook introducing the concept of the Tarot as a mirror for the personality and the self. Early chapters offer particularly good exercises for investigating and experiencing the meaning of the cards.

MacGregor, Trish and Phyllis Veta. *Power Tarot*. New York: Fireside, 1998. Offers over a hundred different spreads, all of which can be adapted for a variety of brainstorming exercises.

O'Neill, Robert V. *Tarot Symbolism*. Lima, OH: Fairway Press, 1986. This rare paperback brings sanity and objectivity to the study of Tarot's symbolism and origins. Scholarly in tone, it provides a thorough introduction to the philosophical, religious, artistic, cultural, and social forces that gave rise to Tarot cards.

Riley, Jana. *Tarot Dictionary and Compendium*. York Beach, ME: Samuel Weiser, Inc., 1995. This concise work pulls together card meanings and associations as defined by as many as a dozen different commentators. Varying interpretations help new users see the same card from many different angles. An excellent, portable "quick reference."

Thompson, Sandra. *Pictures from the Heart: A Tarot Dictionary*. New York: St. Martin's Griffin, 2003. If you're curious about the meaning behind every sign, symbol, and story behind the images on many Tarot cards, this book will become a treasured addition to your library. In addition to a readable (and down-to-earth) introduction to the cards and a gallery of popular decks, Sandra Thompson takes readers on a guided tour of all things Tarot, from the abyss to the zodiac. I consider the book a "must have."

Internet Resources

Aeclectic Tarot (http://www.aeclectic.net/tarot/). This site, dedicated to "the beauty and diversity of Tarot," offers hundreds of deck reviews, each of which usually contains at least six card images from the deck under consideration. Also offers basic Tarot info, readings, and a Tarot-related community message board.

Comparative Tarot (http://groups.yahoo.com/group/ComparativeTarot/). Definitely the friendliest Internet-based Tarot community online, *Comparative Tarot* unites self-professed "deck-a-holics" with Tarot authors, enthusiasts, and scholars. The list gets its name from founder Valerie Sim's comparative method, which involves observing changes in the tone and content of a reading when corresponding cards are pulled from decks with different illustrations. The companion website, www.comparativetarot.com, archives card essays written by group members and publishes the occasional special feature.

Orphalese Tarot (http://www.orphalese.net). This is, quite simply, the single most useful, flexible, and powerful Tarot software on the market today. No canned readings here - instead, creator Richard Jeffries focused on making this virtual deck as functional as possible. In addition to one-click sorting, shuffling, and dealing, the program allows users to specify any images, from card scans to old vacation photos, as a Tarot deck. All this for less than ten bucks!

Tarot-L (http://groups.yahoo.com/group/TarotL/). Discussion can get lively in this group, which leans toward an evidence-based approach to Tarot and its history. Users with all levels of experience are welcome, but, as with any Internet group, it's a good idea to read posts for a few days before jumping in the discussion.

The Tarot-L History Information Sheet (http://www.tarothermit.com/infosheet.htm). Created and maintained by members of the Tarot-L Yahoo! Group and now compiled and edited by Tom Tadfor Little, this web page organizes in one concise document some of the best available information on Tarot and its origins, with an emphasis on statements that can be supported by documentation and evidence.

Tarot Passages (http://www.tarotpassages.com). Now updated twice monthly (or more!) by webmistress Diane Wilkes, *Tarot Passages* offers the Internet's most accessible collection of Tarot book and deck reviews. This is the ultimate "try before you buy" site, and my first stop when I'm looking for information on a deck I've never encountered.

TarotTools.com (http://www.tarottools.com). The companion web site for this book offers additional resources, informative articles, and interactive demos. It's the first site on the web exclusively dedicated to promoting Tarot as a visual brainstorming tool.

Index

ORDER LLEWELLYN BOOKS TODAY!

Llewellyn publishes hundreds of books on your favorite subjects! To get these exciting books, including the ones on the following pages, check your local bookstore or order them directly from Llewellyn.

Order Online:

Visit our website at www.llewellyn.com, select your books, and order them on our secure server.

Order by Phone:

- Call toll-free within the U.S. at 1-877-NEW-WRLD (1-877-639-9753). Call toll-free within Canada at 1-866-NEW-WRLD (1-866-639-9753)
- We accept VISA, MasterCard, and American Express

Order by Mail:

Send the full price of your order (MN residents add 7% sales tax) in U.S. funds, plus postage & handling to:

Llewellyn Worldwide
P.O. Box 64383, Dept. 0-7387-0444-X
St. Paul, MN 55164-0383, U.S.A.

Postage & Handling:

Standard (U.S., Mexico, & Canada). If your order is:
Up to $25.00, add $3.50
$25.01 - $48.99, add $4.00
$49.00 and over, FREE STANDARD SHIPPING
(Continental U.S. orders ship UPS. AK, HI, PR, & P.O. Boxes ship USPS 1st class. Mex. & Can. ship PMB.)

International Orders:
Surface Mail: For orders of $20.00 or less, add $5 plus $1 per item ordered. For orders of $20.01 and over, add $6 plus $1 per item ordered.

Air Mail:
Books: Postage & Handling is equal to the total retail price of all books in the order.
Non-book items: Add $5 for each item.

Orders are processed within 2 business days. Please allow for normal shipping time.
Postage and handling rates subject to change.

Tarot for Beginners

An Easy Guide to Understanding
& Interpreting the Tarot

P. Scott Hollander

The Tarot is much more than a simple divining tool. While it can—and does—give you accurate and detailed answers to your questions when used for fortunetelling, it can also lead you down the road to self-discovery in a way that few other meditation tools can do. *Tarot for Beginners* will tell you how to use the cards for meditation and self-enlightenment as well as for divination.

If you're just beginning a study of the Tarot, this book gives you a basic, straightforward definition of the meaning of each card that can be easily applied to any system of interpretation, with any Tarot deck, using any card layout. The main difference between this book and other books on the Tarot is that it's written in plain English—you need no prior knowledge of the Tarot or other arcane subjects to understand its mysteries, because this no-nonsense guide will make the symbolism of the Tarot completely accessible to you. You will receive an overview of of the cards of the Major and Minor Arcana in terms of their origin, purpose, and interpretive uses as well as clear, in-depth descriptions and interpretations of each card.

1-56718-363-8, 352 pp., 5 ¼ x 8, illus.   **$12.95**

Spanish Edition
Tarot para principiantes
1-56718-399-9, 288 pp., 6 x 9, illus.   **$12.95**

To order by phone call 1-877-NEW WRLD
Prices subject to change without notice

The Robin Wood Tarot Deck

created and illustrated by Robin Wood
instructions by
Robin Wood and Michael Short

Tap into the wisdom of your subconscious with one of the most beautiful Tarot decks on the market today! Reminiscent of the *Rider-Waite* deck, *The Robin Wood Tarot* is flavored with nature imagery and luminous energies that will enchant you and the querant. Even the novice reader will find these cards easy and enjoyable to interpret.

Radiant and rich, these cards were illustrated with a unique technique that brings out the resplendent color of the prismacolor pencils. The shining strength of this Tarot deck lies in its depiction of the Minor Arcana. Unlike other Minor Arcana decks, this one springs to pulsating life. The cards are printed in quality card stock and boxed complete with instruction booklet, which provides the upright and reversed meanings of each card, as well as three basic card layouts. Beautiful and brilliant, *The Robin Wood Tarot* is a must-have deck!

0-87542-894-0, boxed set: 78-cards with booklet   **$19.95**

Tarot Awareness

Exploring the Spiritual Path

Stephen Walter Sterling

With its powerful imagery, hidden meanings, and sometimes earth-shattering revelations, the Tarot can surprise you like a sudden lightning flash across the evening sky. It can open the way to a more aware and vibrant communication with the inner self, the divine spark within.

Through the study of the Tarot, you can find your way back from the mad carnival of the outer world to the natural inner world of Awareness. This book encourages a spirit of dedicated introspection and practical application that will bring you to the very Source of your strength and well-being. When this happens, problems are solved and goals are reached.

You will study the meaning behind Tarot symbolism, as well as the Tarot reading, an interpretation of the patterns of a group of cards in a particular moment in time. Readings are, above all, a challenging, daring, and intriguing entryway into the subtle realms.

1-56718-676-9, 384 pp., 7 ¹/₂ x 9 ¹/₈, 82 illus.   **$17.95**

Tarot Companion

An Essential Reference Guide

Tracy Porter

While some people are so psychically gifted they can give an accurate tarot reading without any formal training, most of us need to develop our inherent intuition. The first step in doing that is to study the symbolism imbedded in the cards. This book is a complete reference to those symbols for all tarot readers, beginning through advanced.

The different symbol systems covered in this book include the following: (1) astrology, which was central to the development of the Major Arcana; (2) numerology which is fundamental to understanding the tarot as each card was placed in its sequence for a particular reason; (3) cabala, which is essential if you want to progress from novice to the more advanced stages; (4) the I-Ching and runes, which evolved separately from the tarot, but which can help you align harmoniously with world-wide philosophies; (5) colors and chakras, which will help you understand the nuances in the scenes and the backgrounds.

1-56718-574-6, 264 pp., 5 ³/₁₆ x 8   **$12.95**

The Sacred Circle Tarot

A Celtic Pagan Journey

Anna Franklin
illustrated by Paul Mason

The Sacred Circle Tarot is a new concept in tarot design, combining photographs, computer imaging, and traditional drawing techniques to create stunning images. It draws on the Pagan heritage of Britain and Ireland, its sacred sites and landscapes. Key symbols unlock the deepest levels of Pagan teaching.

The imagery of the cards is designed to work on a number of levels, serving as a tool not only for divination but to facilitate meditation, personal growth, and spiritual development. The "sacred circle" refers to the progress of the initiate from undirected energy, through dawning consciousness, to the death of the old self and the emergence of the new.

The major arcana is modified somewhat to fit the pagan theme of the deck. For example, "The Fool" becomes "The Green Man," "The Heirophant" becomes "The Druid," and "The World" becomes "The World Tree." The accompanying book gives a full explanation of the symbolism in the cards and their divinatory meanings.

1-56718-457-X, Boxed Kit: 78 full-color cards; 288 pp. book, 6 x 9   **$29.95**

To order by phone call 1-877-NEW WRLD
Prices subject to change without notice

Tarot for the Healing Heart

Christine Jette

Health and happiness are in the cards for you

Tarot for the Healing Heart introduces a new way to use the tarot. Discover how to promote healing in yourself through the use of mind-body techniques and visualization with the cards.

Wellness is body, mind, and spirit in balance. Illness is a neutral, direct message focusing our awareness on issues that need attention. We are either in a life lesson (imbalanced energy / disease) or life wisdom (balanced energy / healing) mode. The tarot can reveal areas that are out of balance and uncover ways to support the healing process. Through the suits of the tarot, you will explore illness and healing as they relate to the four levels of existence—physical (pentacles), emotional (cups), psychological (swords), and the spiritual (wands). The major arcana cards represent the higher insight of disease, and the court cards are the healers of the tarot.

Activities include ten original tarot layouts, tarot meditations for releasing the healer within, exploring healing as a lifestyle, breaking the pain cycle, contacting your healing guide and developing psychic ability through sacred play with tarot cards. No prior knowledge of tarot is needed.

0-7387-0043-6, 7½ x 9⅛, 264 pp. $14.95

To order by phone call 1-877-NEW WRLD
Prices subject to change without notice

Tarot for All Seasons

Celebrating the Days & Nights of Power

Christine Jette

Working with the tarot cards is a simple but powerful way to create a seasonal connection with the Goddess. The universal pictures of tarot awaken the voice of inner knowing as you align yourself with the larger forces of the universe and embrace the cycle of the seasons.

Part spellbook, part ritual guide, *Tarot for All Seasons* describes how to extract seasonal energy throughout the Wheel of the Year to improve all areas of your life—relationships, making money, establishing a career, and choosing healthful lifestyles. Useful for both solitary practice and coven group wisdom.

- This is the first book devoted solely to how Tarot relates to the Wheel of the Year

- Addresses the common concerns and developmental stages of young women

- Combines ritual, Wiccan history, mystery and lore, focused intention (magic), and seasonal tarot layouts

- The twelve original layouts capture the spirit of the full moon esbats, waxing and waning moons, and eight solar holidays

- Readers are empowered to "change the cards to change reality"

0-7387-0105-X 144 pp., 6 x 9, 12 illus. $12.95

Understanding the Tarot Court

Foreword by Rachel Pollack

Mary K. Greer & Tom Little

Just who are those kings, queens, knights, and pages in the Tarot deck? Generally considered the most difficult part of the Tarot to interpret, they actually represent different characters or personalities that are aspects of ourselves. They also serve as teachers or projections of our own unacknowledged qualities.

Two esteemed Tarot scholars unmask the court cards with details not found in any other book. Discover your significator and your nemsis. Compare the differences among the cards in well-known decks. Match the court cards with the zodiac signs, the Myers-Briggs personality types, and the Jungian archetypes. Learn a variety of spreads that reveal childhood issues, career destiny, and a storytelling spread to spark the creative writing process.

Available April 2004!
0-7387-0286-2, 360 pp., 6 x 9, illus.   **$14.95**